Blake, Ethics, and Forgiveness

Blake, Ethics, and Forgiveness

Jeanne Moskal

THE UNIVERSITY OF ALABAMA PRESS
TUSCALOOSA & LONDON

The University of Alabama Press
Tuscaloosa, Alabama 35487-0380

Manufactured in the United States of America

designed by Paula C. Dennis

∞

The paper on which this book is printed meets the minimum requirements of American National Standard for Information Science-Permanence of Paper for Printed Library Materials, ANSI Z39.48-1984.

Library of Congress Cataloging-in-Publication Data

Moskal, Jeanne.
Blake, ethics, and forgiveness / Jeanne Moskal.
p. cm.
Includes bibliographical references (p.) and index.
ISBN 0-8173-0678-1
1. Blake, William, 1757–1827—Ethics. 2. Forgiveness in literature. 3. Ethics in literature. I. Title.
PR4148.E8M67 1994
821'.7—dc20 93-11799

British Library Cataloguing-in-Publication Data available

For Larry

Contents

Illustrations

A Note on References

All quotations from William Blake's works follow the newly revised edition of David V. Erdman, *The Complete Poetry and Prose of William Blake* (Berkeley and Los Angeles: University of California Press, 1982), and will be cited parenthetically in the text, prefaced by E.

All quotations from the Bible follow the Authorized Version of 1611, the translation known by Blake, and will be cited parenthetically in the text.

Biographical references are cited from *Blake Records*, edited by G. E. Bentley, Jr. (Oxford: Clarendon Press, 1969). Such references will be given parenthetically in the text, prefaced by *BR*.

Acknowledgments

My thanks to Hazard Adams, who directed my dissertation on Blake at the University of Washington and thus got me started on this project. For help in ethical issues, my thanks to Stanley Hauerwas, who expressed continual skepticism about Blake. John E. Grant, W. J. T. Mitchell, Roland E. Murphy, and Aileen Ward made critiques of sections of the book; Donald D. Ault and Mark L. Reed generously read the entire book and offered comments that improved it.

I am grateful for permission to reprint in chapters 1, 2, and 5 versions of articles that appeared in *Religion and Literature* 20, no. 2 (1988): 19–39; *Studies in Philology* 86 (1989): 69–86; *South Atlantic Review* 55, no. 2 (1990): 15–31; and *Philological Quarterly* 79 (1991): 317–37.

This project was supported in part by a fellowship in the Institute for the Arts and Humanities at the University of North Carolina at Chapel Hill. The University Research Council provided support for the publication of the illustrations.

Some research for this project was conducted at the Library of Congress. My thanks particularly to Bruce Martin and Victoria C. Hill of the library's staff. Thanks also to my graduate assistants, Patty McRae, Christine McPherson Morris, and Christine Sneed, and to the secretarial staff of the Department of English at the University of North Carolina at Chapel Hill: Frances Coombs, Rhonda Jeffries, Tobi P. B. Schwartzman, and Nina Wallace. Nicole Mitchell and the staff of The University of Alabama Press have helped me with their patience and good humor.

I am grateful for the support of my friends during this project: Reid Barbour, Doris Betts, Laurence Cooper, Pamela Cooper, Virginia Sickbert, and David Valtierra. My particular thanks go to Joseph J. Tiernan for a decade of friendship and guidance. My husband, Lawrence Zelenak, has seen this book through from its beginning: he deserves the lion's share of my gratitude.

Introduction

William Blake has a reputation as one of our culture's greatest immoralists. This reputation is based, in the mind of the public, on Blake's numerous aphorisms that outrage common morality, such as "Sooner murder an infant in its cradle than nurse unacted desires" (E, 38), and on his vociferous advocacy of sexual freedom and political rebellion. A more refined version of this reputation—Blake as immoralist—has become the received opinion about Blake's ethics among scholars of the British Romantic period and among literary scholars generally. Indeed, the received opinion about Blake's ethics rightly aligns him with the antinomian Protestant sects such as the Quakers and Ranters of seventeenth- and eighteenth-century England, since both Blake and the sects advocated breaking the laws of church and state in order to achieve freedom from these laws.

While the received opinion is true, as far as it goes, it is limited, even distorted, by the assumptions about ethics accepted by the culture at large and by literary scholars, despite searching questions raised by specialists in ethics. Questions of ethics have been unfashionable in literary studies for several years, because of the fear that ethical matters would become thematized into monolithic and logocentric "meanings" of texts, "meanings" that would deny indeterminacies in the text or differences between historical periods.[1] In one recent recovery of ethics for literary study, Laurence S. Lockridge has historicized the major Romantic thinkers' ethical concerns within the context of eighteenth- and nineteenth-century European ethical debates. Two of the most exciting strands of recent work on ethics make a substantial contribution in the understanding of Blake and of Romanticism as a whole.

The first of these is a group called variously "ethicists of character" or "ethicists of virtue." Primary among this recent work is the polemical history of ethics constructed by Alasdair MacIntyre in *After Virtue.* MacIntyre makes the large claim that crucial terms for ethics—the Aristotelian vocabulary of character, virtues, and dispositions—have been lost both in the Enlightenment emphasis on duty and also in its mirror image, the post-Enlightenment rejections of duty by Søren Kierkegaard and Friederich Nietzsche, among others. Stanley Hauerwas, another leader of the ethicists of character, usefully names our cultural inheritance of this Enlightenment version of ethics "the standard account," suggesting that in its emphasis on duty and obligation as they pertain to all individuals interchangeably, the standard account alienates each individual from his plans, metaphors, and stories. Since most literary scholars have accepted the standard account of ethics, they have no ground from which to question the received opinion about Blake and antinomianism.

This study challenges that dominant standard account, placing the work of Blake in the context of recent work on the ethics of character and particularly of MacIntyre's polemical history. I employ MacIntyre's historical plot of the relation between teleological ethics (roughly, based on character) and deontological ethics (roughly, based on obligation) rather than conceiving these terms as timeless and neutral frames of reference for Blake's "immorality" and "morality." In contrast to the received opinion of Blake's antinomianism, which perceives Blake's struggle to subvert obligation's coercive power, I argue that Blake is an ethical *bricoleur*, Claude Lévi-Strauss's improvising bricklayer, who seeks to construct an ethics of character in the absence of Aristotelian vocabulary described by MacIntyre. I elaborate on Lockridge's argument that Romantic writers display "an ethical play of mind more directed to the articulation of values than to their subversion" by tracing in the case of Blake a convoluted course of subverting some ethical systems and articulating others, somewhat partially.[2] This course is convoluted because Blake, like most other thinkers in his time and circle, lacked a coherent account of the virtues and hoped to substitute for it a thoroughgoing critique of duty and obligation.

I draw my main lines of argument about Blake and ethics from MacIntyre's analysis of the relation between obligation and virtue. MacIntyre argues that the current state of ethical discourse is in disarray, consisting in an incommensurability between the language of rights and of obligations. He traces the legacy of this disarray to the revolution in ethics wrought by Kant. Though Kant himself lived in a culture with considerable consensus about what constituted the human good, and largely shared that consensus, his ethical formalism concentrated attention on doing right, on the weighing of conflicting obligations, and on proper performance of duties arising from these obligations. Moreover, Kant's categorical imperative, by which one understands what is right, assumes the priority of the universal individual; that is, any one person decides about the right on the basis of a concept of individuality that includes what is essential, what the individual shares with all other individuals, and that excludes the peculiar. The categorical imperative produces a stripped-down version of the self. Nietzsche rightly rejected such a pared-down version of ethics as merely the assertion of power, for the social and teleological justifications of such a version of the right had been made invisible, with only the formal justifications explicit.

MacIntyre's originality lies in plotting Kant's revolution in ethics as a loss of Aristotelian categories, among them the dispositions (both virtues and vices), the character formed by the dispositions, and the goal or *telos* that organizes the dispositions. As MacIntyre points out, not all virtue-based ethical systems are teleological, for Homer accounts for virtues by means of roles, not ends; and not all teleological accounts agree about ends, with Aristotle privileging human goods attainable in this world, and the New Testament choosing otherworldly goods.[3] Kantian ethics loses any teleological justification by which human goods or a single human good can underwrite decisions and actions.

Corollary to this loss is the eclipse of the vocabulary of dispositions, virtues, and character: a vocabulary that frames individuals within their social roles and conscious choices and, more important, within their everyday lives. Led by MacIntyre, the ethicists of character have several related goals—to make visible the principles of ethics that inform everyday life, as contrasted with the high-profile ethics of rights and obligations that inform debates over moral quandaries; to reestablish the claims of community over a previously exclusive focus on the unembedded individual stripped of his peculiar properties and roles, as formulated by Kant; and to rehistoricize the major thinkers in the history of ethics.[4]

A more traditional way of posing the opposition between Aristotle and Kant is to look at the formal distinction between teleological and deontological ethics as timeless and neutral. According to William Frankena's authoritative introduction to ethics, teleological theories hold that "the basic or ultimate criterion or standard of what is morally right, wrong, obligatory, etc., is the nonmoral value that is brought into being. The final appeal, directly or indirectly, must be to the comparative amount of good produced."[5] Deontological theories, by contrast, "assert that there are, at least, other considerations which may make an action or rule right or obligatory besides the goodness or badness of its consequences—certain features of the act itself."[6] Teleological theories, of course, can take several forms, including utilitarianism's search for "the greatest good for the greatest number" as well as Aristotelian and Thomistic aims for the human good of contemplation. Deontological theories are best represented by Kant's categorical imperative, "Always act on that maxim which you would will to be a law for all other beings," an imperative that depends on fulfilling formal criteria for rightness without any specification of the good sought.

There is much that is historically accurate about the current consensus about Blake's antinomianism, in that it places Blake in the company of his contemporaries, the heterodox Ranters and other religious sects. Moreover, this consensus implicitly recognizes Blake's opposition to the rule-boundness of the Church of England during his time, an era that, historians agree, was singularly arid in its exclusive emphasis on duty, obligation, and reason. Some of the eccentric twists in Blake's treatment of human forgiveness were caused historically, I think, by the domination of ethical discourse in his time by theories of duty, obligation, and universal law over theories of sympathy and benevolence.[7] But with the aid of MacIntyre's historicization of that era in ecclesiastical and intellectual history, we can see the force of Blake's opposition. The fact remains that Blake committed himself to some form of Christianity, most often conceived as primitive, prophetic, and individualistic. However eccentric Blake's Christianity might be, the commitment informs his ethical stance and statements. Both virtues and obligations are implicated in this commitment. The ethical implications of this commitment are best described by Paul Ricoeur: "The prophetic moment in the consciousness of evil is the revelation in an infinite measure of the demand that God addresses to man. It is this infinite demand that creates an unfathomable distance and distress between God and man. But as this infinite demand does not declare itself in a sort of preceding void, but applies itself to a preceding matter, that of the old Semitic 'codes,' it inaugurates a tension characteristic of all Hebrew ethics, the tension between an infinite demand and a finite commandment. It is this polarity that must be respected . . . this dialectic of unlimited imagination and detailed prescription."[8] Ricoeur elegantly sets out the division between obligation and virtue, a division that pervades not only Hebrew ethics but those ethical systems derived from it. In casting Blake as ethical *bricoleur*, my study depends not only on resituating Blake in the history of ethics proposed by MacIntyre but also on granting the historical fact that Blake committed himself to some form of Christianity, however eccentrically conceived, and thus was an inheritor of the tension described by Ricoeur between infinite demand and finite commandment. Out of this quarry Blake did his work.

I do not claim that Blake himself was an Aristotelian. One of the best-known elements of Aristotle's ethics, the notion of virtue as a golden mean between vicious extremes, clearly will not suit the aphorist who claims that "Exuberance is Beauty" (E, 38). Moreover, what Blake explicitly says about Aristotle suggests a lifetime of outright dislike. In the *Marriage* he caricatures "analytic" philosophers as monkeys and baboons; in his last work, the Dante illustrations, he places Aristotle with Homer at the center of Dante's error. Closer examination reveals that Blake's knowledge of Aristotle was probably based on scant acquaintance with his texts, and probably Blake rejected the Aristotle he knew as part of his wholesale rejection of the classics: "The Classics, it is the Classics! & not Goths nor Monks, that Desolate Europe with Wars" (E, 270). Thus I do not claim that Blake used Aristotle as a source, nor that Blake, unbeknownst to himself, really "was" an Aristotelian. Rather, I claim that the eclipse of an Aristotelian ethics of character in Blake's time complicated Blake's struggle with ethics and human forgiveness.

The second group of ethicists whose work I find illuminating for Blake are those concerned with an ethics of alterity. This line of thinking in ethics—like the resurgence of interest in dispositional ethics, a reaction against the prevalence of deontological ethics—focuses less on the individual as the locus of ethical scrutiny (for whether the ethicist inquires about obligations or virtues, usually the discrete individual is still the object of inquiry) than on relationships. On the most concrete level, such ethicists concern themselves with social policies aimed at alleviating the suffering of groups with a defined need. On the more theoretical level, however, the ethics of care depends on the ethics of alterity, on the accounts we offer for the encounter with the other or with otherness. The phenomenological philosophy of Martin Heidegger and Martin Buber are crucial documents here in their accounts of "letting be" and of the distinction between "I-Thou" and "I-It" relationships.[9] The important figures in defining my approach to an ethics of alterity are primarily Emmanuel Levinas and Luce Irigaray. Levinas proposes an important qualification of the view of the disclosure of the other presupposed by Heidegger and Buber. Levinas contends that their accounts of disclosure presuppose an other that is merely a replication of the self; he believes it is essential to keep the other as exterior, as a phenomenological nonobject which cannot be assimilated to the self but which remains exterior to the self.[10] Levinas critiques as "totalizing" that mode of consciousness which seeks to reduce the exteriority of the other. Irigaray raises the question of the autonomy and genderedness of the other: Is the other merely another version of the self? For the purposes of Blake, the questions raised by Levinas and Irigaray provide an alternative point of view on the ethics of the latter half of Blake's life, particularly the vision of the self that he creates.

In posing these questions about ethics, I wish to clarify my assumptions about the total picture of Blake's life and thought. The question of the internal consistency of Blake's work has received several answers. An early answer, which prevailed among scholars until the 1940s, divided Blake's work into two phases, an initial period of clarity and a late period of incoherence. Against this prevailing view, Northrop Frye proposed the maxim which governed Blake criticism for decades, that the engraved works form an internally consistent whole, a whole which demands that proportional attention be given to the major prophecies. (Curiously, the critics who described Blake's ethics as "antinomian" predated Frye and had little knowledge of Blake's major prophecies. Yet Frye and the later critics did not examine the question of Blake's ethics in the light of his prophecies.) A third influential position was developed by Morton D. Paley, who argued for a decisive change in Blake's allegiances from energy to imagination at about 1803, when Blake made a deeply felt, if eccentric, return to the Christianity of his youth.[11] The view of Blake became fragmented as some Blake critics subdivided his oeuvre into ever-smaller stages, arguing for his coherence at each stage, while other critics questioned even this latter version of coherence. Recently, W. J. T. Mitchell has argued that Blake critics have overemphasized his coherence and his benignity, losing sight of his madness, obscenity, and, sometimes, incoherence. In general, I shall rely on Paley's account of Blake's career. However, I am compelled to agree with Mitchell that moments of intractable contradiction and incoherence emerge over and over.[12]

In my judgment Paley's two-phase account of Blake's career best explains the effect of the series of devastating events in Blake's life beginning in about 1800, events that are familiar to Blakeans: the identity crisis with his patron William Hayley, the dearth of readers for his poetry, the failure of his only exhibition, the struggle to find commissions for engraving his designs. Chief among these woes was his sedition trial in 1803, arising from Blake's expulsion of a Private Schofield from his garden in Felpham. Paul Youngquist has recently reexamined the Schofield incident, conceding that much in the accusation of Private Schofield may have been accurate, though Blake himself remained silent during the trial while his lawyer prepared a statement praising Blake's loyalty to the monarchy.[13] Though the statement was not read,

Youngquist rightly emphasizes "the enormous psychological tension required for him to maintain a private allegiance to his vision while denying it in public."[14] For my purposes it is central that Blake himself marked the watershed quality of the sedition trial by a renewed concern with forgiveness. Blake's intense engagement—even obsession—with forgiveness during the later years of his life led Alfred Kazin to ask, "What was it that made him long at the end, above everything else, for 'forgiveness'? What was it that he had to be 'forgiven' for?"[15] While Youngquist suggests accurately but briefly that Blake sought forgiveness for publicly denying his private vision, I will develop this theme with some care, for the internal pressures that account biographically for Blake's concern with forgiveness also distort his use of the concept.

Thus the onset of a passionate concern for forgiveness corroborates Paley's sense that a new epoch begins for Blake in the shift from energy to imagination as the centerpiece of his thinking. In terms of ethics, the shift from energy to imagination can be described in this way. In the early Blake, up until 1802–3, the major good that Blake praises is not so much energy but the contrariety he envisions when reason ceases its war against energy: the valorization of energy, which seems to be Blake's ostensible purpose, is placed in its contrary context by the titles of two of the most important works from those days, *The Songs of Innocence and of Experience, shewing the Contrary States of the Human Soul,* and *The Marriage of Heaven and Hell.* The ethical imperative in the second half of Blake's career is forgiveness, or the identification of the imagination of the individual with Los and/or Jesus, the two figures Blake variously uses to signify the exemplar of virtue.

Why does forgiveness function as the magnetic pole of my realignment of the terms *Blake* and *ethics*? Throughout this book I am concerned most with ethical forgiveness, that is, the problem of human beings forgiving each other, rather than the theological problem of God forgiving human beings. The term *forgiveness,* like an individual word in Ferdinand de Saussure's linguistics, not only has a referential meaning to specific human or divine acts; it also possesses a structural meaning, functioning within a conceptual system and shifting its meaning when transplanted to a different system. As I will be using it here, the concept of forgiveness functions within three different ethical frames—which are not of course mutually exclusive—the ethics of obligation, the ethics of virtue, and the ethics of care and alterity. My basic definition of forgiveness is derived from Hannah Arendt, who writes that in forgiveness "*what* was done is forgiven for the sake of *who* did it." She contends that forgiveness establishes an eminently personal relationship organized by love, for, she continues, "only love has the power to forgive. For love, although it is one of the rarest occurrences in human lives, indeed possesses an unequaled power of self-revelation and an unequaled clarity of vision for the disclosure of *who,* precisely because it is unconcerned to the point of total unworldliness with *what* the loved person may be, with his qualities and shortcomings no less than with his achievements, failings, and transgressions" (original emphasis).[16]

This exposition of forgiveness begins with its place in the interstices of the systems of obligation and virtue: in drawing attention to *what* was done, it serves as part of the redress for the violation of obligations—crimes, sins, and so forth. Arendt further suggests the function of the virtues in an act of forgiveness: it is an act of love for the other, and, moreover, an act of creativity: forgiveness is "the only reaction which does not merely re-act but acts anew and unexpectedly, unconditioned by the act which provoked it and therefore freeing from its consequences both the one who forgives and the one who is forgiven."[17]

Forgiveness, then, interweaves the accounts of obligation and virtue. Part of the reason for the usefulness of forgiveness as a magnetic pole, or, to switch metaphors, as a fault line, is that forgiveness provides a useful line of demarcation between Aristotelian and New Testament ethics. Aristotle dismisses the practice of forgiveness, writing in the *Nicomachean Ethics:* "If a man accepts another man as good, and he turns out badly and is seen to do so, must one still love him? Surely it is impossible, since not everything can be loved, but only what is good. . . . But the man who breaks off such a friendship would seem to be doing nothing strange."[18] As MacIntyre points out, such a conclusion makes sense given Aristotle's definition of friendship as shared allegiance to the good.[19] Furthermore, forgiveness requires "that the offender already accepts as just the verdict of the law upon his action and behaves as one who acknowledges the justice of the appropriate punishment." Added to this conceptual acknowledgment is the acceptance of the claim of personhood: "The practice of forgiveness presupposes the practices of justice, but there is this crucial difference. Justice is characteristically administered by a judge, an impersonal authority representing the whole community; but forgiveness can only be extended by the offended party. The virtue exhibited in forgiveness is charity."[20] It is in the imperative to charity, that is, to forgiveness, that the New Testament departs the most from Aristotelian ethics.

For our purposes, the final strand of ethical system implicated in the definition of forgiveness is the ethics of alterity. Arendt's emphasis on the revelation of the self and disclosure of the other in the act of forgiveness fits logically into the systems of ethics that concern themselves with the possibility of an authentic encounter of self with other. In this elaborated account, then, forgiveness, like the death of Oedipus's father, lies at the place where three roads meet: the ethics of obligation, in the matter of forgiving what was done; the ethics of virtue, in the matter of the motive of love and the virtue of creativity; and the ethics of alterity, in implying a deep and abiding concern for the other who is disclosed. In this elaborated account, forgiveness serves as an index of the strengths and the limits of Blake's two sequential ethical systems as a whole, and especially of his engagement with the ethics of obligation, opposition to which had no public spokesman in his time. Fundamentally, in the first part of his career, Blake opposed the ethics of obligation in terms implicitly similar to the recovery of an ethics of virtue: most notably the primacy of individuality (what he called contrariety) over universalizability.

But in the second part of his career, Blake, in a sense, defected, by practicing a version of the fault in obligation-based ethics that he earlier deplored—that is, its emphasis on the universalized individual. In preferring the metaphors of brotherhood, readership, and friendship, he privileged same-sex reconciliation and thus, in excluding the female figures, seems to exile the principle of otherness. For theorizing about forgiveness continually acknowledges the personhood of the one forgiven. Forgiveness, as Arendt writes, discloses to us the who, the person, for whose sake we forgive what was done. Forgiveness thus reveals the other person in his or her radical otherness.[21] Forgiveness depends on a certain emotional traffic that runs both ways. When we see the other, who has offended us, as a suffering human being, we project outward our own experience of suffering, an experience that we know intimately only when it is our own suffering, onto the other. Then we feel compassion for him as for ourselves. And, in the other direction, when we see the offense, the evil the other has done, as a possibility for ourselves, we project inward into ourselves the evil that we feel most keenly when it is imposed on us from outside, from another. As Reinhold Niebuhr has written, forgiveness is "the demand that the evil in the other shall be borne without vindictiveness because the evil in the self is known."[22] Niebuhr's formulation allows for self-knowledge, knowing the evil in oneself as a basis for forgiving the other's. But in Niebuhr's formulation, since those two evils need not be the same evil, the otherness of the other is maintained. Thus for Niebuhr, the identification with the other goes only so far as the recognition that self and other both do evil, though our specific vices may differ. Forgiveness serves as an occasion of recognizing otherness—a step Blake takes with great ambivalence and reluctance.

The central irony of Blake's emerging concerns with friendship and forgiveness in the second half of his career is that his mythology increasingly led him to formulations that minimize or deny altogether the intractable otherness of other human beings. It is not only that, as Paley and Damrosch have both written, Blake was a dualist who wished he were a monist—such a position on Blake has ample justification and applies to numerous strains of his thought. It is also that Blake's individualism dominates his pluralism completely. As Laurence S. Lockridge writes, "his mythology of the self, even because of its profundity, makes problematic the extension of the self to social world."[23] To Lockridge's observation that "Blakean psychology inhibits full acknowledgement of other lives,"[24] I can add that the late treatment of forgiveness demonstrates the pervasiveness of that inhibition.

To help the reader anticipate the whole, I shall summarize the outline of this essay. Here I employ the notion of forgiveness as a fault line for the two successive ethical models Blake took on. In the first half of his career, when he was most engaged with critiquing the flaws of duty and obligation, Blake's work partially took on the problem of the unity of the virtues. Chapters 1 and 2 examine this partly solved problem in Blake. This first chapter looks at Blake as antinomian, with the unstated but implied position that resistance to rules is itself the unifying principle of ethics. (Jesus broke all ten of the commandments and acted from impulse, not from rules.) The second chapter looks at Blake's explorations not of the unity of the virtues, but of the possibility of unifying the vices under the rubric of "error." Blake never quite took the step that knowledge or enlightenment provides the unifying virtue to counteract this vice.

Chapters 3, 4, and 5 constitute the second conceptual division of my study, in which I argue that forgiveness is a fulcrum that allowed Blake to balance two contradictory impulses in his life and thought. As several important Blake scholars have demonstrated, the problem of dualism and unity plagued Blake throughout his life and came to particular intensity in the late period of his life, when the ethical ideal of contrariety no longer seemed to serve by itself. Three influential Blake critics summarize the problem. Paley first opened up discussion of this question by his contention that "Blake was a monist who found his mythology entrapping him in a dualistic position"; Damrosch read the philosophical underpinnings of Blake and concluded, "Blake is a dualist who wishes he were a monist." Morris Eaves, who does not take the dualistic line on Blake that Paley implies and Damrosch espouses, in reading the metaphors of Blake rather than the philosophy, states that "commentators who confuse metaphors of identity with metaphors of transaction inevitably fail at explaining theories of art such as Blake's."[25] Eaves's distinction between meta-

phors of identity and metaphors of transaction proves extremely fruitful for examining the question of dualism and monism in Blake. For forgiveness is a metaphor that Blake wanted to serve both purposes, to stand the middle ground between transaction and identity. In its most common acceptance, forgiveness assumes a relation of transaction between individual, historically conditioned and differentiated human beings. In this line of thinking, human forgiveness remedies the problem of human failings in such relationships. Blake referred to these concepts, deliberately echoing this set of nuances. Yet, on the other side, Blake took forgiveness as the very process by which the transaction is changed into an identity. He imagined forgiveness as the process by which a person, often a reader or a writer, becomes identified with his exemplar, either Jesus or Los. In the late poems, then, I shall argue, forgiveness became absolutely central to Blake because it bridges the contradiction between transaction with an other and identity with him. Since the theorizing of Levinas and Irigaray becomes pertinent in the second half of the study, I will postpone a fuller discussion of them until chapter 3. For the time being we can focus on the conflict of virtue and obligation in Blake's treatment of forgiveness, mostly in the first half of his career.

Forgiveness
"Written Within & Without" Law

The title of this chapter alludes to *Milton*, when Jesus descends with "The Clouds of Ololon folded as a Garment dipped in blood / Written within & without in woven letters" (*M* 42:12–13; E, 143). I intend this allusion in a couple of different ways. First, any design, whether it be letters or other patterns, will be woven both "within" and "without," that is, it will show on both the inside and the outside of the piece of cloth. The "within" and the "without" will present mirror images of each other. I submit that this metaphor of the woven garment fittingly describes Blake's complex attitude toward law and antinomianism, and that in fact Blake came to a position critiquing antinomianism as merely the obverse of law and obligation. Second, Blake's use of the figure of the garment frequently alludes to the rending of the veil of the Temple at Jesus' crucifixion and thus to the dawning of a new dispensation.[1] I adopt this sense of the metaphor to underline that in his later work Blake came to view forgiveness as a new dispensation, along the lines of an ethics of virtue, almost achieving an independent conceptual status, written successfully "without" the dispensation of law.

In this chapter I examine the segment of Blake's oeuvre usually cited to support the claim that his ethical position most resembles that of the antinomians. While this generalization holds true, by and large, for the first half of Blake's career (until 1803), I find that even in his most antinomian passages, Blake simultaneously approves antinomianism and critiques the logical trap into which antinomianism falls: namely, that any lawbreaking depends, logically and temporally, on prior lawgiving; thus, it has no independent conceptual foundations. In addition, I find that Blake's famous celebrations of female sexual "transgressions" frequently present a distorted form of the antinomian logic that inspired them, distorted by Blake's ambivalences about sexuality. In antinomian logic any violation of the law is as good as any other, for the point is to break the rule of law and be free. However, Blake sometimes allowed advocacy of sexual freedom to dominate the stage, so that sexual acts become the normative expression of freedom rather than just one alternative among several. My final discovery in relation to Blake's antinomianism is that, in the second half of his career, Blake recast both these themes, the critique of antinomianism and the celebration of female sexual "transgressions," in terms approaching an ethics of virtue. Blake attempted this recasting most fruitfully in his 1818 fragment, *The Everlasting Gospel*.

Before proceeding to Blake, it may be useful to review the historical conditions of antinomians in the 1780s and 1790s, including the relation of antinomianism to various religious movements, the place of sexual transgression in the logical structure of antinomianism, and the overall logical premises of the ethics of antinomianism.[2] According to A. L. Morton, the term *antinomianism* was sometimes applied to a specific sect but more generally referred to a tendency in several religious sects—Ranters, Seekers, Muggletonians, Traskites, Shakers, and Quakers—which had survived in England since the Commonwealth. They persisted among the working classes of London until Blake's day, in keeping with a tradition of sympathy for political revolution fostered during the English civil wars and later during the 1790s. They described politics in the language of religious revolution, hoping for the dawn of a new age. The specific framework of this millenarianism comes from the Italian mystic Joachim of Flora, who "taught that the history of the world fell into three ages, those of the Father, the Son, and of the Holy Ghost. The first was the age of fear and servitude, and ended with the death of Christ, the second was the age of faith and filial obedience, and the third, which was to be expected shortly, was the age of love and spiritual liberty for the children of God. The scripture of the first age was the Old Testament, of the second the New Testament. In the coming age of the Spirit the full truth of the Everlasting Gospel will be revealed, not in a new sacred book but in a new revelation of the spiritual sense of the Bible with which God will illuminate the hearts of men."[3] These antinomians believed that God existed in human beings and sometimes that God had no other existence. They further believed that the moral laws resulting from the earlier stages of human history were no longer binding on them, as they had already passed into a third dispensation, the

"Age of the Holy Spirit." This third age, partly already realized in them and partly still to be realized, would be characterized by a new kind of morality in which liberty would replace obedience.[4]

In the interval between the English Revolution and the French Revolution, the antinomianism latent in some sects, such as Quakers, became more inward, as the practitioners began to wait for the kingdom within and "patiently to suffer from the world."[5] Thus antinomianism persisted in some forms even in the increasingly respectable dissenting sects, though the more unruly strain of antinomianism persisted as well. John Wesley noted in his *Journal* for 1768 that in Somersetshire he found "a mixture of men of all opinions, Anabaptists, Quakers, Presbyterians, Arians, Antinomians, Moravians and what not."[6] In the 1790s fear and hope about the French Revolution and its potential for ushering in the millennium strengthened antinomian sentiment among the artisans and working classes in London. Two millenarian movements gained considerable currency: those of Richard Brothers (1757–1824), the "Prince of the Hebrews" who told the English Parliament in 1792 that the war against France was the war predicted in the Book of Revelation; and Joanna Southcott (1750–1814), who also preached a new age, broke with Brothers in 1802, and in the final years of her life claimed she would give birth to the new Messiah, Shiloh. The strength of these movements, Paley suggests, demonstrates that the pursuit of the millennium did not stop with the seventeenth-century antinomians but flourished in Blake's time and beyond; further, Blake knew about these matters from his acquaintance John Gabriel Stedman, his friend William Sharp, and the public press.[7]

Antinomianism, for all its energy and appeal, remained riddled with logical contradictions. As Gertrude Huehns observes, these contradictions arose from the antinomians' combination of "the clear-cut alternative of Calvinism, damnation or salvation, with the Arminians' belief that assurance as to one's place on earth in the final scheme of things may well be gained here on earth."[8] In other words, antinomians felt themselves saved or damned and believed that, once assured of their election, they could not act in any way to annul it. There is no question of perfectibility, for they saw perfection as instantaneous. Huehns further argues that the antinomians placed exclusive emphasis on the infusion of grace as an emotional experience, so that once they possessed that emotional conviction, no other principle of ethics could be consulted to question it, as they discarded the notions of reason and of ecclesiastic tradition. For the purposes of this argument, the crucial matter is that the antinomians could never distinguish an independent principle of action, as Huehns writes: "They carried into every relation of life the ambiguity of their attitude towards the 'law,' denying it and affirming it almost simultaneously."[9] This ambiguity is manifested in the seventeenth-century antinomian Thomas Collier, who writes that Christians shall "live above the Law in the Letter, even of the Gospel, yet not without it, for they have it within them . . . and so they are a Law to themselves."[10] Thus the very logical structure of antinomianism replicates the ambiguity of its name, which always contains the principle of *nomos*, or law. Antinomianism, interwoven with law, consistently re-presents the obverse image of the system it seeks to escape.

When it is written only within the context of law and antilaw, "nomianism" and antinomianism, forgiveness runs the risk of becoming what Blake later calls "false forgiveness," an operation that merely reproduces the status quo of an ethics of obligation. In other words, within a system of obligation, forgiveness functions parasitically to perpetuate the system. Blake always valued certain goods for human beings, among them the vision achieved through sensual enjoyment and the recognition of individual genius in contrariety. As long as laws infringed on those goods, disobeying them remained a positive action, because of the end (vision or contrariety) achieved in the action itself, the action that happened incidentally to be forbidden. But, when the antinomian position implies that the essence of human good lies in the very violation of the law, then the antinomian position has reached its logical limit, a limit Blake gradually came to recognize. Blake recognized an analogous logical problem in his remarks about the doctrine of the atonement: "Thinking as I do that the Creator of this World is a very Cruel Being & being a Worshipper of Christ I cannot help saying the Son O how unlike the Father First God Almighty comes with a Thump on the Head Then Jesus Christ comes with a balm to heal it" (E, 565). As Blake acutely realized, the "balm" here has no absolute effect or goodness; it is only a remedy for a previous wrong. The paradox is that it depends on the previous thump on the head for its efficacy.

The potential for logical contradiction, already considerable within antinomianism, grows greater when the privileged example of lawbreaking is sexual activity. Although the resurgence of antinomianism in the 1790s also addressed the questions of democracy and monarchy, the primacy of sexuality differentiates this phase of antinomianism from the earlier one. Among all the political controversies and unrest of the 1790s—the Reign of Terror, food shortages of 1795, and the crises of the Napoleonic Wars, antinomian sects were also confronted directly with a society examining marriage laws. There is a streak of antinomianism in Emanuel Swedenborg, in the proposition that "all have a capacity to be regenerated, because all are redeemed," echoed in the

New Jerusalem Church's Proposition 33, "Now it is allowable to enter into the Mysteries of Faith," and on the inscription over the door of the Swedenborgian New Jerusalem Church in Eastcheap: "Now it is allowable."[11] Sexuality figured prominently in the controversies of the day over what was now "allowable." The Swedenborgian church itself, in its "concubinage dispute," suffered division over what was allowable sexually. As Paley explains, the dispute arose over plans for religious practice and governance in a proposed Swedenborgian colony.[12] This proposal offered a compromise when the ideal of a marriage between two Swedenborgian believers could not be met: believing men with nonbelieving wives could take a believing concubine (while refraining from sexual relations with their wives), and believing men who legally married nonbelieving women were said to be living in concubinage. Even though this proposal merely articulated a mechanism for a practice allowed by Swedenborg himself, the New Jerusalem Church in England rejected it, probably to dissociate itself from all kinds of radicalism, following the English reaction to the French Revolution and to Jacobin morality. As a result, several prominent Swedenborgians were expelled from the community. Thus in the 1790s the antinomian potential in Swedenborg's writings was obviated by his followers in deference to English marriage laws.

In addition, the 1780s had seen substantial controversy over marriage laws, in the form of agitation for the repeal of the Clandestine Marriage Act of 1753, an act that required that "all Banns of Matrimony shall be published in an audible manner on the three Sundays preceding the marriage."[13] This law was generally perceived, as E. B. Murray has shown, as a rich man's law "to keep young heirs (young heiresses were less likely victims) from the clutches of the hostler's daughter by a precipitate marriage the morning after a night in bed."[14] Controversy over this law was stirred up by a Methodist preacher, Martin Madan, in a polemic entitled "Thelyphthora; or, a Treatise on the Female Ruin." Madan argued that the sexual act was in fact a marriage, and that "any man who seduced a virgin, *even if he was already married*, had, in effect, wed her and should be held accountable to her for all his days" (Murray's emphasis).[15] Despite Madan's evident concern for the female victims of ruin and seduction, his numerous and voluble opponents found him a villain, not a hero; focusing on the imputed humiliation of the British woman under a polygamous system, they bristled at the implication that polygamy was allowable, nay, inevitable, under biblical law. His polemic engendered substantial outcry, creating his reputation as the "polygamous parson," and, in short, keeping the matter of what was allowable in marriage steadily in the public eye for three years as the House of Commons debated the law's repeal.

Thus, in the decades of the 1780s and '90s, the matters of law and antilaw, *nomos* and antinomianism, became deeply enmeshed with the paradoxes of sexuality, marriage, and gender, so much so that Blake often writes of sexual experience as a privileged mode of freedom. Harold Bloom has underlined Blake's vision of the connection between the two: "Sexual excess leads to antinomian perception."[16] Logically, of course, Blake, like his antinomian predecessors, viewed repressive marriage laws as part of a more fundamentally corrupt institution, the law itself. Sometimes, however, within this ethic of law (*nomos*) and its mirror image in an antinomian ethic of defiance, defiance of sexual laws, rather than other laws, takes on a disproportionately important place. In the mixed context of sexuality and law, Blake's antinomian response to forgiveness partakes of some blind spots common to his day.

The ambivalence Blake manifests toward sexuality has been examined by Susan Fox, Alicia Ostriker, and Anne K. Mellor. Ostriker presents four sets of Blakean attitudes toward women and sexuality, and usefully explains that Blake sometimes held contradictory attitudes simultaneously, not simply sequentially. The early antinomian poems I shall be examining are usually grouped unproblematically in Blake's antinomian camp, Ostriker's Blake Number One who believes sexuality should be unfettered. At times, however, strains of Ostriker's Blake Number Four emerge even in this early period, the Blake who contends that the proper study of woman is the happiness of her man. This Blake Number Four distorts the portrayal of Oothoon in *Visions of the Daughters of Albion* and skews the portrayal of forgiveness there along gendered lines.

It is within this profoundly messy context that Blake treats law and antinomianism in his early works. In *The Marriage of Heaven and Hell* and in *Visions of the Daughters of Albion*, Blake simultaneously advocates the antinomian course of disobeying law in order to be free of it and also critiques the inextricable interweaving of antinomian actions with a system of obligation-based ethics. This picture is complicated by the distortions that obtain when Blake, unlike the seventeeth-century antinomians, takes women's sexual "transgression" as the proving ground of his antinomian case. These works also demonstrate Blake's emerging protrayal of accusation as a vice, a tendency that leads him in the later works to define forgivingness as a virtue along the lines of a disposition-based ethics.

Blake's deeply antinomian work *The Marriage of Heaven and Hell* consistently opposes religious authorities, the priests and churches who claim to dispense divine forgiveness to human beings.[17] While Swedenborg comes under particular fire, Blake also takes aim at the very foundation of religious hierarchies in plate 11. There he recounts a mythic past in which poets endowed the world with names, "Till a system was formed, which some took advantage of & enslav'd the vulgar by attempting to realize or abstract the mental dieties [*sic*] from their objects: thus began Priesthood" (*MHH* 11; E, 38). These priests, motivated by the desire for power, "enslav'd the vulgar," alienating them from the source of religious and imaginative life: "Thus men forgot that All deities reside in the human breast" (*MHH* 11; E, 38). With such persons controlling the discourse of law and transgression, forgiveness is naturally suspect, either as the "false forgiveness" that an unjust society metes out to its unfortunates, or as the last resort of weaklings and victims.

This latter sense of forgiveness, from the victim's point of view, provides a partial explanation for Blake's first presentation of "forgiveness" in the *Marriage*. Among the seventy Proverbs of Hell, Blake presents this maxim: "The cut worm forgives the plow" (*MHH* 7:6; E, 35). A parallel proverb soon follows: "A dead body revenges not injuries" (*MHH* 7:16; E, 36). Both proverbs address the plight of the victim, an exceptionally helpless victim. As Martin Nurmi points out, the Proverbs of Hell "are told from the point of view of infernal wisdom, not advocating contrariety but advocating energy."[18] From this partisan point of view, both proverbs suggest that to forgive means to refrain from revenge, not out of deliberate renunciation of it, but out of the utter helplessness of death. The corpses forgive because they cannot do otherwise. Thus in both cases the act of forgiveness is not, properly speaking, an act at all, but merely the passive complicity of victims in their own oppression—a possibility that will arise again in Oothoon's forgiveness of her oppressive lover Theotormon. While these proverbs do take into account the victim's suffering,[19] they also show a certain contempt for the passivity of the victims they pity, an attitude that Blake the poet does not necessarily share.

The advocate of energy who speaks in the Proverbs shows mixed pity and contempt for the passive victim, but he admires the active plowman unreservedly. This admiration for plowing and for active work in general manifests itself in the entire group of proverbs concerning plowing.[20] The other proverbs in this group are "Drive your cart and your plow over the bones of the dead" (*MHH* 7:2; E, 35); "As the plow follows words, so God rewards prayers" (*MHH* 9:43; E, 37); and "Prayers plow not! Praises reap not! / Joys laugh not! Sorrows weep not!" (*MHH* 9:59–60; E, 37). Perhaps the proverb "Where man is not nature is barren" (*MHH* 10:68; E, 38), in its concern for fertility, also belongs to this group.[21] As a group, the proverbs take the point of view of the energetic plowman, whose work surpasses in importance the sanctity of burial grounds.[22] This plowman, moreover, actually achieves through his work what prayers and praises fail to accomplish, and in so doing, the active plowman receives the answer from God denied to the passive repeaters of prayers. Blake's praise of the plowman follows a venerable literary tradition beginning with Jesus' saying, "No man, having put his hand to the plow, and looking back, is fit for the kingdom of God" (Luke 9:62), and continuing through Chaucer's Plowman (for whom Blake expresses admiration). In his later works Blake contributes the plowman Palamabron to this tradition. From energy's point of view, then, the proverb celebrates the ability of the severed earthworm to divide into two worms, and so to overcome any seemingly harmful effects of the bold plowman.[23] Blake's proverb includes both his protest against the social forces that give victims a passive "forgiveness" as their only choice, and also a certain contempt for that passivity in favor of active energy. Forgiveness by victims, then, is tainted.

Others of the Proverbs of Hell imply Blake's position that sexual acts are central to the expression of energy, such as "Sooner murder an infant in its cradle than nurse unacted desires" and "Prudence is a rich ugly old maid courted by Incapacity" (*MHH* 10:67, 7:4; E, 38, 35). Nonetheless, they also admit interpretations that Blake advocates other actions besides sexual ones, resulting in the implication that sexual expression takes its place as one act among several possible choices of freedom from law.

This exposition of the antinomian theme that it is violation itself that matters, not the violation of any particular commandment, takes pride of place at the end of the *Marriage*, in a "Memorable Fancy" which has the effect of converting its angelic hearer to the devil's party. Blake's Devil speaks: "now hear how [Jesus Christ] has given his sanction to the law of ten commandments: did he not mock at the sabbath, and so mock the sabbaths God? murder those who were murderd because of him? turn away the law from the woman taken in adultery? steal the labour of others to support him? bear false witness when he omitted making a defence before Pilate? covet when he pray'd for his disciples, and when he bid them shake off the dust of their feet against such as refused to lodge them? I tell you, no virtue can exist without breaking these ten commandments: Jesus was all virtue, and acted from impulse, not from rules" (*MHH* 23–24; E, 43). Here Blake's speaker reads black where authorities read white, in a passage that may indeed shed more heat than light.[24] The speaker contends that the Ten Commandments, and all other laws, repress persons of greatest genius, such as Jesus. One escapes that bondage by breaking the laws, and in so doing, discerning one's own gifts and finding the vision that religions promise but fail to deliver. Jesus, the person of "impulse," serves as a model of activity, which passive victims in the situation of the cut worm can emulate.

Yet the poet suggests the limits of the speaker's words, revealing the curiously parasitic relationship between lawgiving and lawbreaking, in which antinomian practices "without" law are deeply interwoven with obligations "within" law. Blake, if he were to "speak straight," might contend that Jesus' active exercise of vision and of sexuality are themselves praiseworthy, and that the breaking of the law is not praiseworthy in itself. For if, as the speaker contends, Jesus' actions are motivated by the desire to break each of the commandments, then law merely governs his actions in reverse. "Impulse" provides no relief from "rules" because impulse has no independent motive. Impulse functions as a parasite in the body of the host of rules. A similar logical problem arises in the passage about Jesus breaking the commandments. Any freedom achieved through Jesus' lawbreaking always logically depends on a previous lawgiving.

Such an impasse has serious implications for any version of forgiveness. The antinomians hoped to achieve liberty from the law by breaking it, scorning forgiveness as a means for lawgivers to consolidate their power. Yet unless antinomianism finds some independent principle, other than violation of the law for its own sake, on which to base its action, no real liberty is achieved. The failure to find a principle independent of law similarly fetters anyone who would like to forgive. Without it, continual forgiveness depends parasitically on continuous transgression. Thus Blake reveals the logical dead end of antinomianism, articulated in Saint Paul, "Shall we then continue in sin, that grace may abound?" (Rom. 6:12).

In *Visions of the Daughters of Albion*, Blake continues in his complex relation with antinomianism: on the one hand endorsing the lawbreaking as valuable while at the same time revealing the interweaving of lawbreaking and lawgiving. And the poem further suggests the distorting power of the example of women's sexual transgression in representing the problems of law, antinomianism, and forgiveness.

Blake's advocacy of the antinomian position for breaking laws emerges in the portrayal of Oothoon, who achieves prophetic insight along with her first sexual act. Oothoon travels to her betrothed, Theotormon, in a flush of affection and desire. On her way, she is raped by the slavemaster Bromion. Upon discovering the rape, Theotormon broods over Oothoon's "sin" and cannot forgive her. Oothoon laments the system that has kept her mind and her senses locked up. In this work Blake views laws of sexual repression and laws promoting conformity, in his characteristically synchronic way, as identical and, similarly, views as identical assertions of sexuality and assertions of individual genius, since they undermine (or overthrow) that unjust law. In *Visions* Oothoon discovers and expresses her sexuality and her individual genius as part of the same unified action.

Blake's critique of antinomianism takes shape in the interweaving of the lawgiver Theotormon and the lawbreaking Bromion. In fact, Oothoon once addresses Theotormon as Urizen, "mistaken Demon of heaven" (*VDA* 5:3; E, 48), in a prolepsis of Blake's later myth of the Four Zoas. The illustrations show him consistently isolated and self-absorbed: clasping his head and hiding his eyes in the frontispiece; head on his knees in plate 4; tormenting himself with a cat-o-nine-tails in plate 6.[25] Theotormon torments not only himself; he "severely smiles" when Oothoon cries for his eagles to "prey upon her flesh" (*VDA* 2:18, 13; E, 46).[26] Despite Oothoon's initial attempts to appease him by claiming she is pure, and despite her later attempts to provide a social critique of the supposed virtue of modesty, Theotormon remains unresponsive most of the time, "fold[ing] his black jealous waters round the adulterate pair" (*VDA* 2:4; E, 46). When he does speak, he laments only his own woe and loss, "a present sorrow and a night of pain" (*VDA* 4:7; E, 48), neglecting to consider Oothoon's sorrow and pain. Throughout the poem he accepts Bromion's evaluation of Oothoon as "Bromions harlot" (*VDA* 2:1; E, 46). While Theotormon does not accuse Oothoon explicitly, in his passivity he assents to Bromion's accusing epithet "harlot." Moreover, his silent, severe smile speaks volumes about his approval of Oothoon's self-recriminations.

In fact, one of the most interesting parts of the poem is Blake's portrayal of the logical paradox of antinomianism in the interweaving of Bromion and Theotormon. The burden of the poem is that Theotormon's offense, of accusing Oothoon, is by far the more serious matter. In fact, Blake suggests that Bromion enacts the repressed desires of Theotormon, so that Bromion's offense in breaking the law is, curiously, an integral part of Theotormon's offense in promulgating the law and accusing Oothoon in its terms.

Blake further stresses the interweaving of Bromion and Theotormon in Oothoon's speeches, which reveal clearly the dependence of lust on repression, of lawbreaking on lawgiving:

> . . . the youth shut up from
> The lustful joy. shall forget to generate. & create an amorous image
> In the shadows of his curtains and in the folds of his silent pillow.
> (*VDA* 7:5–7; E, 50)

Theotormon, who has shut himself up from lustful joy, has created an amorous image and would like to act as Bromion has done. As D. G. Gillham observes, in relation to Oothoon, Theotormon and Bromion represent the two halves of a divided male personality, "a man composed, not of desires and satisfactions, but of lusts and restrictions." Gillham continues, "As Bromion, he rapes his wife Oothoon, and as Theotormon he makes both Oothoon and himself suffer in revulsion at what they have done."[27] Like the Jesus who acted from impulse, not from rules, Bromion merely accepts the sovereignty of those rules, in reverse. Further indications of their similarity are their common complicity in the slave trade[28] and their common assumption that a hostile god or law controls them.[29] One would expect that only Theotormon, the one tormented by theology, pictures the afterlife as punishment. Yet this picture comes from the mouth of Bromion:

> And is there not one law for both the lion and the ox?
> And is there not eternal fire, and eternal chains?
> To bind the phantoms of existence from eternal life?
>
> (*VDA* 4:22–24; E, 48)

Bromion here denies the contrariety of lion and ox as part of the theological torment of "eternal fire, and eternal chains." Consistently, then, Bromion exemplifies what is implicit in Theotormon; they are part of the same system. The complicity of Bromion and Theotormon, lawbreaking and lawgiving, fits with Blake's critique of the logical paradox of antinomianism's dependence on a prior law.

When we examine Oothoon more closely, however, we see some of the problems in Blake's assumption that sexual "transgression" is a privileged form of antinomian activity. This distortion is exposed when we see that, on the most straightforward level, the plot of *Visions* ignores the most grievous crime, Bromion's rape of Oothoon. Even Oothoon in her best attempts at forgiveness remains locked in the system of lawgiving and lawbreaking created by Theotormon and Bromion.[30] Blake suggests the imprisonment of all three characters by the same mind-forged manacles, indeed within the same mind, in the frontispiece to *Visions*[31] (see figure 1). There Blake depicts them naked and paralyzed, Bromion manacled, his arms restraining Oothoon, who kneels before the brooding Theotormon. As Erdman observes, Blake masses the rocks, clouds, and sun to suggest a human face in the sky, with Bromion, Oothoon, and Theotormon grouped at the jaw, neck, and base of the skull.[32] This configuration suggests that all of them are contained within the "religious caves" of one mind.[33]

FIGURE 1.
Frontispiece to *Visions of the Daughters of Albion*
(The Tate Gallery, London/Art Resource, N.Y.)

Blake's peculiar emphasis on the status of sexually transgressive women skews the ethical implications of the poem, emphasizing the falseness of the false forgiveness Theotormon might offer Oothoon for her sexual activity, and eclipsing completely any consideration of the genuine forgiveness Oothoon might offer Bromion for the genuine harm done to her in rape. Blake expresses little interest in Oothoon's forgiving Bromion, the man who raped her. One would think that Bromion's offense provided the most obvious, and the most difficult, opportunity for forgiveness in the whole scenario. Blake does not see it quite that way, however.

The frontispiece foreshadows the frustration of Oothoon's attempts to forgive Theotormon later in the poem. Despite her superior insight, Oothoon's forgiveness remains ineffective because, to some extent, she cannot break free of the discourse of lawgiving and lawbreaking. To be sure, she approaches autonomy more closely than does Bromion, whose lawbreaking logically feeds on Theotormon's lawgiving. But forgiveness remains hampered by law and its categories.

Oothoon's instincts are generous, but she has no vocabulary other than that of lawgiving and lawbreaking by which to describe her vision of forgiveness. She says,

> But silken nets and traps of adamant will Oothoon spread,
> And catch for thee girls of mild silver, or of furious gold;
> I'll lie beside thee on a bank & view their wanton play
> In lovely copulation bliss on bliss with Theotormon:
> Red as the rosy morning, lustful as the first born beam,
> Oothoon shall view his dear delight, nor e'er with jealous cloud
> Come in the heaven of generous love; nor selfish blightings bring.
> (*VDA* 7:23–29; E, 50)

Here we see Oothoon at her generous best, as a prophetic character, her moment of desire functioning as a prototype for the later prophetic actions of Los and Milton.[34] Oothoon's earlier declamation of the Blakean doctrine of contrariety and her present attempt to forgive set her in prophetic company. Despite the dominant tone of approval for Oothoon and her attempt to forgive Theotormon, her vision of forgiveness has some disquieting recessive features. One of them is that Oothoon remakes Theotormon in the image of Bromion. He will break the same law he currently upholds, but, as Blake's analysis of Bromion has made clear, he will remain subject to that law. Transferred from the category of lawgiver (and accuser) to the category of lawbreaker,

Theotormon will copulate "bliss on bliss" with girls of "mild silver" or "furious gold." From Blake's point of view, of course, Oothoon admirably rises above sexual jealousy.[35] Her vision reveals the renunciation of any sexual jealousy such as Theotormon has so annoyingly exhibited throughout. Yet in this vision she herself remains excluded, as a voyeur, loving perhaps but not beloved. Her vision thus imitates the flaws in the situation she has been given. Currently Theotormon the lawgiver shuns her; Theotormon as lawbreaker still will not love her. Oothoon reads black where Theotormon reads white.

The intrusion of Blake's view of women's subservience begins to distort Oothoon's vision of forgiveness. In addition to making over Theotormon in the image of Bromion, she does the same for herself. Thinking that she is promoting "free love," she acts like the violent Bromion, trapping the girls of silver and gold just as Bromion trapped her. Thus free love is anything but free. Her first remark reveals her readiness to entrap:

> But silken nets and traps of adamant will Oothoon spread,
> And catch for thee girls of mild silver, or of furious gold."
>
> (*VDA* 7:23–24; E, 50)

As Blake himself made clear in his poem "How sweet I roam'd," silken nets confine as surely as iron cages. This love that Oothoon imagines is hardly free for the "girls" so entrapped. Thus Oothoon's vision of forgiveness and free love is limited by the same resort to compulsion that characterized Bromion's violence toward her.

Oothoon's forgiveness, in effect, substitutes the ethics of the lawbreaker Bromion for those of the lawgiver Theotormon. Yet Blake had already deliberately shown that Bromion's and Theotormon's ethics merely mirror each other. In depicting Oothoon's forgiveness, Blake advanced to a little patch of new ground, though its logical underpinnings remain complicit in the law, complicit like the Jesus who broke all the commandments and the Bible reader who merely reads black where the law reads white. The work's final plate holds in balance both Oothoon's prophecy and also her limits. Blake shows her flying freely like the figurehead of a ship, borne by the clouds that had formerly served as her bed of torment.[36] Yet the sense of imprisonment evoked in the frontispiece remains in the closing line, a refrain throughout the poem: "The Daughters of Albion hear her woes. & eccho back her sighs" (*VDA* 2:20, 5:2, 8:13; E, 46).

Despite the logical frustration of Oothoon's forgiveness, Blake's thinking

about forgiveness here looks forward to some important themes in the prophecies. Theotormon has nothing, really, to forgive. Oothoon is blameless, even praiseworthy. But for Theotormon to realize that fact would require him to perform an act that feels like forgiveness. Oothoon, by contrast, does have something evil to forgive, or at least the glimmer of something evil—complicity in an ethic of accusation. Despite Blake's avoidance of the word *forgiveness,* here he anticipates a paradox fully articulated in the prophecies, that accusation of another's sin is itself the sin most in need of forgiveness.

Blake's concern with the practice of forgiveness subsides in *The Book of Urizen*.[37] He focuses on Urizen's laws of universal conformity, and so provides further analysis of the character of the accuser. Insofar as Blake does treat the theme of forgiveness explicitly, he implies that the institutions of law compromise and defeat any attempt at forgiveness.

Blake's development of the portrait of the accuser complements the earlier portrait in *Visions of the Daughters of Albion*. In *Visions* Blake revealed the sexual repression that motivates Theotormon, the accuser of one who violates sexual prohibitions. In *Urizen* Blake shows that denial of contrariety, that is, of individual genius, lies at the root of accusation.[38] The "Preludium" links Urizen to the accusers Blake mentioned in the *Marriage* when it declares its subject matter: "Of the primeval Priests assum'd power" (*BU* 2:1; E, 70). And early in the poem Urizen expresses his desire to escape the contraries of life:

> I have sought for a joy without pain,
> For a solid without fluctuation.
>
> (*BU* 4:10–11; E, 71)

Urizen's desire to homogenize the emotions and the physical universe has a corollary in the legislation of conformity on a group of individuals.

Within the context of Urizen's early denial of contrariety comes the sole mention of forgiveness. Having founded his own church on

> This rock, plac[ing] with strong hand the Book
> Of eternal brass
>
> (*BU* 4:31–33; E, 72)

in a parody of the foundation of Christianity, Urizen legislates

> Laws of peace, of love, of unity:
> Of pity, compassion, forgiveness.
>
> (*BU* 4:34–35; E, 72)

He continues:

> Let each chuse one habitation:
> His ancient infinite mansion:
> One command, one joy, one desire,
> One curse, one weight, one measure
> One King, one God, one Law.
>
> (*BU* 4:36–40; E, 72)

Urizen's benevolent beginnings deserve note: he begins by seeking peace, love, unity, pity, compassion, and forgiveness. It is customary to read this passage as a revelation of Urizen's hypocrisy, in which the demand for conformity is his true motive.[39] But Urizen's speech suggests instead a corollary to a theme we saw in *Visions*, the theme of the frustration of forgiveness.

This frustration is due in part to the inadequacy of Urizen's terms. He seeks these goods by means of laws, which always have the potential to repress. Moreover, Urizen equivocates about the meaning of *unity*. He declares his intention to establish "Laws of peace, of love, of unity" (*BU* 4:34; E, 72). All the other terms in this series—peace, love, pity, compassion, forgiveness—presuppose a relationship between two or more persons. If *unity* is to belong in this series, it must be the kind of unity-in-diversity that respects the otherness of the other, a respect implied in the metaphor of marriage, which Blake used earlier, or the metaphor of brotherhood, which he adopts later. But Urizen takes up the conceptually simpler version of unity, in which all are uniform, and this uniformity is the leitmotif of his next lines: "Let each chuse one habitation: / His ancient infinite mansion." In direct contrast to Jesus' hope of many mansions in the Father's house (John 14:2), Urizen houses everyone in the same facilities. Thus "unity" has become uniformity.

What are the consequences for forgiveness of this slip from unity to uniformity? In his rage for order, Urizen has lost the legitimate reconciliation of others that "laws of forgiveness" might bring about, in favor of enforcing that very otherness out of existence. Upon further reflection, it becomes clear that Urizen's oxymoron, "laws of forgiveness," may lie at the root of the problem. In the *Marriage* we observed a portrait of Jesus in which Blake explored the possibility that antinomian violation might free one from the law, raising the problem that such violation seems to be governed in reverse by the same law. In *Visions* Oothoon's forgiveness was frustrated because she could imagine it only in terms that depended, like violation, on a previous structure of oppressive law. Urizen has less good will than Oothoon, and his weaker benevolence, like hers, fails to break free of the oppressive conceptual terms of the universal law. As W. J. T. Mitchell writes, in *Urizen* the creation of the law is the primal crime.[40] This is true because the creation of the law dictates the terms for any attempts to escape it.

Urizen functions as a containing character or ground for the action of the poem and for the other characters, much as Theotormon had functioned in *Visions*. Nelson Hilton has observed that Blake suggests even Los's dependence on the terms set by Urizen.[41] Urizen himself is the "death" (for the eternals so name him) upon which life depends, as he recognizes in his statement that "life liv'd upon death" (*BU* 23:27; E, 81).[42] Further, Blake's typography presents Urizen's speech as "Here alone I in books formd of metals" (*BU* 4:24; E, 72), a configuration of words and lines which suggests that all creativity, all books, are formed out of the raw material of "me," that is, of Urizen, the speaker.[43] Finally, Urizen's arrival on the scene anticipates and contains the arrival of Los by means of several anagrams of Los's name, such as "Obscure, shadowy, void, *sol*itary," "Self-*clos*'d, all repelling," and "That *sol*itary one" (Hilton's emphasis).[44] Urizen seems indeed to be determining the shape of things to come, even of Los, his apparent contrary.

One possible rationale for Blake's showing Los's dependence on Urizen may be his desire further to examine the relation between law and mercy that he hinted at in the *Marriage*. Blake's dismal creation scene, all critics acknowledge, recalls the book of Genesis. Leslie Tannenbaum has observed, further, that Blake drew from the biblical commentators who recognized the two separate creation accounts, modeling Urizen after the Elohim ("judges") and Los after the impulsive Jehovah. In early drafts of *Paradise Lost*, which Blake may have read, John Milton dramatized conflicting divine impulses at the creation as a debate between Justice, which accuses the human race, and Mercy, which pleads for it.[45] In the light of this background, it is possible that Blake suggested Los's dependence on Urizen as part of an ongoing doubt, a doubt that so-called mercy merely repeats the strictures of the law, reading black where justice reads white.

Be that as it may, it is more certain that Blake addressed the dependence of pity, frequently a motive for forgiveness, on the preexisting structure of the law. Los and Urizen each make serious efforts to express their pity. The difference between the two forms of pity is significant. Blake had earlier seen to the heart of the social uses of pity.[46] In *The Songs of Innocence and of Experience* he writes:

> Pity would be no more,
> If we did not make somebody Poor.
>
> (*SIE* 47:1–2; E, 27)

Like forgiveness, pity is inextricably linked with oppressive social institutions. Moreover, "pity divides the soul" (*BU* 13:53; E, 77) because the flowing out of emotion toward the other colludes with the love of one's own social superiority and of one's own apparent benevolence. Urizen's pity is of this type, stemming from his desire for an exclusive holiness.[47]

Blake places Urizen's pity in the context of a compensation. Urizen has just given up on his previous attempts to legislate uniformity on his children.

> . . . he curs'd
> Both sons & daughters; for he saw
> That no flesh nor spirit could keep
> His iron laws one moment.
>
> (*BU* 23:23–26; E, 81)

He renounces his laws in favor of another tactic of control, a net of pity and religion:

> And he wept, & he called it Pity
> And his tears flowed down on the winds.
>
> 7. Till a Web dark & cold, throughout all
> The tormented element stretch'd
> From the sorrows of Urizens soul
> And the Web is a Female in embrio
> None could break the Web, no wings of fire.
>
> 8. So twisted the cords, & so knotted
> The meshes: twisted like to the human brain
>
> 9. And all calld it, The Net of Religion.
>
> (*BU* 25:3–4, 15–22; E, 82)

The pity of Urizen, made palpable in the Net of Religion, never achieves an independent status. Urizen's pity also becomes "A cold shadow follow[ing] behind him" (*BU* 25:11; E, 82)—a significant metaphor because a shadow merely reduplicates the outline of the body, just as Urizen's pity "shadows" his law. Urizen created it only as a substitute for his own iron laws and based it, just as he based his laws, on the assumption of his own superiority or exclusive holiness.[48] Yet ultimately Urizen's children find the net of religion as uncomfortable as the iron laws: "They called it Egypt, & left it" (*BU* 28:22; E, 83). Urizen's pity, and the forgiveness that might follow, fail to escape the law; to be free, Fuzon and the others must escape both law and pity.

By calling Urizen's pity a "female in embrio," Blake links it with an earlier instance of pity, when Los exudes pity for Urizen, and that pity takes the form of "the first female now separate" (*BU* 18:10; E, 78).

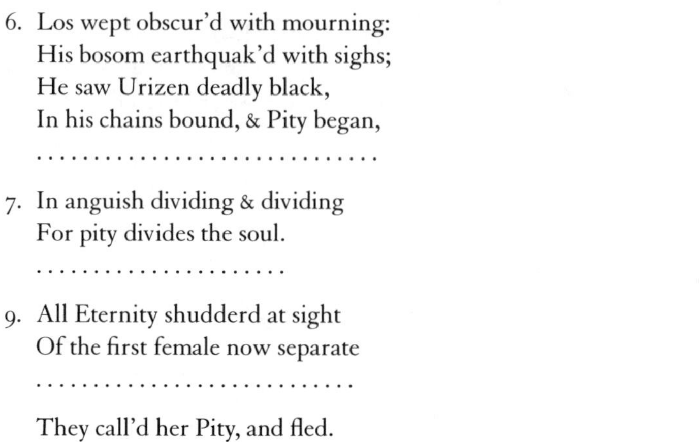

6. Los wept obscur'd with mourning:
His bosom earthquak'd with sighs;
He saw Urizen deadly black,
In his chains bound, & Pity began,

. . . .

7. In anguish dividing & dividing
For pity divides the soul.

. . . .

9. All Eternity shudderd at sight
Of the first female now separate

. . . .

They call'd her Pity, and fled.

(*BU* 13:48–53, 18:9–15, 19:1; E, 77–78)

Once again we see Blake facing a curious paradox, one congruent with the one we observed in *Visions*, the paradox that most accusers have no legitimate reason to take offense, and that only their own offense of accusation truly calls for forgiveness. Here, Urizen had exhibited a false form of pity for his children, one that he meant to keep them enslaved. As such an inveterate accuser, Urizen himself is the proper object of pity. Despite the sorrow and evil that attends Enitharmon's separation from Los, the fact that she takes a human form seems hopeful, in contrast to the Net of Religion which Urizen's pity becomes. As such, Enitharmon joins the list of emanations, including Oothoon, Leutha, Ololon, and Jerusalem, who embody conceptions such as forgiveness, repentance, and self-sacrifice.

Forgiveness was not among Blake's major concerns during the 1790s. Nonetheless, we may extract from the works of the period the following conclusions. Blake profoundly detested the laws of sexual repression and of universal conformity. "Forgiveness" of those who broke these laws was clearly suspect. Moreover, Blake tended to side with the antinomian position that violation of these laws produced freedom from them. Yet his works sometimes imply that such violation fails to escape the logical limits of the law. As Blake comes to examine the oppression of law less as a logical problem and more as a vice of accusation in the accuser, he hints at the possibility that a genuine form of forgiveness can overcome that accusation, and so produce freedom from the law. The problem, however, is to find a logical ground for forgiveness that is independent of the terms of the law and of its violation.

Why did forgiveness, rather than, say, generosity or humility, become the central ethical term for Blake? Clearly his choice was governed partly by his own experience of accusation as a profound injustice. Yet Blake's choices were quite slim. It is striking how much Blake disliked conventional moral terms. In a provocative inscription Blake writes that prudence, justice, fortitude, and temperance, the traditional four cardinal virtues, are "the Four Pillars of Tyranny." Like pity, these "virtues" were used by state authorities, inculcated into citizens in order to make them more malleable. Political use, then, made moral terms distasteful. Moreover, the Church of England in Blake's day was fundamentally compromised, ignoring the experience of religious emotion (a need filled by John Wesley and George Whitfield) and stressing instead rational, practical morality. As a consequence of the profoundly compromised nature of ethical vocabulary in Blake's day, Blake needed a concept relatively uncontaminated by compromise. He turned to forgiveness.

A further reason for the usefulness of forgiveness to Blake is its adaptability to both internal and intersubjective processes. In intersubjective forgiveness, two enemies are reconciled; in internal forgiveness, Blake could keep his earlier sense that an accuser needed to renounce his tendency to accusation. (By "internal forgiveness" I mean that general process by which the character strives to achieve good, and not the process by which one forgives oneself for past offenses or vices.) In the more traditional, Aristotelian discourse about ethics that Blake rejected, such internal processes would have been described as the cultivation of various virtues, such as the four "tyrannous" ones already named. Blake interposed forgiveness into this void, coming to picture the internal life as a constant struggle to overcome the disposition to accuse another by what we might call the disposition of "forgivingness," but which Blake called "self-annihilation." Perhaps Blake was intrigued by the verbal possibilities in *forgive*, namely, the potential pun "give for."[49] That aspect of our character which we "give for" others he called the "selfhood."

In the major prophecies Blake represented both intersubjective forgiveness and internal forgiveness by the same symbol system. By making accusation the paradigmatic offense, Blake stressed a central insight about forgiveness, that any evil in the other must be recognized as a possibility for the self. But in the process of compressing his vocabulary for the sake of emphasis, Blake translated all conflicts, intersubjective and internal, out of the traditional moral vocabulary with its multitude of virtues and vices to a binary opposition between accusation and forgiveness.

During the years of Blake's most intense reflection on forgiveness, 1802–18, he experiments with the idea that Jesus can represent this principle of forgiveness, which is independent of the law and also independent of its mirror image, antinomianism. As we shall see, he develops a notion of Jesus as the human individuality, the principle of forgiveness in each person, which needs to be freed from the state of accusation. As such, Jesus represents a disposition, an alternative way of looking at the moral life from the grid of obligations and duties used by promulgators of universal laws. As part of this experiment with the idea of Jesus as the representative of dispositions, Blake returns later in his life to the themes of law, repression, and violation.

One may discern further indications of Blake's desire to free forgiveness from the vocabulary of the law in a watercolor painting he produced in about 1805. That painting, *The Woman Taken in Adultery*, formed part of the illustrations to the Bible Blake executed for his friend and patron Thomas Butts (see figure 2). Blake based the painting on John 8:1–11. In the antinomian manifesto on Jesus and the law that we examined earlier, Blake's devilish speaker had claimed that in this incident, Jesus "turn[ed] away the law from the woman taken in adultery" (*MHH* 23; E, 43). Significantly, the story provides multiple instances of accusation. The Pharisees accuse the woman as part of a larger scheme: they bring the woman for Jesus to judge "that they might have to accuse *him*" (John 8:6; emphasis added). The story continues:

> But Jesus stooped down, and with his finger wrote on the ground, as though he heard them not. So when they continued asking him, he lifted up himself, and said unto them, He that is without sin among you, let him first cast a stone at her. And again he stooped down, and wrote on the ground. And they which heard it, being convicted by their own conscience, went out one by one, beginning at the eldest, even unto the last: and Jesus was left alone, and the woman standing in the midst. When Jesus had lifted up himself, and saw none but the woman, he said unto her, Woman where are those thine accusers? hath no man condemned thee? She said, No man, Lord. And Jesus said unto her, Neither do I condemn thee: go, and sin no more.
>
> (John 8:6b–11)

The biblical story thus presents the woman as a pawn in a game of mutual accusations between the Pharisees and Jesus: the Pharisees intend to use her as a mere instance of violation of the law, "in order to accuse [Jesus]." The memorable close of his story, the "punchline," is that Jesus turns the accusation

Figure 2.
The Woman Taken in Adultery,
watercolor over traces of pencil on paper, about 1805, 35.5 x 35.8 cm.
(Museum of Fine Arts, Boston)

back on them with the statement, "He that is without sin among you, let him first cast a stone at her."

Blake changes the force of the incident considerably by focusing on the exchange between Jesus and the woman after the Pharisees leave. With the departure of the Pharisees, the impasse of reciprocal accusation dissolves. Blake's painting depicts Jesus bending forward, beginning to write on the ground. The accusers have turned to leave, and the woman, hands bound behind, waits for Jesus to write. Blake's strategic choices in this painting correspond with an interest in making the figure of Jesus not merely reverse the law but become independent of it and, with him, the principle of forgiveness that he represents. As Christopher Heppner has observed, Blake alters the tradition followed by many painters, that Jesus wrote on the ground the same words he spoke, "He that is without sin among you, let him first cast a stone at her."[50] Blake shows the accusers already leaving, so presumably they have already heard that pronouncement which accuses them and forgives her. Here again, Blake stresses the paradox that most accusers have no legitimate reason to take offense, and that only their own offense of accusation truly calls for forgiveness.

Blake's picture focuses on Jesus' relation to the woman who has "trangressed" sexually, but the dignity in her bearing suggests that she committed no sin at all. In other words, Blake seems to celebrate the sexual energy which in her overflowed the bonds of marriage. Blake further modifies tradition in his portrayal of the woman. Many painters showed her trying to cover herself and achieve a semblance of modesty. This woman stands upright, dressed in white as Jesus is, and waits for the words he will write. Her unconventional lack of shame suggests Blake's continued commitment to the principle that the expression of sexuality is part of the expression of genius, and that it is accusation which alone deserves censure.

Blake's concern that forgiveness free itself from the vocabulary of law also shows in the picture's use of light. Heppner notes the apparent inconsistency in the shadows, an inconsistency that vanishes if Jesus' halo is seen as the source of light. Blake's placement of the source of light here makes the halo, rather than the words on the ground, the focus of attention. It accords with our sense that Blake, in depicting a principle of forgiveness, moves away from a forgiving text addressed to those who cite accusing texts. Instead, the human form divine, independent of writing, functions as the source of a separate forgiveness.

In chapter 3 of *Jerusalem*, Blake returns to his antinomian theme of the fundamental goodness of women's sexual "transgressions" and the futility of imagining that they need forgiveness. He takes an original tack in making Jesus almost literally a son of forgiveness. There he modifies the story of Joseph's discovery that Mary has conceived Jesus by the Holy Spirit (Matthew 1:18–25). Blake changes the story, making Mary an adulteress in order to stress that Joseph's forgiveness of her is the act that makes the child divine. Apart from the obvious attack on the orthodox doctrine of the virginal conception of Jesus, Blake's aim is to portray Jesus' divinity (a human divinity) as the result of human forgiveness.[51] At first glance, this passage seems to duplicate the logical impasse of the antinomians, that continual forgiveness of sins depends logically on the continual commission of sins.[52] But closer examination suggests that Blake has begun to see his way out of the limits of the antinomian terms.

Blake presents the incident as a vision seen by the character Jerusalem:

> She looked & saw Joseph the Carpenter in Nazareth & Mary
> His espoused Wife. And Mary said, If thou put me away from thee
> Dost thou not murder me? Joseph spoke in anger & fury. Should I
> Marry a Harlot & an Adulteress? Mary answerd, Art thou more pure
> Than thy Maker who forgiveth Sins & calls again Her that is Lost
> Tho She hates. he calls her again in love.
>
> (*J* 61:3–8; E, 211)

Significantly, Mary accepts the terms of the law that accuses her. Joseph calls her a harlot and an adulteress, and she herself admits that she is sinful, lost, and impure. In fact, she insists on her impurity as a condition of forgiveness: "if I were pure, never could I taste the sweets / Of the Forgive[ne]ss of Sins!" (*J* 61:11–12; E, 211). Mary's paradigm supposes that forgiveness of sins depends on commission of sins, and if Blake plans to make Joseph's forgiveness the source of the child's divinity, then Blake would seem to let stand the verdict that Mary's adultery was sinful. Yet clearly Blake sees Mary in the same light as Oothoon, who deserves praise for her assertion of individual genius and of sexuality. How can Joseph's forgiveness of Mary be definitive if she committed no genuine offense? Blake has met this impasse before.

Blake's formulation of Joseph's response suggests that this time he has found a way out of the impasse. The response is deceptively simple— "Ah my Mary" (*J* 61:14; E, 211)—and yet it generates an outpouring of affection, including an embrace, a familiar Blakean sign of forgiveness. Blake's phrasing here suggests that Joseph's forgiveness consists in recognizing Mary's individuality, here suggested by her name, rather than in pardoning the specific infraction. As Blake writes in addressing "The Accuser who is The God of This World":

Truly My Satan thou art but a Dunce
And dost not know the Garment from the Man
Every Harlot was a Virgin once
Nor canst thou ever change Kate into Nan.

(*FS;* E, 269)

Joseph's recognition "Ah my Mary" functions as a recognition of the intractable individuality of Mary, the kind of recognition the dunce Satan cannot make, since he always tries to change Kate into Nan. The use of names suggests that forgiveness consists in part in the revelation of the other as a *who*, a person needing to be forgiven, as constrasted with the *what*, the offense to be forgiven, as Arendt observes.[53] Harlotry, Blake suggests here, is only a garment for an individual woman. Joseph remains in the state of accusation as long as he calls her by such abstract conceptual names, "a Harlot & an Adulteress." To see her as "my Mary," however, is to see her individuality. This way of formulating Joseph's response to Mary avoids the logical trap that continual forgiveness depends on continual sin, because Joseph forgives by recognizing Mary's individuality in any of her actions, not by ignoring her annoying ones. Moreover, this formulation links the concepts of individuality and forgiveness with Jesus, an association Blake makes throughout *Jerusalem*. In the light of Blake's previous reflection on law, transgression, and forgiveness in the 1790s, it appears that Joseph has performed an act of forgiveness in the borrowed sense; that is, he has undergone a process of psychological adjustment that feels to an accusing person like forgiveness of an offender but actually means simply accepting something he should have accepted in the first place.

Blake goes farther. He takes up the line of inquiry suggested in Mary's recrimination of Joseph, "Art thou more pure / Than thy Maker who forgiveth Sins?" Moving from the practice of human forgiveness to the theory of divine forgiveness, Blake offers a long explanation, in which offenses against sexual prohibitions ("Pollution") are linked with the metaphor of sins as debts:

. . . Doth Jehovah Forgive a Debt only on condition that it shall
Be Payed? Doth he Forgive Pollution only on conditions of Purity
That Debt is not Forgiven! That Pollution is not Forgiven
Such is the Forgiveness of the Gods, the Moral Virtues of the
Heathen, whose tender Mercies are Cruelty.

(*J* 61:17–21; E, 212)

The false forgiveness described in the opening lines is that practiced by the state deities and their priests, forgiveness that retains a permanent sense of the offense, either as debt or as pollution, and "forgives" it only on conditions of repayment or purity, that is, terms that perpetuate the definition of the initial offense. Here we have the dilemma of the antinomians repeated. Rather than simply opposing the terms of the law with their mirror opposites, debt with repayment and so forth, Blake sidesteps the terms completely and comments on their inadequacy. His explanation of the theological model of forgiveness continues:

> . . . But Jehovahs Salvation
> Is without Money & without Price, in the Continual Forgiveness of Sins
> In the Perpetual Mutual Sacrifice in Great Eternity!
> (*J* 61:21–23; E, 212)

Blake here declares that a more adequate model of theological forgiveness completely dismisses the metaphor of money and the conception of sins as debts. He invokes the authority of Isaiah: "Every one that thirsteth, come ye to the waters, and he that hath no money; come ye, buy, and eat; yea, come buy wine and milk without money and without price" (Isaiah 55:1). In its original context, the rejection of a system of exchange is directly connected to a promise of forgiveness: "Let the wicked forsake his way, and the unrighteous man his thoughts: and let him return unto the Lord, and he will have mercy upon him; and to our God, for he will abundantly pardon" (55:7). Blake's version of such a forgiveness, which forgoes the idea of debts and money and price completely, is "the Continual Forgiveness of Sins / In the Perpetual Mutual Sacrifice in Great Eternity." In other words, "the Continual Forgiveness of Sins" consists in the "Perpetual Mutual Sacrifice in Great Eternity," that is, when each person annihilates his selfhood and accusation in falsely accusing others who are exerting their proper talents and genius. Joseph's forgiveness of Mary is such an act. Unlike the false forgivenesses, which demand sacrifice on only one side, the more adequate model of forgiveness is "Mutual"—one in which neither party assumes the position of moral superiority that can lead to accusation.

From this borrowed sense of forgiveness as the acceptance of the other's talents and genius and sexuality emerges one of Blake's few approbative uses of chastity. In protest, Los cries out:

> How can the Female be Chaste O thou stupid Druid . . .
> Without the Forgiveness of Sins in the merciful clouds of Jehovah

And without the Baptism of Repentance.
(*J* 63:26–28; E, 214)

Blake here suggests the possibility that forgiveness can exist independently of a system of laws and violations. It can lead to the cultivation of virtues, such as chastity, which form motives with their own integrity for action, as contrasted with the sheer desire to violate laws which prompted that Jesus of 1793 who acted from "impulse, not from rules."

In *The Everlasting Gospel*, written in 1818, Blake again takes up the challenge of establishing an independent motive apart from the violation of law. Again, he seeks to identify this independent motive for action with Jesus, who personifies for Blake the principle of forgiveness of sins. Blake makes this stress on forgiveness clear in a remark he wrote in pencil at the beginning of *The Everlasting Gospel*: "There is not one Moral Virtue that Jesus Inculcated but Plato & Cicero did Inculcate before him[.] what then did Christ Inculcate. Forgiveness of Sins[.] This alone is the Gospel & this is the Life & Immortality brought to light by Jesus. Even the Covenant of Jehovah, which is This[.] If you forgive one another your Trespasses so shall Jehovah forgive you That he himself may dwell among you[.] but if you Avenge you Murder the Divine Image & he cannot dwell among you . . . because you Murder him he arises Again & you deny that he is Arisen & are blind to Spirit" (E, 875). Blake's choice of the curious phrase "the everlasting gospel" as his title suggests that he intends this poem as a direct response to the antinomians with whom he allied himself in the 1790s. The antinomians used this term in stressing the inner light of the new morality, a gospel that is not a new sacred book but "a new revelation of the spiritual sense of the Bible with which God will illuminate the hearts of men."[54]

The Everlasting Gospel has left scholars unsatisfied both aesthetically and conceptually[55] and has seemed to Erdman, its most thorough scholar, an anomalous throwback to Blake's earlier iconoclasm.[56] Blake's ambivalence toward the ethical category of forgiveness accounts for some of its oddities. Between 1818 and 1820, Blake wrote in his Notebook several fragments about the character of Jesus and the importance of forgiveness. One fragment bears the title "The Everlasting Gospel," and editors have extended that title by courtesy to the whole effort, consisting of twelve fragments and a reference to another piece, presumably lost.[57] The fragments fall logically into three groups: Blake's preliminaries on forgiveness, two fragments on chastity and love, and three fragments on humility and pride. These sentences about forgiveness are the earliest-written portion and the "seedbed" of the entire effort: "There is not one Moral Virtue that Jesus Inculcated but Plato & Cicero did Inculcate before him[.] what then did Christ Inculcate. Forgiveness of Sins[.] This alone is the Gospel & this is the Life & Immortality brought to light by Jesus" (E, 875).[58]

In the work as a whole, Blake mixes his protest against obligation-excusing forgiveness with his search for a name for a disposition to replace them. His two candidates—not entirely successful ones—are love and pride.

Blake consistently opposes classical writers' sense of moral virtues, which, he claimed, disrupted literary form with a moral "like a sting in the tail" (*On Homers Poetry*; E, 269), and which, he claims, depended on oppressive social structures: "You cannot have Liberty in this World without what you [the Ancient Greeks] call, Moral Virtue" (*VLJ*; E, 564). The words *moral* and *virtue* are almost always pejorative in Blake. In *The Everlasting Gospel* passage on forgiveness, he implies that Plato and Cicero inculcated an inferior category of ethical concepts. In looking for the uniqueness of Jesus' message, Blake focuses on forgiveness of sins. He implies that the forgiveness of sins is somehow the precondition of all the attributes praised by Plato, Cicero, and Jesus. This is so because it imparts "life and immortality" and so changes the source from which the virtues spring—no longer do they need to be "inculcated."

In this line of thinking, forgiveness is closely linked with love, frequently described as the form of all the virtues. Blake's sense of forgiveness as the wellspring of the virtues is reinforced by another passage on forgiveness which begins the narrative portions of the poem:

> Then Jesus rose & said to [*men*] Me
> Thy Sins are all forgiven thee
> Loud Pilate Howld loud Caiphas Yelld
> When they the Gospel Light beheld.
>
> (*EG*; E, 876)

Erdman eloquently notes that "the change of 'men' to 'Me' changes parable into drama" (E, 876). For Blake, Pilate and Caiaphas represent lawgiving, which is here disrupted by Jesus' act of forgiveness, not by an act of lawbreaking.

It is not surprising that Blake would turn to the concept of love in his search for an alternative to lawgiving and lawbreaking. No doubt Blake's praise of love in *The Everlasting Gospel* derives in large measure from the traditional distinction between love and law. The New Testament would give Blake an alternative authority from which to criticize that of lawgiving. So would Saint Augustine's maxim, "Love, and then do what you will."

In addition to the distinction between love and law, it is useful to distinguish possible contents of the word *love*. As is well known, the English term *love* includes three ideas usefully separated in Greek: *agape, eros,* and *philia*. Blake is concerned only with the ambiguity between the first two: this ambiguity allows him to express two meanings simultaneously. The first is that love, equated with free expression of *eros*, provides an alternative to an ethic of obedience to lawgiving. However, it falls into the opposite problem of defining itself as a violation of those laws, and so antinomianism remains a parasite in the host of law. The second is that love, equated with *agape* as a disposition of the agent, can provide a new basis for morality. However, Blake never quite sorts the two meanings out in a satisfactory way.

In *The Everlasting Gospel* Blake relates love to sexuality again, in the first draft of the chastity section, which begins, "Was Jesus born of a Virgin Pure?" Here he takes the antinomian line in *Jerusalem* much further: Jesus' mother should be a habitual offender against chastity, a "harlot":

> Was Jesus Born of a Virgin Pure
> With narrow Soul & looks demure
> If he intended to take on Sin
> The Mother should an Harlot been.
>
> (*EG*; E, 877)

Mary Magdalen would have been more suitable, in Blake's view, because she violated the commandment against adultery more often than the Virgin Mary. Here he reaches the logical extreme of advocating violation of obligation for its own sake, a more radical stance than in the parallel scene in *Jerusalem*. Blake's purpose in speculating on this kind of incarnation, however, is not mere shock value, but a desire for a compassionate Jesus:

> Or what was it which he took on
> That he might bring Salvation
> A Body subject to be Tempted
> From neither pain nor grief Exempted
> Or such a body as might not feel
> The passions that with Sinners deal.
>
> (*EG*; E, 877)

Blake's substitution of a lawbreaker, Magdalen, as Jesus' mother is part of an effort to humanize Jesus by seeing him as subject to temptation and passion. In so doing, Blake makes Jesus more truly "the Friend of Sinners" (*J* 3; E, 145). By this point in the text, however, Blake's direction has changed. He initially redefined Mary. Now he wants to redefine Jesus. Thus his next line, "Yes but they say he never fell," suggests that Blake wants to refute chastity with an action in which Jesus, not Mary, "falls" by giving way to sexual passions. Blake finds no appropriate biblical story, so this section wanders directionless, with couplets on various stories and a gratuitous anti-Semitic remark. Then the fragment breaks off with a mention of the woman taken in adultery.

> And from the Adulteress [he] turnd away
> Gods righteous Law that lost its Prey.
>
> (*EG*; E, 878)

The "Virgin Pure" fragment ends with this couplet, not because Blake has hit a dead end but because he has thought of a new place to begin. His composition habits suggest an influx of enthusiasm. Erdman surmises that Blake at this point began writing section *f* ("Was Jesus Chaste?") (*EG*; E, 878). Blake switched from a loose sheet to his notebook, Erdman notes, and began to write more rapidly. The story of the woman taken in adultery solves Blake's problem, because Jesus, not Mary, is the central character.

Thus the second chastity section is far more focused. It recounts one dramatic action, Jesus' forgiveness of the woman taken in adultery. Blake names the adulteress Mary, thus combining the Virgin Mary, Mary Magdalen, and Mary the sister of Lazarus.[59] He probably hoped to shock his reader, as in his earlier draft. Still, the plot follows familiar lines. Accusers bring Mary before Jesus as an adulteress; Jesus declares her forgiven. Blake's Jesus then goes on to state the principle behind his forgiveness. He has not merely granted clemency to a convicted harlot but undermines the principle by which she is convicted:

> Good & Evil are no more
> Sinais trumpets cease to roar
> Cease finger of God to Write
> The Heavens are not clean in thy Sight
> Thou art Good & thou Alone
> Nor may the sinner cast one stone
> To be Good only is to be
> A Devil or else a Pharisee.
>
> (*EG*; E, 521)

The antecedent of "Thou" is a bit tricky. Perhaps Blake intends an allusion to Jesus' remark that God alone is good (Luke 18:19).[60] In this case "God" would be the antecedent. Or perhaps Blake means his Jesus to address Mary, in which case she, her own individuality, is a new "Good," which is "Good *alone*." The Pharisaic law she violates, however, is "To be Good *only*" (emphasis added), which makes one "A Devil or else a Pharisee" (*EG*; E, 521). Blake had originally written, "A *God* or else a Pharisee" (emphasis added).[61] The substitution of *Devil* for *God* suggests that Blake himself is not sure when he is using *God* ironically, to refer to the Nobodaddy worshipped by the churches, or when he means it straightforwardly.

Despite Blake's efforts to focus on the character of Jesus, the character of Mary the adulteress steals the show. She shifts the terms of discussion to love:

> But this O Lord this was my Sin
> When first I let these Devils in
> In dark pretence to Chastity
> Blaspheming Love blaspheming thee
> Thence Rose Secret Adulteries
> And thence did Covet also rise.
>
> (*EG*; E, 522)

The "sin" that Mary confesses is not adultery, a public violation, but "Secret Adulteries," or a disposition by which she implicitly blasphemed love. Moreover, she identifies love as Jesus by her parallel phrasing, "Blaspheming love blaspheming thee." By implying that love is a person, that is, identifiable with Jesus, Mary comes to another foundational sense of a virtue or vice as the wellspring of action.

Blake is still stuck, however. He wants to show that Mary is praiseworthy because she violated a false obligation. But Jesus' forgiveness here depends on Mary's previous violation of an obligation, and so forgiveness remains parasitic on law. Faced with this problem, Blake unsatisfactorily makes Mary a sinner of a different stripe, namely, a hypocrite. Clearly this revision does not solve the problem, and Blake wrote at the top of this section: "This was Spoke by My Spectre to Voltaire Bacon &c" (*EG*; E, 525). Blake's attribution of these lines to his Spectre shows his frustration with the argument.[62]

Blake has better luck with his second candidate, pride. The concept of pride gives Blake both the antinomian protest against conventional advocacy of humility and also the conceptual advantage of denoting a disposition independent of law rather than an action of lawbreaking dependent on the law. In this latter way, particularly, the concept of pride fits Blake's purpose better than the concept of love. Love, as we saw in Mary's discourse, denoted a specific act of erotic expression as well as a disposition. In turning to the concept of pride,

Blake draws on a traditional language of dispositions, both virtues and vices. Aristotle praises pride as "magnanimity," the just recognition of one's strength.[63] Scripture, however, condemns pride as the root of sin, trusting in oneself instead of God.

Blake's use of the concept of pride draws from the consensus, on both sides of this traditional debate, that pride denotes a disposition. So pride becomes his second candidate for an escape from the vocabulary of lawgiving and lawbreaking. This exploration occurs in a second group of fragments, one on gentility and two on humility. It has already been suggested that the gentility section is a preliminary draft of the humility section, abandoned in favor of the more biblical language of pride and humility.[64] Textual scholars concur that this group of fragments contains the poem's collapse; specifically, they locate it in the second version of the humility section, despite the fact that this fragment received Blake's mark of approval—a title. I would like to reassess this section as an advance. In the notion of "honest triumphant pride," Blake begins to break free from the grip of lawgiving and lawbreaking to an independent account of virtue.

The first two fragments, the one on gentility and the first one on humility, can be quickly discussed. In both fragments Blake recounts the story of the child Jesus remaining behind in the Temple. In "gentility" Jesus violates the imperatives of filial obedience and good manners. Obligation is not questioned. The duty to the divine parent merely trumps the duty to the earthly one, as Blake's Jesus says,

> No Earthly Parents I confess
> My Heavenly Fathers business.
>
> (*EG*; E, 523)

Throughout, Blake protests society's cooptation of religious ideas for its own ends. Jesus follows up:

> Obedience is a duty then
> And favour gains with God & Men.
>
> (*EG*; E, 523)

Blake thus exposes his society's praise of obedience in order to train socially acceptable members, who are "gentle" and who gain favor with God and men. Blake's version of the temptation of Jesus makes even more clear the destructive force of the imperative to obey, by putting it in the mouth of Satan:

Come said Satan come away
Ill soon see if youll obey
John for disobedience bled
But you can turn the stones to bread
Gods high king & Gods high Priest
Shall Plant their Glories in your breast
If Caiaphas you will obey
If Herod you with bloody Prey
Feed with the Sacrifice & be
Obedient fall down worship me.

(*EG*; E, 523)

Blake's Jesus subdues this tempter with wrath:

And in his hand the Scourge shone bright
He scourgd the Merchant Canaanite
From out the Temple of his Mind
And in his Body tight does bind
Satan & all his Hellish Crew
And thus with wrath he did subdue
The Serpent Bulk of Natures dross.

(*EG*; E, 524)

Blake attributes wrath to Jesus here to designate a disposition that guides Jesus' action, instead of praising his mere violation of the law of obedience.[65] In the "gentility" section, then, Blake progresses from merely trumping one obligation with another, leaving the notion of obligation unquestioned, to articulating a specific disposition, wrath, that motivates Jesus. Blake's next attempt, the first "humility" section, merely retells the story of the disobedient child Jesus. Its major significance for the development of Blake's thought is that Blake shifts the term from gentility to humility.

In the second humility section, Blake even more fully arrives at a dispositional sense of pride. Blake attacks the conventional sense of humility, redefining it as falsehood: "Did [Jesus] Boast of high Things with Humble tone?" (*EG*; E, 518) asks Blake, implying that to speak of high things "humbly" is to lie. As in the gentility and first humility sections, Blake retells the story of Jesus in the temple. But this time Blake omits the taunt of Jesus' parents. Blake's Jesus simply states the truth as he perceives it:

No Earthly Parents I confess
I am doing my Fathers business.

(*EG*; E, 518)

From this practice of truthtelling emerges the category of pride:

> He was too *proud* to take a bribe
> He spoke with authority not like a Scribe.
> (*EG*; E, 519; emphasis added)

Pride is a synonym for integrity, or, as Blake suggests in the next line, authority. In using this term, Blake alludes to Matthew 7:29, which contrasts Jesus' authority with the scribes and emphasizes the wellspring or motive of his teaching. Unaccountably, in the next lines Blake switches back to the "humble" Jesus he despises:

> He says with most consummate Art
> Follow me I am meek & lowly of heart.
> (*EG*; E, 519)

Perhaps by this time Blake has realized his contradiction: when his Jesus says, "He who loves his Enemies betrays his Friends," Blake asserts in his own voice: "This is surely not what Jesus intends" (*EG*; E, 519). The paper in Blake's Notebook shows signs of very heavy erasure under these lines. This erasure suggests a great deal of tinkering in a piece that was, for the most part, rapidly composed. For Blake is at the crux of his problem: Is Jesus humble or proud? Blake's contempt for the church's manipulative use of the concept of humility makes it hard for him to call Jesus humble. Instead, Blake distinguishes between two kinds of pride. The first one, "sneaking pride," is fulfillment of obligations; the second, "honest triumphant pride," refers to disposition. Then Blake attributes the hypocrisy of loving enemies rather than friends to:

> . . . the sneaking Pride of Heroic Schools
> And the Scribes & Pharisees Virtuous Rules[.]
> For [Jesus] acts with honest triumphant Pride
> And this is the cause that Jesus died.
> (*EG*; E, 519)

The "sneaking Pride of Heroic Schools" is based on obligation, "the Scribes & Pharisees Virtuous Rules." The Jesus of "honest triumphant Pride," however, is independent of obligation, an independence implied in Blake's remark, "And this is the cause that Jesus died." Here Blake cites an action, Jesus' death, which does not itself violate one of the Ten Commandments. In this it is unlike the catalog of violations in the *Marriage*, and unlike the forgiving of the adulteress and the running away from home.[66] Curiously, we have come round full circle to love again, for Blake surely knew the more traditional ascription of Jesus' motive in submitting to death: "Greater love hath no man than this, that a man lay down his life for his friends" (John 15:13). Honest triumphant pride may then be equivalent to such love. Moreover, Blake almost explicitly identifies his newly discovered disposition, pride, and his long-beloved faculty of imagination. He places these words in the mouth of his opponent Sir Isaac Newton:

> And as for the Indwelling of the Holy Ghost
> Or of Christ & his Father its all a boast
> And Pride & Vanity of Imagination
> That disdains to follow this Worlds Fashion.
> (*EG*; E, 519)

Newton suggests, by indirection, that the pride that motivated Jesus has a counterpart in each person's imagination, which is for Blake "the Indwelling of the Holy Ghost." Pride resembles the motive of Blake's ancient poets, the prompting of the deity that resides in the human breast.

The relationship of the disposition of "honest triumphant pride" to the theological idea of the indwelling of the Holy Ghost is significant. It provides an important caveat in reading the most famous couplet in the poem,

> Thou art a Man God is no more
> Thy own Humanity learn to adore.
> (*EG*; E, 520)

It is too easy to assimilate Blake to Nietzsche here[67] by forgetting the context. Blake does not mean that God is dead, but that the opposition between lawgiving God and obedient man has been replaced by one's own "Humanity," the deity in one's breast, or by the honest triumphant pride that comes from "the Indwelling of the Holy Ghost." This much seems clear, though Blake in the next few lines vacillates about whether humility is praiseworthy or not. On the one hand, Jesus was "Humble to God Haughty to Man" (*EG*; E, 520). On the other hand, Blake implies that Jesus' humility was a mistake: "If thou humblest thyself thou humblest me," says God the Father, "Thou also dwellst in Eternity" (*EG*; E, 520).

Despite Blake's equivocations about humility, we may draw some conclusions about the meaning of "honest triumphant Pride" in Blake's *Everlasting*

Gospel. It hearkens back to an earlier, approbative sense of pride in the *Marriage*: "The pride of the peacock is the glory of God" (*MHH* 8; E, 36). Moreover, the significance of *The Everlasting Gospel* lies in Blake's distinction between the disposition of pride from law-derived "sneaking Pride of Heroic Schools." This distinction clarifies Blake's warning in the prophecies against "Cruel Pride" (E, 325) or "Pride & Self-righteousness" (*J* 8:30; E, 151). Not all pride is itself cruel and self-righteous. Blake realized it was not enough simply to invert the received values of his culture, reading black where they saw white, or, in moral terms, "What they called Humility I called Pride" (*EG*; E, 518).

In this chapter we have examined several familiar sites of Blake's antinomianism. The works from the Lambeth period reveal Blake's ability to penetrate the logical problems associated with an antinomianism pure and simple. However, by the time Blake came to write *The Everlasting Gospel* in 1818, he had behind him almost two decades' worth of thinking about forgiveness. By that time, Blake was well aware that antinomianism as a principle had its logical limits. Moreover, much of the work in which Blake is usually described as an antinomian reveals on closer inspection that Blake exposes the limits of this ethical position. Simply put, the contradiction is that, on this view, Blake's advocacy of "continual forgiveness of sins" depends, paradoxically and parasitically, on a continual supply of commission of sins on which forgiveness feeds.[68] If we look at contrariety as the ground of Blake's later advocacy of forgiveness, this logical quandary is avoided. The paradigm, instead, looks like this: persons continually commit acts of imagination according to their own genius; many of us tend to take on the state of negation, that is, judging all others by the "One Law" derived from our own peculiar inclination and character. For us to put aside that negating attitude is to achieve forgiveness or generosity; thus "continual forgiveness of sin" is achieved in the face of good, namely, the continual exposure to the individual genius of others, to their contrariety.

Blake's critique of his society's abuse of forgiveness in the 1790s, we have seen, is derived logically from his sense that the so-called "offenses" are correctly seen as good, as expressions of individual genius and sexuality. Insofar as Blake admitted a source of human evil, he attributed it to error. To the relation between error and forgiveness we now turn.

2

Error and Forgiveness

The shift in Blake's thinking in about 1803 had a profound effect on another mainstay of Blake's thought in the 1790s: the idea that human offense is attributable to error. Like Blake's antinomianism, the attribution of human offense to error relies on a theory of evil as privation or falling off from the good, as contrasted with a dualistic theory that grants evil a genuine reality. Theories of evil as privation of good have a long tradition, both as cosmology or theology, which try to explain evil in the world at large, and in ethics, which tries to explain evil or offense within human beings and human society. The notion of knowledge as remembering, of course, was shared by Plato and the Neoplatonists.[1] Thomas Aquinas gave a classic formulation to the theory in stating, "Blindness is in the eye."[2] Like Blake, Thomas linked error closely with the sense of sight, a position implied in Blake's couplet in the Auguries of Innocence,

> We are led to Believe a Lie
> When we see not Thro the Eye
>
> (*AI* 125–26; E, 492)

and in his Proverb of Hell, "A fool sees not the same tree that a wise man sees" (*MHH* 7:9; E, 35).[3] In Blake's own time, a prominent spokesman for the view of human offense as error was William Godwin. In his *Enquiry Concerning Political Justice*, Godwin writes, "Vice and weakness are founded upon ignorance and error."[4] His position follows logically from a view of the self as fundamentally unified. Godwin makes precisely such a claim: "We are no longer at liberty to consider man as divided between two independent principles, or to imagine that his inclinations are in any case inaccessible through the medium of his reason. We find the thinking principle within us to be uniform and simple . . . [and] susceptible of unlimited improvement."[5] While Blake was probably only on the periphery of the circle of Godwin, Joseph Johnson, and others (*BR*, 41), the popularity of Godwin in the 1790s would make it likely that Blake knew the general outlines of his theory.

Error makes the process of forgiveness unnecessary, because error is an offense against an impersonal standard, truth, and errors, at worst, are "wrongdoing." Forgiveness presumes the violation of a relationship between offender and victim, a violation of wronging another human being.[6] We must reconcile Blake's attribution of human offense to error with his advocacy of forgiveness.

Many Blake scholars opine that Blake conceives of human offense primarily as error. This consensus has been challenged by Damrosch, who notes some important inconsistencies in Blake's use of the term. Damrosch writes that, at the beginning of his career, "instead of 'sin' Blake prefers the Platonic conception of 'error.' But he is increasingly driven back upon a conception which comes close to the traditional idea of sin."[7] Damrosch rightly observes that Blake sometimes holds that human evil is illusory, as a notion of error would imply, while sometimes holding the apparently opposite view that human evil is genuine, as a notion of sin would imply. And yet the map of these inconsistencies is not entirely as Damrosch implies. During the 1790s Blake did rely on a notion of human offense as attributable to error, a position implied in statements such as "All Bibles or sacred codes. have been the causes of the following Errors" (*MHH* 4:1; E, 34) and the infernal proverb, "Every thing possible to be believ'd is an image of truth" (*MHH* 8:38; E, 37). Though the early Blake may have an implied theory of error, as Damrosch suggests, in fact Blake uses the term *error* more frequently in works produced in his maturity, namely, Night the Ninth of *The Four Zoas*, *A Vision of the Last Judgment*, and *Jerusalem*.[8] Blake's notion of error, however, is not the all-inclusive category most Blake scholars have taken it to be. In the period before the 1790s, Blake protests outright against a theory of human offense as wrongdoing against a principle and advocates a theory of offense as wronging another person: the paradigm necessary for forgiveness. And in the period after the 1790s, Blake qualifies the notion of error by limiting its frame of reference.

Let us begin with a backward glance, to some very early writing of Blake's, the annotations to Johann Caspar Lavater's *Aphorisms on Man*, annotations written in 1788.[9] The annotations come from a period of early allegiance to Christianity, which Blake says he renewed in 1800.[10] In general, Blake approved of Lavater's ideas, showing his approval by writing his name below Lavater's on the title page and drawing a heart around both names. But on the nature of human offense, Blake registered disagreement. Whereas Lavater conceives human offense as error or lying (in either case, an offense against the impersonal standard of truth), Blake responds by stressing the resentment of a personal victim and, hence, the definition of human offense as the violation of a relationship.

Lavater relies on a paradigm of human offense as wrongdoing, in which the offender commits a moral transgression against a collective entity such as society, or against an impersonal principle, such as truthtelling.[11] But Blake relies on a model of human offense as wronging, that is, the classic case of "those who trespass against us," in which the offender acts immorally toward the injured party and hurts him: a principle is violated, and a relationship is harmed.[12] Only in this case is "forgiveness" truly appropriate for the injured party, for forgiveness requires both that the offense violate an objective principle and that the victim overcome his feelings hurt by the violation of a relationship.

Blake disagrees when Lavater insists that lying rather than sin is the paradigmatic offense, because lying offends principle and not persons. Lavater in effect makes all "wrongs" against persons into "wrongdoings" against truth. We can see this logical shift in the following aphorisms. In Aphorism 165 he finds "the race of sophists"—offenders against truth—less improvable, more intolerable, and more oppressive, than thieves or murderers. And he explicitly names the object of their offense. "They are intolerable," he says, "against all nature, against all that is called *general, demonstrated truth*" (emphasis added). And Aphorism 39 makes lying a paradigmatic offense: "Who, without pressing temptation, tells a lie, will, without pressing temptation, act ignobly and meanly." In Lavater's view, a liar is capable of any other heinous act: once his fidelity to truth has been disrupted, no holds on vice are barred. Finally, Lavater almost identifies lying with evil itself in Aphorism 333: "Between passion and lie there is not a finger's breadth." Here Lavater describes his villain, lying, as a bedfellow of the traditional moral villain, passion. Lavater's definition of offense as wrongdoing against the truth precludes consideration of the wronged personal victim, thus circumventing the possibility that human failing can consist in violating a relationship.

When Lavater does consider the victims of others' failings, he recommends that the victim become merely a detached observer, ignoring his own personal injuries. Often Lavater recommends that the victim—now become spectator—correct the offender's error, as in Aphorism 399: "He is more than great who *instructs* his offender whilst he forgives him." So, too, in Aphorism 82, "Who can love him, in the moment of *correction*, is the most amiable of mortals." The former victim now becomes the instructor and corrector of the offender. Lavater recasts victim as teacher even more explicitly in number 38: "He, who boldly interposes between a merciless censor and his prey, is a man of vigour: and he, who, mildly wise, without wounding, *convinces him of his error*, commands our veneration" (emphasis added in all examples). We should admire the person who averts an evil action by "convinc[ing]" the wrongdoer of his error. Lavater's reader should observe others and measure his own progress by his response: "Let the unhappiness you feel at *another's errors*, and the happiness you enjoy in their perfections, be the measure of your progress in wisdom and virtue" (no. 278). Lavater's reader is cast as the disinterested spectator of other people's character—especially of their "errors." In another aphorism (no. 242), Lavater equates the moral instructor with a connoisseur of paintings—the spectator par excellence. The emphasis is always on intellectual correctness and error; victims are either spectators or instructors.

Blake consistently objects to Lavater's equation of all offense with error or with wrongdoing against a truth. In response to number 39, Blake writes: "a man may lie *for his own pleasure*," a remark which implies that lying, perhaps as the lowest form of creativity, is pleasurable, and, as such, is permissible. He then adds an important qualification: "*but if any one is hurt* by his lying will confess his lie" (Ann. Lavater; E, 585, emphasis added). Only when someone is hurt, only when a relationship is violated, Blake suggests, does any real harm arise. Blake makes the same distinction in his response to Aphorism 248. It reads, in part: "Know that the great art to love your enemy consists in never losing sight of MAN in him: humanity has power over all that is human."[13] Blake responds: "none can see the man in the enemy[.] if he is ignorantly so, he is not truly an enemy[.] if maliciously not a man[.]" (Ann. Lavater; E, 589). Again Blake criticizes Lavater's translation of wronging into wrongdoing. To paraphrase Blake: If my enemy harms me ignorantly, as is the case in most of Lavater's examples, he is not my enemy; he offends against truth, not against me. But if he harms me maliciously (a case which Lavater never allows), his humanity has been forfeited. Blake goes on in this vein: "I cannot love my enemy for my enemy is not man but beast & devil if I have any. I can love him as a beast & wish to beat him" (Ann. Lavater; E, 589). Blake now shifts explicitly to the victim's own feelings about the enemy, beginning by rejecting Lavater's advice, "I cannot love my enemy." From the point of view of resentment, the offender truly is "beast & devil." Thus Blake, speaking on behalf of resentment, writes: "I can love him as a beast & wish to beat him."[14]

Blake insists the more on the gravity of violating a relationship because Lavater denies it. All of the reconciliations depicted by Lavater occur at the scene of fresh offense, where the victim would most naturally feel resentment. His skepticism is directed particularly against those aphorisms that depict immediate forgiveness at the scene of fresh offense. Lavater has written, "Who *begins* with severity, in judging of another, ends commonly with falsehood" (no. 36; emphasis added). Blake responds, "Severity of judgment is a great virtue" (Ann. Lavater; E, 585). In this case, Blake praises "severity of judgment" because it truthfully names the offense: no one can help his initial response of hurt and resentment against a wrong inflicted by an enemy. Blake's other skeptical comments function similarly as a corrective to Lavater's picture of fresh offense. If we reexamine Blake's response, "this I cannot concieve [*sic*]" (Ann. Lavater; E, 592), we may surmise that Blake took Lavater to be describing a scene of fresh offense when he praises "a manner of forgiving so divine, that you are ready to embrace the offender for having called it forth" (no. 400). One may well surmise that the offender has just this moment "called forth" forgiveness by the offense itself (though the aphorism would also bear the reading that he calls it forth by an apology). But since Lavater omits any reference to the offender's repentance or apology, Blake would be justified in reading this aphorism as another account of fresh offense. Another of Blake's responses to Lavater illustrates his selective disagreements only with Lavater's descriptions of fresh offense. Lavater has counseled, "judge with lenity of all" (no. 630), a maxim in which no particular offense is named. Blake responds generously: "Whoso dwelleth in love dwelleth in God & God in him. & *such an one cannot judge of any but in love*" (Ann. Lavater; E, 599; emphasis added). Blake does not think resentment's "severity of judgment" should last forever, but there are times when love is the appropriate motive for judgment. Thus he objects to Lavater's omission of resentment because it hides the violation of bonds of relationship, falsely sanitizing the messy emotions in human forgiveness.

One of Blake's long marginalia offers an account of the relationship violated by human offense, supplementing that which Lavater had omitted by focusing on error. In linking human forgiveness to brotherhood, Blake praises the person who judges by love. Blake there responds to Lavater's recommendation to "judge with lenity of all" (no. 630) by indicating the source of such "lenity" or generosity in judgment: "It is the God in *all* that is our companion &

friend, for our God himself says, you are my brother my sister & my mother; & St John. Whoso dwelleth in love dwelleth in God & God in him. & such an one cannot judge of any but in love. & his feelings will be attractions or repulses" (Ann. Lavater; E, 599; original emphasis).

Having established a notion of human offense entirely different from that of Lavater, Blake also provides a rubric whereby this offense can be forgiven: regeneration. One cannot help but be struck by Lavater's inability to forgive and his unwillingness to acknowledge that the offender might change. Lavater's omission of regeneration profoundly affects his presentation of forgiveness. Lavater divides the world into two camps, the good honest truthtellers and the lying knaves. He sees forgiveness as the habitually honest person forgiving the intractably dishonest—but with no hope of his regeneration. In Lavater's view, the offender will always remain a knave, and so the prudent victim remains distant. Further, Lavater's model implies that it is a species of truthtelling to persist in accurately labeling the dishonest as such. In precluding regeneration, Lavater creates a world forever divided between sheep and goats: "Some characters are positive, some negative" (no. 104). Moreover, diametrically opposed behavior characterizes these groups: "As the *good* love thee, the *bad* will hate thee" (no. 261). Lavater once hedges a bit by conceding that the groups may *appear* to overlap. "Good may be *done* by the bad," he says, but quickly reasserts the reality of the split—"but the good alone can *be* good" (no. 362; original emphasis).[15] Blake explicitly rejects this grouping of persons into permanent classes. One of his most direct criticisms of Lavater occurs here: "this aphorism seems to me to want discrimination" (Ann. Lavater; E, 596). Blake objects again, when, in Aphorism 636, Lavater shows his suspicions: "Receive no satisfaction for premeditated impertinence—forget it, forgive it—but keep him inexorably at a distance who offered it." Blake, more tactfully this time, notes, "This is a paradox" (Ann. Lavater; E, 600); the wariness of keeping the offender "inexorably at a distance" is not what anyone would call forgiveness. And when Lavater writes about "assign[ing] to each class and each individual its own peculiar fit of vice or folly" (no. 533), Blake responds: "knaveries are not human nature[.] knaveries are knaveries" (Ann. Lavater; E, 596). Blake implies that no one is permanently and by nature a knave—to use the language of Blake's later works, knavery is a state into which an individual may fall.

Blake uses the word *regeneration* sparingly in his early writings; it and its cognates occur only twice outside his prophecies, both times here, in the annotations to Lavater.[16] The concept of regeneration was familiar to Blake

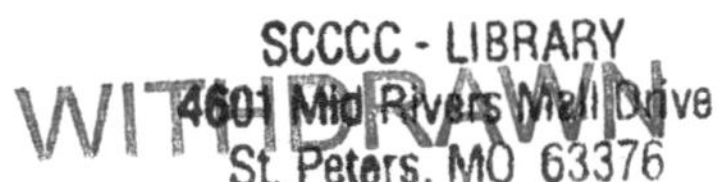

from the Methodist preachers George Whitfield and John Wesley, whom Blake praises as servants and prophets of God (*M* 24:61; E, 118) and from the Lutheran mystic Jacob Boehme, whom Blake praises in the *Marriage* (*MHH* 22; E, 43).[17]

Regeneration and its emotional turmoil do not suit Lavater's taste. Lavater tends to condescend to those who experience emotional turmoil. In number 607 he writes, "Him who is hurried on by the furies of immature, impetuous wishes, stern repentance shall drag, bound and reluctant, back to the place from which he sallied: where you hear the crackling of wishes expect intolerable vapours or repining grief." Lavater seems to intend the traditional term *repentance* as a synonym for "repining grief," which he attributes to an "immature" person. There is no hint that Lavater sees it as divinely inspired. Perhaps Lavater's omission of regeneration stems from his distrust of fanaticism, emotion, and mystery.[18] Blake invokes the concept of regeneration in response to Aphorism 20, which reads:

> Distinguish with exactness, in thyself and others, between *wishes* and *will*, in the strictest sense.
>
> Who has many wishes has generally but little will. Who has energy of will has few diverging wishes. Whose will is bent with energy on *one*, *must* renounce the wishes for *many* things. Who cannot do this is not stamped with the majesty of human nature. (No. 20; original emphasis)

The aphorism's concluding sentence was underlined by Blake, as a mark of approval: "The energy of choice, the unison of various powers for one is only will, born under the agonies of self-denial and renounced desires" (no. 20). Lavater's tone is ambivalent here: on the one hand he seems to praise the single-willed person as bearing the stamp of human majesty, and he goes on in this vein in the next aphorism, number 21, which begins, "Calmness of will is a sign of grandeur"; thus he seems to disapprove of those caught in emotional turmoil. On the other hand, he seems to acknowledge the "agonies of self-denial and renounced desires" as a necessary preliminary to singleness of will. Blake's response has none of Lavater's ambivalence: to the last sentence he appends one word, "Regeneration" (Ann. Lavater; E, 584), which describes the process as a divine one. Blake's resistance to Lavater at this point is further registered in his "uneasy" response to Lavater's praise of "Calmness of will" (Ann. Lavater; E, 584).

Lavater's paradigm thus precludes regeneration of the offender: Blake insists on mentioning it, insists that by regeneration the offender is made a new person, and demands it as a precondition for forgiveness. For this reason

Blake is especially hard on repeat offenders, those whose actions make it hard for us to believe in their regeneration. His note to Aphorism 256 reads: "Such a one I can never forgive *while he continues such a one*" (Ann. Lavater; E, 589). In response to Lavater's number 606, "The public seldom forgive twice," Blake writes; "let us take their example" (Ann. Lavater; E, 598). To Aphorism 477 he adds "& never forgive him *till he mends*" (Ann. Lavater; E, 594); to number 309, "to hell *till he behaves better*" (Ann. Lavater; E, 590); and to number 401 "forgiveness of enemies can only come *upon their repentance*" (Ann. Lavater; E, 592; emphasis added in all examples). In the aphorisms to which Blake is responding, Lavater has portrayed these offenders as intractable knaves who are likely to be repeat offenders. Blake agrees with Lavater that *proven* repeat offenders, whom the public censures, do not deserve forgiveness. But Blake more generously hopes for regeneration in the case of first offenders. This generosity deserves note, even if Blake seems harsh in demanding repentance as a precondition of forgiveness. More important, Blake consistently assumes that offenders can "repent," "mend," and "behave better." His reliance on the idea of regeneration emerges even more clearly in his note that he cannot forgive an offender "while he continues such a one." This way of putting it suggests that the offender may *not* continue "such a one" but become a new, or regenerate, "one." It makes further sense of Blake's remarks about beating his enemy which I quoted at the beginning. Here is Blake's whole comment:

> none can see the man in the enemy[.] if he is ignorantly so, he is not truly an enemy[.] if maliciously not a man
>
> I cannot love my enemy for my enemy is not man but beast & devil if I have any. I can love him as a beast & wish to beat him.
>
> (Ann. Lavater; E, 589)

In comparing the unregenerate offender to a "beast & devil" and the regenerate to a "man," Blake implies that the regenerated really are new "ones," that is, members of a new species. It also suggests that Blake tends to see human forgiveness as the forgiveness of *a person*, who has been changed, rather than of a person's *sins* or infractions. His description implies that the victim forgives what his enemy *is,* instead of what he does.

Blake's second explicit mention of regeneration forms one of the longest marginalia in the book. He is responding to Lavater's Aphorism 489, in which Lavater somewhat qualifies his customary either/or view of human nature. The aphorism reads: "An entirely honest man, in the severe sense of the word, exists no more than an entirely dishonest knave: the best and the worst are only approximations of those qualities. Who are those that never contradict themselves? yet honesty never contradicts itself: who are those that always contradict themselves? yet knavery is mere self-contradiction. Thus the knowledge of man determines not the things themselves, but their proportions, the quantum of congruities and incongruities" (E, 594). Lavater first concedes the abstractness of his moral terms, by claiming that neither entirely honest men nor complete knaves exist. But then he invokes his customary division of honesty and knavery in the principle of self-contradiction. Blake here makes one of his rare direct criticisms of Lavater, showing that the aphorist omits regeneration: "this aphorism seems to consider man as simple & yet capable of evil . . . but if man is considerd as only evil. & god only good. how then is regeneration effected which turns the evil to good. by casting out the evil. by the good" (Ann. Lavater; E, 594). Blake revises Lavater's usual split between good and evil persons. Blake locates the split between good and evil in what Lavater had called the "proportions" within the individual: "Man is a twofold being. one part capable . . . of good[.] that which is capable of good is not also capable of evil. but that which is capable of evil is also capable of good" (Ann. Lavater; E, 594). Regeneration implies a mysterious process by which a person's character is renewed. Blake's description of it implies that there is no immutably evil person or part of a person, for "that which is capable of evil is also capable of good." By implying that the same human faculty is capable of both evil and good, Blake allows for a process that converts it from evil to good. Blake sees it as divine mercy whereby the good in human nature effects regeneration suddenly, "by casting out the evil by the good." Blake then compares regeneration to Jesus casting out devils (Matthew 12:26–29). Presumably this exorcist can cast out the "beast & devil" in one who has offended us.

The Lavater annotations thus provide some important precedents for a theory of human offense that is more complex than mere intellectual error: instead, we have precedents for Blake's two later ideas about forgiveness, that individuals pass through "states" and that offenders should undergo a fundamental remaking of their character, here "regeneration," later "self-annihilation."

Throughout the 1790s Blake did tend to think that human evil could be attributed to error. Yet curiously Blake uses the word *error* most frequently after the 1790s. In general, one can plot Blake's transition from a privative to a dualistic view of evil by means of his employment of the two villains, Urizen and the two spectres, Satan and the Spectre of Urthona. In *The Four Zoas* Blake initially wrote a resolution, in Night the Ninth, in which Urizen renounces his errors and is restored to his proper place. Later Blake interposed Night the Eighth, which attributes Urizen's sinister behavior to the "prester serpent," the evil of which must be exorcised. In *Milton* Blake's hero, Milton, must first wrestle with Urizen, who personifies the errors in *Paradise Lost*; he must then confront the evil in himself, his selfhood, personified in Satan. Despite the curious statement in the Bard's Song that "Satan is Urizen" (*M* 10:1; E, 104), the villains Urizen and Satan imply fundamentally different views of the nature of human offense, as error or as genuine evil. Blake's use of both villains in *The Four Zoas* and *Milton* suggests a desire to combine the two, to preserve the earlier, benign view, in the face of an increasing shift of conviction toward the more sinister view. In *Jerusalem* Urizen, for all practical purposes, disappears.

Night the Ninth of *The Four Zoas* provides an effective synthesis of Blake's middle view of offense as error and his representation of that view in his treatment of Urizen. This final night, which presents the renovation of Urizen, contains all the instances of the word *error* anywhere in *The Four Zoas*. A fundamental point of the privative theory of evil, as Thomas Aquinas and Blake both state it, is a dependence of error on faulty perception. Urizen's status as the reason, the faculty capable of error, is clear from Luvah's statement "Urizen who was Faith & Certainty is changd to Doubt" (*FZ* 27:15; E, 318) and from the final statement of the result of Urizen's renovation: "The dark Religions are departed & sweet Science reigns" (*FZ* 139:10; E, 407). Blake's dislike of religion here also suggests an earlier strain of his thought, in which, as Bentley notes, Blake made a frontal attack on Christianity.[19]

In accordance with a privative theory of evil, the goal of Night the Ninth is to rehabilitate all the Zoas. The Eternal Man, Albion, cries out to the Zoas, calling Urizen to rediscover his previous glory:

> O Prince of Light where art thou I behold thee not as once
> In those Eternal fields in clouds of morning stepping forth
> With harps & songs . . .
> . . . .
> See you not all this wracking furious confusion
> Come forth from slumbers of thy cold abstraction come forth
> Arise to Eternal births shake off thy cold repose
> Schoolmaster of souls great opposer of change arise.
> (*FZ* 120:14–16; 18–21; E, 389)

The eternal man calls Urizen to wake up "from slumbers of . . . thy cold abstraction," like the slumber from which the eternal man has awakened. The terminology of error and knowledge, or in Blake's terms, "dark Religions & sweet Science," continues as the Eternal Man criticizes Urizen's religion as

> The first author of this war & the distracting of honest minds
> Into confused perturbation & strife & honour & pride.
> (*FZ* 120:43–44; E, 390)

He further condemns Urizen's false science: "Thy self destroying beast formed Science shall be thy eternal lot" (*FZ* 120:40; E, 390). In response to this rhetoric of error and knowledge, religion and science, Urizen repents of his error:

> Urizen said. I have Erred & my Error remains with me
> What Chain encompasses in what Lock is the river of light confind
> That issues forth in the morning by measure & the evening by carefulness
> Where shall we take our stand to view the infinite & unbounded.
> (*FZ* 122:21–24; E, 391)

Urizen's sense that the river of light cannot be confined by a lock (or a Locke) reflects the sense that once error is cast off, one may see "the infinite & unbounded." Along with rehabilitation of Urizen at the end of the poem, the "End of the Dream" which includes the departure of the dark religions and the reign of sweet science, Blake replaces error in the world:

> The Expanding Eyes of Man behold the depths of wondrous worlds
> One Earth one sea beneath nor Erring Globes wander but Stars.
> (*FZ* 138:25; E, 406)

Yet Blake did not let the synthesis of Urizen as reason and offense as error stand. The Eternal Man had threatened to cast out Urizen, invoking a principle that Blake normally uses when writing about the spectre or the selfhood. This rhetoric of casting out seems to have hit a nerve, for later Blake added some lines in which error is described in terms far more pernicious than we have seen previously:[20]

> With Mystery the Harlot & with Satan for Ever & Ever
> Error can never be redeemd in all Eternity
> But Sin Even Rahab is redeemd in blood & fury & jealousy
> That line of blood that stretchd across the windows of the morning
> Redeemd from Errors power. Wake thou dragon of the Deeps.
> (*FZ* 120:47–51; E, 390)

In this addition Blake reverses the position he has held heretofore, that error, not sin, is forgivable. The Eternal Man seems to be addressing Urizen as an accuser, one who cannot forgive sexual "sins." This is why Blake mentions Rahab, the prostitute who aided Moses' spies: her sin is forgivable and she is free from error's power by joining the followers of Moses. The only reason the Eternal Man would proclaim the forgiveness of a prostitute is that he wants to shame the accuser. Thus, insofar as the Eternal Man here rebukes Urizen, it is in his function as accuser and not as reason.

Blake further qualifies the presentation of offense as error by adding subsequent layers to the manuscript. Although Night the Ninth of *The Four Zoas* is the last section of the poem, it was almost certainly not the last to be written.[21] In fact, it seems to belong to an earlier strain of Blake's thought, one in which Blake strives to show "that all parts of the self must be rehabilitated and harmonized."[22] In Night the Eighth, Blake interrupts this earlier model, by presenting the evil in Urizen as the "prester serpent." Significantly, Urizen's renunciation of his error can come only after the Eternal Man casts out this more pernicious force. He exorcises the prester serpent, the evil form that took over Urizen:

> Arise O stony form of death O dragon of the Deeps
> Lie down before my feet O Dragon Let Urizen arise.
> (*FZ* 120:28–29; E, 389)

This later layer of the manuscript places Urizen's renunciation of error in a new context: that first one must be freed from this spectral form, and only then can he renounce his errors.

Blake's later inclusion of new layers of narrative around the initial presentation of Urizen presents a modified position, that errors are a lesser evil. Urizen's errors are the errors of bad science, but the endeavor of science is itself active and hence positive. Blake wrote in the Lavater annotations: "As I understand Vice it is a negative . . . all Act is Virtue" (226:4, 12; E, 601). And yet the revisions to the Ninth Night of *The Four Zoas* imply a new twist on that view: that renunciation of the privative evil of one's errors demands an exorcism of the genuine evil of the selfhood.

The Four Zoas implied that the category of error applies only to activities which are fundamentally good. Blake experiments with this possibility further in his Notebook's prose fragments, called by his editors *A Vision of the Last Judgment*. Blake implies a thematic link between Night the Ninth, subtitled "Being the Last Judgment" (*FZ* 117; E, 386), and his *Vision* of the same event.

Vision is frequently cited by those who believe that Blake saw human offense primarily as error. Yet close examination of this curious document reveals that it invokes error only in the context of bad art.[23] All Blake's references to error in *Vision* occur in the final section, that is, from page 83 of the Notebook to the end. In the first half Blake had described the scene of the Last Judgment and the respective fates of the just and the unjust. In the second half, Blake repeats himself somewhat, reinterpreting the Last Judgment as a decision about art and artists.

In an early version in a letter to Ozias Humphry, Blake describes baptism and Holy Communion in a fairly conventional manner: "On the Right hand of the Throne of Christ is Baptism On [*his*] the left is the Lords Supper the two introducers into Eternal Life Women with Infants approach the Figure of an aged Apostle which represents Baptism & on the left hand the Lords Supper is administerd by Angels from the hands of another [*aged*] Apostle" (E, 553–54). The recapitulation begins when Blake confronts the rationale for a last judgment, "A Last Judgment is Necessary because Fools flourish" (*VLJ* 84:16; E, 561). When Blake returns to this image in the second part of the document, he reinterprets it as referring to art. He writes: "Around the Throne Heaven is opend & the Nature of Eternal Things Displayd All Springing from the Divine Humanity All Beams from him. . . . He is the Bread & the Wine he is the Water of Life accordingly on Each Side of the opening Heaven appears an Apostle that on the Right Represents Baptism that on the Left Represents the Lords Supper" (*VLJ* 84:33–38; E, 561–62). The diction shows a subtle shift. Instead of "Christ," Blake uses his own preferred name for Jesus, "the Divine Humanity." Earlier he stressed the outward ceremony of baptism, in which a woman brings an infant, and the outward ceremony of communion, administered by an apostle. In the later version, the Divine Humanity is "the Bread & the Wine" and "the Water of Life." Thus Blake gives an internal significance to the outward signs. The statement that the nature of eternal things is, like a group of paintings, "Displayd" suggests an artistic allusion.

But Blake then interprets the sacraments as simultaneously the battles of truth and error and also the struggle of the artist. "All Life consists of these Two," he writes, having just referred to the two sacraments. He then renames them: "Throwing off Error <& Knaves from our company> continually & recieving [*sic*] Truth <or Wise Men into our Company> Continually" (*VLJ* 84:39–41; E, 562). He summarizes this interpretation of his own picture: "Thus My Picture is a History of Art & Science [*fits*] <the Foundation of Society> Which is Humanity itself" (*VLJ* 84:46–47; E, 562). Here again he uses science in the sense we saw in *The Four Zoas*; the Last Judgment and its revelation of error addresses the errors of bad science, as we saw earlier, and the present situation of bad art. Even the inferior genres of fable and allegory are "Seldom without some Vision" (*VLJ* 68:10; E, 554).

Blake makes a similar remark in his Annotations to Reynolds, a debate between two artists which, understandably, centered on professional issues. Blake's acid responses to Sir Joshua are motivated in part by Blake's sense of personal injury.[24] It is also motivated by Blake's objection to Reynolds's artistic theory, which, as Hazard Adams writes, attempts a "compromise between an empirical and a Platonic stance" on general beauty, both components that deny Blake's fundamental commitment to minute particulars.[25] Within this context of a professional dispute, Blake responds to Reynolds's statement, "The errors of genius, however, are pardonable," with the remark: "Genius has no Error it is Ignorance that is Error" (111; E, 652).

Blake's complaints about bad art were prompted by considerable professional hardships. Other artists were flourishing; he was not. As Aileen Ward observes, Blake was particularly hurt by the repeated rejection of his paintings by the Royal Academy.[26] (He could not be accepted as engraver because he refused to accept the Royal Academy's designation of engraving as a reproductive, not an original art.) Blake may have overreacted in his charges against the academy, Ward concludes; but, by "setting a standard that by and large had benefited English art, the Academy had also gained a power to exclude, and Blake had not yet learned to bear the sense of exclusion and neglect."[27] These, then, were the fools whose flourishing demanded a Last Judgment. The fact that Blake limits his invocation of error to the section on art suggests that art, like science, has a privileged place. Even bad art is necessary: "No man can Embrace True Art till he has Explord & Cast Out False Art" (*VLJ* 84: E, 562). Thus one function of the Last Judgment, in terms of one person's relationship to truth and art, is the casting out of error: "Whenever any Individual Rejects Error & Embraces Truth a Last Judgment passes upon that Individual" (*VLJ* 84: E, 562).[28]

Bad art may be necessary, even desirable, on the individual level. But Blake has no patience with bad artists, sometimes personifying them as the error they produce. When Blake continues, "to be an Error & to be Cast out is part of Gods Design" (*VLJ* 84: E, 562), he begins the identification of the error with the offender, an identification that begins to undo all the advocacy of bad art's value. Indeed Blake begins to betray his resentment: "this is A Last Judgment when Men of Real Art Govern & Pretenders Fall. . . . A Last Judgment is not for the purpose of making Bad Men better but for the Purpose of hindering them from opressing the Good with Poverty & Pain by means of Such Vile

Arguments & Insinuations" (*VLJ* 84: E, 561). The Last Judgment Blake imagines here is not at all a gentle one in which errors are corrected. The Last Judgment will not make "Bad Men better" but will simply remove their power to accuse good men by means of "Vile Arguments & Insinuations." Thus, if error is cast out of bad men at the Last Judgment, their error looks remarkably like the disposition of accusation.

The tendency to personify error is linked to one of Blake's own favorite artistic doctrines, the advocacy of minute particulars: "<These> are not only Universal but Particular. Each are Personified There is not an Error but it has a Man for its [*Actor*] Agent that is it is a Man. There is not a Truth but it has also a Man <Good & Evil are Qualities in Every Man whether <a> Good or Evil Man>" (*VLJ* 86:3–7; E, 563). Here Blake softens his earlier resentment toward the pretenders to art. Earlier he had seemed ready to cast them out as if their very being were equivalent to their errors. Here he makes a gesture of forgiveness in the admission that "Good & Evil are Qualities in Every Man whether <a> Good or Evil Man." Blake develops this line of thinking about forgiveness in his major personification of human offense, within and without the self, in the Spectre of Urthona.

Blake's limiting his use of error to the contexts of art and science suggests that Blake rethought his position of the 1790s. As McGann observes, "Because Blake came to grips with the problem of truth as a practising artist, rather than as an academic or a philosopher, his philosophical significance is to be sought, and defined, in his graphic and poetical work, and not in his ideas as such."[29] Moreover, in Blake's view this concentration of truth and error in the endeavor of art applies to the work of other artists, pretenders though they might be, as well as applying to himself: "Art and imagination have more to do with truth and falsehood than do the forms of 'abstract reasoning.' "[30] For Blake error was always a useful category for art, but increasingly not all human endeavors could be described as the active pursuit of the positive values of art and science.

The word *error* occurs only once in *Milton*. Clearly, however, Blake is concerned with the problem of Milton's errors. In the Preface to *Milton*, Blake enumerates Milton's errors and diagnoses their cause: "The Stolen and Perverted Writings of Homer & Ovid: of Plato & Cicero. which all Men ought to contemn: are set up by artifice against the Sublime of the Bible. but when the New Age is at leisure to Pronounce; all will be set right: & those Grand Works of the more ancient & consciously & professedly Inspired Men, will hold their proper rank, & the Daughters of Memory shall become the Daughters of Inspiration. Shakspeare & Milton were both curbd by the general malady &

infection from the silly Greek & Latin slaves of the Sword" (*M* 1: E, 95). Though Blake critics have written about Milton's errors,[31] Blake's dominant metaphor here is of illness and obstacle, not of error. Milton and Shakespeare were "curbd" and "infected," literally, under the influence of pernicious models. For Blake to speak of infection, then, suggests that error is more insidious than previously recognized.

Yet the plot of *Milton* suggests that Blake wants it both ways. As a result, in *Milton* Blake gives Milton two opponents. Once again, Milton's errors, such as they are, are primarily conceptual errors incurred in the process of doing something fundamentally constructive, that is, writing poetry. One error appears as the oppressive Mosaic figure Urizen, who meets Milton at the river and tries to impede his progress. Urizen, as the discussion of *The Four Zoas* revealed, was the Zoa who fell most frequently into error. In *Milton* their struggle is presented with great solemnity:

> Urizen emerged from his Rocky Form & from his Snows,
> And he also darkened his brows: freezing dark rocks between
> The footsteps. and infixing deep the feet in marble beds:
> That Milton labourd with his journey, & his feet bled sore
> Upon the clay now chang'd to marble.
> (*M* 18:51, 19:1–4; E, 112)

Milton does not attempt to subdue Urizen but, as one might with any creative or created form, to reform him, in the literal sense.

> Milton took of the red clay of Succoth, moulding it with care
> Between his palms: and filling up the furrows of many years
> Beginning at the feet of Urizen, and on the bones
> Creating new flesh on the Demon cold, and building him,
> As with new clay a Human form in the Valley of Beth Peor.
> (*M* 19:10–14; E, 112)

Like the errors of false art that Blake discussed in *Vision of the Last Judgment*, the errors of *Paradise Lost*, personified in Urizen, are raw material to be reshaped. In fact, Blake's comparison of Urizen to the artistic medium of clay emphasizes this raw potential that exists in all erroneous art and science.

The other enemy allocated to Milton is Satan, the Spectre of Milton. But Blake treats more harshly that other part of Milton's false self, Satan, the Spectre of Milton, who needs to be annihilated at the end of the poem. We will return to the figure of Milton's Spectre, Satan, in chapter 4. For the time being, let it suffice to say that in *Milton* Blake's cast divides up the depiction of Milton's past, Urizen personifying his savable errors and Satan personifying that accusing disposition in the character, that part of Milton's own energy which he exiled to hell—a hell that turned out to be a furnace.

Milton's two villains, then, present Blake's desire to preserve a sense of offense as merely intellectual or artistic error that can be overcome and reshaped, and also a concurrent sense that evil is genuine and volitional, demanding "self-annihilation." When Blake moved into *Jerusalem*, his sense of the pernicious corruption of the will had become stronger, and he rewrote the notion of error to reflect this more pessimistic and suspicious sense.

The transition between Blake's attribution of offense to error and the attribution of offense to a genuine evil can be seen in a simpler form in the following poem from the Notebook:

> Anger & Wrath my bosom rends
> I thought them the Errors of friends
> But all my limbs with warmth glow
> I find them the Errors of the foe.
>
> (E, 503)

At first this poem seems to record a simple reversal, by which Blake abandons the idea that those who offended him were his friends and recognizes them now as foes. Yet the peripeteia is more complex: formerly he attributed errors to "friends"; now he assigns them to a single, monolithic foe. The first couplet suggests the benign view that offenses are merely errors that do not destroy relationships, because the offenders are still "my friends." The second couplet reveals a sense of a more sinister agent, one whose concerted efforts organized all the individual affronts offered by friends. Thus the "Errors" of the foe in the second couplet are errors of a far different order from the errors of friends recorded in the first.

In *Jerusalem* Blake comes to use *error* in both of those senses, errors as the mistakes of Albion, Los's friend, and also error as a pernicious force, governed by an overarching foe. The problem arises, in this double use, that the entire mitigating force of error as an excuse for offense is lost, so that error is just as bad as sin—as Blake wrote in one of the later additions to *The Four Zoas*, error can never be redeemed in all eternity.

In a couple of instances, Blake places the idea of offense as error in a deliberate rhetorical context. One case is a speech by the character Jerusalem. As she protests Albion's rejection of her, she longs for an earlier time in which she and Albion lived, "forgetting error, not pondering on evil" (*J* 20:7; E, 165). Later, she protests Vala's advocacy of remembering and revenge, as encapsulated in the image of captives "number[ing] moments over and over; / Stringing them on their remembrance as on a thread of sorrow" (*J* 20:7; E, 165). Then Jerusalem offers this alternative view:

> O Vala what is Sin? that thou shudderst and weepest
> At sight of thy once lov'd Jerusalem! What is Sin but a little
> Error & fault that is soon forgiven; but mercy is not a Sin
> Nor pity nor love nor kind forgiveness!
> (*J* 20:22–25; E, 165)

Significantly, here Blake takes a position much like the one he himself stated earlier and places it in a deliberate dramatic context, that of pastoral. Jerusalem had prefaced this statement with the following protest against Albion:

> Wherefore hast thou shut me into the winter of human life
> And clos'd up the sweet regions of youth and virgin innocence:
> Where we live, forgetting error, not pondering on evil:
> Among my lambs & brooks of water, among my warbling birds:
> Where we delight in innocence before the face of the Lamb:
> Going in and out before him in his love and sweet affection.
> (*J* 20:5–10; E, 165)

This pastoral, idyllic scene, "the sweet regions of youth and virgin innocence," displays many of the hallmarks of Beulah or innocence, such as the birds, lambs, and brooks of water. Moreover, the youth and virgin relate to the Lamb as children, delighting in innocence before his face. Blake wrote in *Milton* that such a Beulistic point of view was appropriate to the emanations, and his placement of the view of sins as error in the mouth of the particular character Jerusalem in the act of recalling this particular pastoral scene may suggest that Blake himself has reflected on his previous position and put it in a place in his comprehensive system. Namely, the attribution of offense to error is the point of view of Beulah or innocence—partially true, but incomplete.

A second time Blake qualifies the notion of human offense as error by presenting it as the point of view of a limited speaker, Oxford. Oxford's speech occurs in the midst of a episode several plates long in *Jerusalem*, chapter 2, an episode in which several personified cities attempt to help their friend Albion. Oxford's speech addresses Albion and diagnoses his problem repeatedly as one of error. He says:

Thou art in Error Albion, the Land of Ulro:
One Error not remov'd, will destroy a human Soul
Repose in Beulahs night, till the Error is remov'd
Reason not on both sides. Repose upon our bosoms
Till the Plow of Jehovah, and the Harrow of Shaddai
Have passed over the Dead, to awake the Dead to Judgment.
(*J* 41:10–15; E, 188)

There may be a certain rightness in having Oxford, the personification of a university town, diagnose Albion's disease as error, as if education alone would eradicate it. (Blake associates Oxford with error once again, near the close of *Jerusalem*. There Los searches for Oothoon, asking, "Where hides my child? in Oxford hidest thou with Antamon? / In graceful hidings of error" [*J* 83:27–28; E, 241]). While the attribution of human offense to error may be a peculiarly academic tendency, Blake makes his qualification of the position clear in other ways. As in the character Jerusalem's discussion of error, Blake associates the definition of offense as error with the condition of Beulah. Oxford, having diagnosed Albion's problem as error, seeks to cure it by the typically Beulistic advice of rest, saying, "Repose in Beulahs night" and "Repose upon our bosoms." Further, Oxford advises Albion to wait for salvation to come from the work of someone else, waiting "Till the Plow of Jehovah, and the Harrow of Shaddai / Have Passed over the Dead." This counsel, of waiting till someone else performs a salvific deed, is one that Blake rejects in other places.[32] Moreover, Blake's alter ego, Los, has just exploded in wrath against the Four Zoas as they advocate such a course. Los

. . . grew furious raging: Why stand we here trembling around
Calling on God for help; and not ourselves in whom God dwells
Stretching a hand to save the falling Man.
(*J* 38:12–14; E, 184)

Blake's portrayal of the efforts of the cities of England to help Albion has been acknowledged as a problematic section of *Jerusalem*. In particular, the portrayal of Bath, the city that speaks before Oxford does, seems quite ambivalent.[33] On the one hand, Blake admires the efforts of Richard Warner, who published a sermon advocating peace with France in 1804, and whom Erdman has identified as Blake's prototype for Bath. Yet on the other hand, Bath's counsel, like Oxford's, promotes a disquieting passivity and what Blake would call false humility. Bath says:

. . . however high
Our palaces and cities, and however fruitful are our fields
In Selfhood, we are nothing: but fade away in mornings breath.
Our mildness is nothing: the greatest mildness we can use
Is incapable and nothing! none but the Lamb of God can heal
This dread disease.

(*J* 40:11–16; E, 187)

While Blake himself may concede part of the truth of Bath's position, that Jesus is necessary to curing Albion's disease, he certainly would conclude not that Albion should therefore conduct himself in passiveness waiting for that salvation, but that he should act, for example, by recognizing the likeness of Jesus in Los his friend, as he does at the end of *Jerusalem*.

As Erdman has pointed out, Blake's ambivalent treatment of Bath is made clearest in Albion's failure to respond to him. The exhortations of a university town have made Albion "studious," but not of himself. He is "studious *of others* in his pale disease: / Brooding on evil"(*J* 42:1; E, 189; emphasis added). The repetition of the theme of Albion's disease further suggests the inadequacy of the error metaphor.

When Los heckles Albion further, to try to convert him, Los adopts the language of error used by Oxford but supplements it with a far harsher set of connotations. Thus the Beulistic view is incorporated into the Edenic:

Los answerd. Righteousness & justice I give thee in return
For thy righteousness! but I add mercy also, and bind
Thee from destroying these little ones: am I to be only
Merciful to thee and cruel to all that thou hatest[?]
Thou wast the Image of God surrounded by the Four Zoa's
Three thou hast slain! I am the Fourth: thou canst not destroy me.
Thou art in Error; trouble me not with thy righteousness.
I have innocence to defend and ignorance to instruct.

(*J* 42:19–26; E, 189)

While Los declares that Albion is "in Error," the condition he describes is precisely that of vengeance, for Los implies that Albion wants Los to commit vengeful acts when he asks, "am I to be only / Merciful to thee and cruel to all that thou hatest[?]" In fact, Los later issues this challenge to Albion: "I defy thy worst revenge" (*J* 42:39; E, 189).

Blake, then, deliberately places the attribution of offense to error in particular contexts, contexts which suggest that they are only partially adequate. Moreover, after the 1790s Blake develops several categories for human offense, categories that he uses simultaneously with error but that cannot be equated with error. Examples are the "Pretenders" to art whom Blake decried in *Vision of the Last Judgment* and the disposition to vengeance in Albion, as Blake portrays it in *Jerusalem*. If Blake's use of the term *error* sufficiently indicates his views of the privative or dualistic nature of evil, then it appears that during the period of the major prophecies, Blake held that offenses in art are privative, while offenses in relationships are genuine.

The increasing importance of forgiveness in Blake's prophecies indicates that the matter of mending broken relationships became as important as, if not more important than, the matter of the individual's relation to truth. And in the matter of human relationships, the difficulty of forgiving the imperfect other emerges. The next two chapters address Blake's struggles to represent that genuine evil as part of the self and as part of the other.

3

States and Individuals

In the second half of his life, Blake used forgiveness as a metaphor to solve a new set of conceptual and psychological issues. His ethical focus shifts as he employs forgiveness as a metaphor to remedy the condition of human otherness, the condition of intractable difference among human beings which he had previously celebrated as "contrariety." Forgiveness offered Blake a powerful metaphor because it implies a story that accounts for both transaction, an intersubjective exchange between two autonomous subjects, and also identity, a psychic fusion of those subjects into what Blake calls "One Man." In Blake's emergent view, it is no longer one party's *offense* that provides the occasion to be forgiven, but *the very fact of his otherness* from the forgiver. Forgiveness, then, becomes the sign of identity, in that the otherness has been overcome or "forgiven." Yet forgiveness retains the trace of transaction, since forgiveness requires the constant fuel of such an "offense" of otherness to be overcome. As Paley and Damrosch have demonstrated, the problem of dualism and monism plagued Blake throughout his life and came to particular intensity in the late period of his life when the ethical ideal of contrariety no longer seemed to serve by itself. Eaves states that "commentators who confuse metaphors of identity with metaphors of transaction inevitably fail at explaining theories of art such as Blake's."[1] Eaves's distinction between metaphors of identity and metaphors of transaction provides the preliminary ground for examining the double role of forgiveness in Blake's dualism and monism; his questioning of self and other. For forgiveness is a metaphor Blake wanted to serve both purposes, to stand the middle ground between transaction and identity, to mediate between an intersubjective transaction between individuals and an intrapsychic coping mechanism. Paradoxically, however, taking forgiveness as intrapsychic denies the recognition of individuality, of otherness, necessary to keeping forgiveness as intersubjective. Forgiveness became absolutely central to Blake because it condenses the two meanings, mediating the contradiction between transaction with an other and identity with him.

Theories of intersubjectivity, of the relation between self and other, can illuminate the ethical import of Blake's turn to human otherness as the object of forgiveness. Phenomenological formulations of the relation between self and other, such as Martin Buber's famous distinction between regarding the other as an It and as a Thou, have long been valued as an attempt to reassert a sense of intersubjectivity in the face of a long tradition of knowing as the subject's dominance over the object.[2] But one must also ask whether the other addressed as Thou is truly other than the self making the address. In this line of thinking, Elizabeth Grosz writes, ethics is "the working out or negotiation between an other (or others) seen as prior to and pre-given for the subject, and a subject. Ethics is a response to the recognition of the primacy of alterity over identity."[3] Within the phenomenological tradition, Levinas proposes an important qualification of the view of the disclosure of the other presupposed by Heidegger and by Buber. Levinas contends that their accounts of disclosure presuppose an other that is merely a replication of the self; he believes it is essential to keep the other as exterior, as a phenomenological nonobject that cannot be assimilated to the self but remains exterior to the self.[4] Levinas describes as "totalizing" that mode of consciousness which seeks to reduce the exteriority of the other. In transferring phenomenological terms to the domain of psychoanalysis, Jessica Benjamin proposes a model in which the mutual recognition of self and other is normative (rather than, say, a model in which a sole self is "autonomous," or in which the other is conceived merely as the mirror or complement of the self). Benjamin writes that the primary advantage of an intersubjective view is that "the other whom the self meets is also a self, a subject in his or her own right."[5] Luce Irigaray has theorized the feminist ramifications of this ethical problem in her responses to Levinas. There she claims that Levinas always defines the feminine as man's other, "the other of the same."[6] For Irigaray, the question of otherness is defined by sexual difference, the question of whether the feminine is accorded its own subjectivity, a true otherness, or merely the status of "the other of the same"—a specious otherness which can be defined as identical with the self or as the opposite or complement of the self, but not as truly other. Postponing until chapter 4 a discussion of Blake's use of forgiveness to define sexual delineations of otherness, in the present chapter I will address Blake's distinction between states and individuals, tracing its function in sometimes permitting and sometimes condemning human individuality and otherness, otherness defined in social and political terms.

Arendt explicitly theorizes intersubjectivity socially to undergird her concept of forgiveness; she is one of the few phenomenological thinkers to address the ethics of forgiveness directly. Her theorizing about forgiveness presents a wide range before the publication of her most famous idea, "the banality of evil," in *Eichmann in Jerusalem* (1963). Earlier, in *The Origins of Totalitarianism* (1951), she concluded that the threshold of the unforgivable had been reached: "Totalitarian regimes have discovered without knowing it that there are crimes which men can neither punish nor forgive. When the impossible was made possible it became the unpunishable, unforgivably absolute evil which could no longer be understood and explained by the evil motives of self-interest, greed, covetousness, resentment, thirst for power, and cowardice: and therefore which anger could not revenge, love could not endure, friendship could not forgive."[7] However, in *The Human Condition* Arendt concluded that forgiveness becomes possible through intersubjectivity, the recognition of the other, which provides the purpose for the endurance of the evil committed by the other. *The Human Condition* presents the ground for forgiveness in a society based on what she calls "the human condition of plurality," that is, "the fact that men, not Man, live on the earth and inhabit the world."[8] Moreover, Arendt's emphasis on the contact with the other as a unique self, rather than as another version of one's own self, accords with her analysis of forgiveness as the springboard for what is genuinely new in human relationships and in human culture. For Arendt, contact with the genuinely other (whom one forgives or encounters through other modes of action) prevents one from constructing the other in one's own image, for, she writes, "plurality is the condition of human action because we are all the same, that is, human, in such a way that nobody is ever the same as anybody else who ever lived, lives, or will live."[9] Arendt's recognition of plurality as the human condition forms the basis of a theory of forgiveness based on intersubjectivity. By contrast, Niebuhr's analysis of forgiveness—that one endures the evil in the other because the evil in the self is known—is formed on the notion of identification, stressing sameness, the commonality of evil in both self and other. It produces the virtue of endurance but runs the risk of constructing a world composed of repetitions of sameness: to invert Arendt's terms, a world composed of Man rather than men. It is this tension—between on the one hand Blake's commitment to what Arendt called plurality and he himself called contrariety, and on the other, Blake's commitment to seeing all men as versions, or repetitions, of the same

Man—that riddles Blake's representations of forgiveness and his theories of states and individuals particularly.

For now I will concentrate on mapping the occlusion of intersubjective in favor of intrapsychic forgiveness in Blake's treatment of "states" and the paradoxical loss of individuality in the notion of "individual" he opposes to "states." Thematically important forgiveness in Blake occurs between characters with little to differentiate them (in *Milton* the male reader Blake forgiving the male poet Milton, for example, or in *Jerusalem* the reader fashioned in the form of Jesus forgiving the male poet Blake).

My argument in this chapter is that Blake attempted to use the distinction between states and individuals as a rubric of forgiveness both intrapsychically (forgiving oneself and understanding one's own propensity to evil actions) and also intersubjectively (forgiving another person and recognizing his or her otherness). Sometimes the states-individuals distinction performs only one of these functions in a text; sometimes the distinction vacillates between both meanings. Fundamentally, the intrapsychic model won out over the intersubjective model, because Blake came to define otherness—the very recognition of which is central to intersubjectivity—as itself an evil.

My distinction between intrapsychic and intersubjective forgiveness illuminates one of Blake's key formulations of human forgiveness, the distinction between "states" and "individuals of (or in) those states"—a distinction that has been oversimplified, seen as univocal rather than referring doubly to intrapsychic and intersubjective forgiveness. With high hopes for this conceptual distinction, Blake invokes the formula several times in moments of crisis. In Night the Eighth of *The Four Zoas,* Los addresses the forces of evil, personified in Rahab: "Learn distinct to know O Rahab / The Difference between States & Individuals of those States" (*FZ* 115:23–24; E, 380). In *Milton* the "Seven Angels of the Presence" instruct the wavering Milton:

> Distinguish therefore States from Individuals in those States.
> States Change: but Individual Identities never change nor cease.

They conclude: "The Imagination is not a State: it is the Human Existence itself" (*M* 32:22–23, 32; E, 132). Blake closes each of *Jerusalem*'s first three chapters with an exposition of the distinction between states and individuals. And Blake's character Jerusalem explicitly declares:

> Learn therefore O Sisters to distinguish the Eternal Human
> That walks about among the stones of fire in bliss & woe

> Alternate! from those States or Worlds in which the Spirit travels:
> This is the only means to Forgiveness of Enemies.
> (*J* 49:72–75; E, 199)

The character Jerusalem's formulation may betray Blake's desperation as well as his hope. Dramatically, her claim that the distinction between states and individuals is "the *only* means to Forgiveness of Enemies" suggests weariness and disillusionment with other, less efficacious means of forgiving enemies, weariness and disillusionment that Blake shared. Despite its dramatic force, however, "only" is conceptually misleading, for the distinction is not univocal but fraught with Blake's desire to stretch his myth over intrapsychic and intersubjective realities. Blake uses the distinction in two ways. In one way of putting it, a *state,* always a single state, is a condition of error or perdition. In the other, *states,* almost always plural, denote types of characters and of individual genius. To put it bluntly, in the first locution an individual must be delivered from a state; in the second, the individual is the state. These uses of the word state are quite distinct, though not so distinct as to have nothing to do with one another.[10] Both uses of *state* provide a logical basis for human forgiveness, and this common purpose, doubtless, motivates Blake to group them together constantly, often mixing the two uses in a single work or passage. Blake uses the word *state* to reconcile and simultaneously to preserve the tension between an intrapsychic ethics of virtue and an ethics of intersubjectivity. Blake thus attempts to unify, through the use of a common term, all efforts to "Humanize / In the Forgiveness of Sins" (*J* 98:44–45; E, 258).

In *Vision of the Last Judgment* Blake uses *states* in an intersubjective sense to denote alterity between self and other and to denote multiple kinds of human individuality. There Blake endows some states with the names of biblical patriarchs: "The Persons who ascend to Meet the Lord coming in the Clouds with power & great Glory. are representations of those States described in the Bible under the Names of the Fathers before & after the Flood" (*VLJ;* E, 559). Here Blake uses *states* in a celebratory way. In this usage, *states* are multiple, and he does not imply that one state is superior to another; variety among the states seems to Blake a good thing. This rubric of states acknowledges the infinite variety among different people. The notion of state, then, allows one to forgive someone who is different from himself, that is, to acknowledge his contrariety and individual genius. In this context *states* remain consistent with Blake's commitment to contrariety, defined in *The Marriage of Heaven and Hell,* and referring primarily to social relations between "the two classes of men, the energetic creators and the rational organizers."[11] Multiple states, where states mean *kinds* of individuality, can here serve as a means to forgiveness of sins in an intersubjective model of forgiveness, because the accuser can forgive the other his otherness in recognizing that not all selves need be alike.

In *Jerusalem,* however, Blake employs *state* primarily as an intrapsychic indicator. For example,

> Then the Divine hand found the Two Limits, Satan and Adam,
> In Albions bosom: for in every Human bosom those Limits stand
> . . . .
> And the appearance of a Man was seen in the Furnaces;
> Saving those who have sinned from the punishment of the Law,
> (In pity of the punisher whose state is eternal death).
> (*J* 31:1–2, 5–7; E, 177)

This passage contains several noteworthy features. One is that Blake equates *state* with the condition of "eternal death," as a part of a strong dichotomy between Satan and Adam. *State* then, denotes a condition Blake condemns, as contrasted with his celebratory attitude toward the various patriarchal states exemplified in biblical characters. A second feature is Blake's focus on Satan and the state of "eternal death" as components of the intrapsychic moral struggle, an ethics of virtue defined by the exemplars Satan and Jesus. At this juncture, differences among individuals—that fundamental truth of intersubjective forgiveness—pales in the light of an intrapsychic truth claimed as universally valid: "for *in every Human bosom* those Limits stand" (emphasis added). Finally, it is significant that Blake attributes "eternal death" to one actively engaged in vengeance, that is, to "the punisher." Blake, then, equates the intrapsychic process with a struggle between forgiveness and accusation—that, in fact, other offenses have been subsumed under the umbrella term *accusation* and other virtues subsumed under the term *forgiveness.*

Viewed intrapsychically, the single state of accusation resembles hierarchical concepts like *level,* which Blake mentions in a famous letter:

> Now I a fourfold vision see
> And a fourfold vision is given to me
> Tis fourfold in my supreme delight
> And three fold in soft Beulahs night
> And twofold Always. May God us keep
> From Single vision & Newtons sleep.
> (*E*, 722)

This vision implies levels of increasingly complete vision. In some contexts Blake relies on all four levels, called Eden, Beulah, Generation, and Ulro.[12] But when Blake addresses the issue of intrapsychic forgiveness, he generally simplifies the four levels of vision to a dichotomy between the dispositions to forgiveness and to accusation.

Blake's use of *states,* then, partakes of the ambiguity that multiple states can describe, nonpejoratively, the variations among human beings related intersubjectively, while also describing, pejoratively, the intrapsychic state of accusation. A similar ambiguity exists, potentially, in Emanuel Swedenborg's writings, which Blake read early in his career. There *states* refer to the proximity of angels to God in heaven. Angels frequently change their states, at times retreating to a state more distant from God in order to rest. The variation between states, Swedenborg writes, is like "the daily changing states of light or shade, warmth and cold, or morning, noon, evening and night in the world."[13] Such variation seems to value all states equally, permitting intersubjective community and acceptance. But the fundamental conception of *states* as nearness to or distance from God permits the other, intrapsychic, sense that some states are inferior or evil. Indeed, Swedenborg locates some states in hell.

Despite his acquaintance with this potential ambiguity in Swedenborg early in his career, Blake does not use the word *state* much before the watershed year of 1802. Before that date a few uses do occur, however. In the Lavater annotations, we noted, Blake remarks that "knaveries are not human nature. knaveries are knaveries." This remark foreshadows the pejorative sense of the word *states*. Since knaveries are not human nature, nothing essentially human is left behind when a person moves from that state to a fuller imaginative identity. Moreover, Blake clearly distinguished knavery from error in the Lavater annotations. Later, *states* connote human variety, making one appearance in *The Songs of Innocence and of Experience,* one of Blake's own favorites among his works, which bears the subtitle, "Shewing the Two Contrary States of the Human Soul" (E, 7). Yet Blake's examples of innocence and of experience suggest their mutual dependence; by naming them "Contraries," he intimates their equal value. Still later, in the Lambeth Books, Blake uses this refrain in his accounts of the Fall: "A first (or second) age passed over, & a state of dismal woe." *State* here seems synonymous with sorrow and materiality, a condition one should flee, as Urizen's sons did: "They calld it Egypt, & left it." Yet no exclusive pattern emerges in Blake's usage of *states* before the period of the major prophecies.[14] In the prophecies Blake condenses the two notions of states in order to create a myth he hoped would be universally valid, accounting for intersubjective and intrapsychic processes. The condensation in the prophecies becomes clearer by contrast with two nonprophetic works from this same period: *Descriptive Catalogue* and *A Vision of the Last Judgment,* in which *state* remains remarkably free from the double duty it performs in the prophecies.

In *Descriptive Catalogue, state* is one of several terms Blake employs to suggest the intersubjective task of recognizing and valuing variations in human individualities. Though Blake does not mention forgiveness in *Descriptive Catalogue,* his use of states as celebrating variations in human individuality is logically fundamental to the process of intersubjective forgiveness theorized by Arendt. Written for his ill-fated exhibition in 1809,[15] *Descriptive Catalogue* asserts the superiority of Blake's own picture of Chaucer's Canterbury Pilgrims over that of Thomas Stothard.[16] In the course of his polemic, Blake claims that Chaucer's pilgrims "represent eternal types in all ages."[17] There Blake insists on the inherence of the class in the individual representative, once writing, "Every Class is Individual" (Ann. Reynolds 63; E, 648). About the pilgrims themselves Blake writes that "Chaucers Canterbury Pilgrims [are] a Complete Index of Human Characters as they appear Age after Age" (*PA;* E, 571).[18] In another place he elaborates the idea of index, proposing various terms for the universal characters depicted by the individual pilgrims. This passage reflects the restless quality of Blake's search for an appropriate term for universality:

> The characters of Chaucer's Pilgrims are the characters which compose all ages and nations: as one age falls, another rises, different to mortal sight, but to immortals only the same; for we see the same characters repeated again and again, in animals, vegetables, minerals, and in men; nothing new occurs in identical existence; Accident ever varies, Substance can never suffer change nor decay.
>
> Of Chaucer's characters, as described in his Canterbury Tales, some of the names or titles are altered by time, but the characters themselves for ever remain unaltered, and consequently they are the physiognomies or lineaments of universal human life, beyond which Nature never steps. . . . I have known multitudes of those who would have been monks in the age of monkery, who in this deistical age are deists. As Newton numbered the stars, and as Linneus numbered the plants, so Chaucer numbered the classes of men.
>
> (*DC;* E, 532–33)

Blake employs several terms for the typicality of these pilgrims: "the *characters* . . . compose all ages and nations"; "nothing new occurs in *identical* existence";

"*Substance* can never suffer change nor decay"; "the *physiognomies* or *lineaments* of universal human life, beyond which Nature never steps"; and "Chaucer numbered the *classes* of men" (emphasis added in all examples). *Class* occurs more often than any of the rest. Frye writes that, for Blake, "a thing may be identified *as* itself, yet it cannot be identified except as an individual of a class. The class is its 'living form,' not its abstract essence, and form in Blake is a synonym for image, or experienced reality. . . . All Blake's images and mythical figures are 'minute particulars' or individuals identified with their total forms."[19] Hazard Adams further clarifies this difficult concept, demonstrating Blake's affinity with Giambattista Vico's idea of an "imaginative universal." "According to Vico," Adams writes, "the earliest people did not possess 'intelligible class concepts of things,' but they nevertheless had to move in thought and expression from particulars to some sort of universals. . . . A Vichean 'imaginative universal' . . . remains animate in its universality by retaining all the qualities of any particular referred to it."[20]

As Blake proceeds through the list of individual pilgrims, his terminology continues to vary. The Knight is "that species of character which in every age stands as the guardian of man against the oppressor"; the Prioress is "of the first rank"; the Plowman is "simplicity itself, with wisdom and strength for its stamina"; and Chaucer himself is "the great poetical observer of men, who in every age is born to record and eternize its acts" (*DC;* E, 533, 533, 536, 534).[21] Within this anaphoric pattern the single use of *state* occurs:

> The Plowman is simplicity itself, with wisdom and strength for its stamina. Chaucer has divided the ancient character of Hercules between his Miller and his Plowman. Benevolence is the plowman's great characteristic. . . .
>
> The Plowman of Chaucer is Hercules in his supreme eternal state, divested of his spectrous shadow; which is the Miller, a terrible fellow, such as exists in all times and places, for the trial of men.
>
> (*DC* 21; E, 536)

Here, the "supreme eternal state" suggests a condition of freedom. In fact, the individual *is* the state. The Hercules of Greek mythology possessed benevolence and strength but was afflicted by "his spectrous shadow," probably, in Blake's view, the shadow of war and empire that afflicted classical culture. Chaucer separates the benevolence and terror in Hercules into the Plowman and the Miller. When Blake remarks on the Plowman as "Hercules in his supreme eternal state," he refers, first, to the condition of typicality, for which many terms have served in this text; he refers also to a condition of imaginative freedom, the state of being freed from the spectre. This use of *state* as an individuality, freed of its spectrous shadow, does not quite square with Blake's use of *state* as the spectral state itself.

Despite Blake's sanguine use of *state* here, the *Catalogue* squarely confronts the problem of human evil which forgiveness tries to remedy. In discussing the Pardoner, Blake borrows back the term *knave* from the Lavater annotations. He writes: "The Pardoner [is] the Age's Knave, who always commands and domineers over the high and low vulgar. This man is sent in every age for a rod and scourge, and for a blight, for a trial of men, to divide the classes of men" (*DC;* E, 535). The Pardoner is unequivocally condemned as "the Age's Knave." Blake's reflections on the Pardoner do not mention his character moving from the state of knavery to a condition of imaginative freedom. Indeed, later in the same document, Blake elaborates on knaves: "Those who say that men are led by interest are knaves. A knavish character will often say, of what interest is it to me to do so and so?" (*DC;* E, 538). Knaves, then, hold a cynical and reductive view of human nature and particularly of artists. Blake's only consoling comment is, "He is suffered by Providence for wise ends, and has also his great use, and his grand leading destiny" (*DC;* E, 535). He exemplifies that "class of men, whose whole delight is in the destruction of men" (*DC;* E, 538), a class to which Blake will devote more attention in the prophecies. Similarly, Blake condemns the Summoner as a "Devil," who like the knave, is "suffered by Providence": "His companion the Sompnour, is also a Devil of the first magnitude, grand, terrific, rich and honoured in the rank of which he holds the destiny" (*DC*; E, 535). In *Descriptive Catalogue,* then, Blake uses the collective terms *class* and *state* to denote a human variety conducive to intersubjectivity as defined by Arendt, Benjamin, and Irigaray, while the personified terms *knave* and *devil* denote those members of society Blake finds evil. By contrast, in the prophecies, the personified term *spectre* denotes an evil primarily conceived as intrapsychic.

The relation between forgiveness and states, conceived intersubjectively as a celebration of human variety, is more explicit in Blake's descriptions of the Last Judgment or Second Coming of Christ, written in his Notebook, probably in 1808–10, and in a letter to Ozias Humphry. The descriptions, like *Descriptive Catalogue,* date from the period Blake worked on his major prophecies, and, like *Descriptive Catalogue,* they exhibit a use of *state* solely in the intersubjective, celebratory sense, rather than the condensed intrapsychic and intersubjective use of *states* in the prophecies. But the dramatic context of the Last Judgment—the paradigm of definitive condemnation or forgiveness, the separation of sheep from goats—makes the connection of states and forgiveness more clear. Here, it is not the distinction between states and individuals, but the notion that multiple states allow multiple kinds of human individuality that permits forgiveness: the descriptions of the Last Judgment imply (but do not declare unequivocally) that Jesus forgives by allowing each sinner his individual character or state, by refraining from judging all persons by the same standards, by practicing the recognition of human variety that undergirds intersubjectivity.

The words *state* and *states* appear far more frequently, twenty-three times, in *A Vision of the Last Judgment,* another work from the same period as the *Descriptive Catalogue.* Here Blake uses *states* to refer to varieties of human character, as in the Plowman's "supreme eternal state." Blake uses other terms, such as *accuser,* to refer to the offender needing forgiveness. As Blake writes, "Forgiveness of Sin is only at the Judgment Seat of Jesus the Saviour" (*VLJ;* E, 565). The description of the last judgment that Blake recorded in his Notebook can be divided into two parts for the purposes of discussion: in the first half, Blake focuses on judging all manners of life; in the second, he thinks through the problem of bad art.

Here Blake uses *states* intersubjectively to refer to various types of characters or to an emotional or psychological condition. For example, Blake mentions morally neutral states, neither blaming nor praising: "Various figures in attitudes of contention representing various *States of Misery* which alas every one on Earth is liable to enter into & against which we should all watch" (*VLJ*; E, 557). At other times *states* are desirable and praiseworthy, as in "a female figure . . . [who] represents *the Solitary State* of those who previous to the Flood walked with God" (*VLJ;* E, 560). The antediluvian patriarchs, who "walked with God," were surely in a condition (or state) of blessedness. Blake repeats this approbative sense of *state* when he claims that "the Persons who ascend to Meet the Lord coming in the Clouds with power & great Glory are representations of *those States described in the Bible under the Names of the Fathers before & after the Flood* (*VLJ;* E, 559; emphasis added in all examples).[22] Blake's emphasis on the association of states with names of biblical figures becomes even more detailed in another section of the work: "<On the Right> Beneath the Cloud on which Abel kneels is Abraham with Sarah & Isaac [&] also Hagar & Ishmael. <Abel kneels on a bloody cloud descriptive of those Churches before the flood . . . even till Abrahams time the vapour & heat was not Extinguishd" (*VLJ;* E, 556). Then Blake links the names of these specific biblical figures, Abraham, Sarah, Hagar, Ishmael, and Abel, with the notion of states: "These States Exist now Man Passes on but States remain for Ever" (*VLJ*; E, 556). As in *Descriptive Catalogue,* individuals represent eternal types: Abel, the

prototypic victim, remains a possibility for other persons as well. So does Abraham, the parent who consented to sacrifice his own child. Like "the great sculptures of Los's halls," these *states* and biblical figures offer what Blake sees as a gallery of timeless human potential. The linking of *states* with names of characters suggests multiplicity, the celebration of human variety necessary to intersubjective forgiveness.

In keeping with the celebratory sense of *state* necessary to intersubjective forgiveness, Blake tropes the relation between the individual and the state as a relation between traveler and place: "He passes thro them like a traveller who may as well suppose that the places he has passed thro exist no more as a Man may suppose that the States he has passd thro exist no more Every Thing is Eternal" (*VLJ;* E, 556). This metaphor of a traveler, which recurs in the prophecies, implies no adverse judgment of any one place. Furthermore, it puns on *state* as a country or government, a connotation particularly important to Blake when he entreats his countrymen to forgive those persons in the state of France. In general, then, in his descriptions of the Last Judgment, Blake uses *states* in the celebratory sense of designating the human variety necessary to intersubjective forgiveness. Nonetheless, Blake suggests an intrapsychic application of this intersubjective version of states in the pictorial composition of some of his "Last Judgments." Mitchell observes that "the early versions of the Last Judgment are organized around a portion or organ of the human form—probably the skull—and the cyclic movement of the figures within that form represents the cycle of consciousness casting off error and embracing truth. The figures are . . . not 'Persons' but mental 'states' which exist inside persons."[23] The variety of figures connotes the intersubjective, celebratory sense of *states,* but Blake's enclosing these figures in one person's skull suggests a simultaneous intrapsychic frame of reference.

The descriptions of the Last Judgment and *Descriptive Catalogue* thus defy the conventional reading of *state* only as an intrapsychic state of accusation. We are familiar with the notion that the traveler may remain forever, while he thinks, mistakenly, "that the places he has passed thro exist no more" (*VLJ;* E, 556). But Blake's insistence that states also "remain forever" suggests the comprehensive function of Chaucer's pilgrims or of the statues in Los's halls—in other words, multiple imaginative universals presented as possibilities for human beings. The equation of states with places illuminates Blake's reference to the accusers of Jesus: "Two persons one in Purple the other in Scarlet are descending [into Hell] <down the Steps into the Pit> these are Caiphas [sic] & Pilate Two *States where all those reside* who Calumniate & Murder <under Pretence of Holiness & Justice"> (*VLJ;* E, 558; emphasis added). Since the states of Pilate and Caiaphas are like residences, the traveler may depart from them as from a place without the painful intrapsychic process of "casting out" a personified part of himself. Because these states as "locations" of the soul are not permanent, Blake explicitly denies that states are a way to separate sheep from goats. Blake here deviates from the use of states usually attributed to him, in which one permanent state connotes ineradicable evil: "I do not consider either the Just or the Wicked to be in a Supreme *State* but to be every one of them *States* of the Sleep which the Soul may fall into in its Deadly Dreams of Good & Evil" (*VLJ;* E, 563; emphasis added). Blake's idea that states are variations of sleep and dreams suggests an infinite variety of such states; the just and the wicked do not exemplify the two states of justice and wickedness, but, Blake says, the just and the wicked are equally asleep.

States as a rubric of infinite human variety promote intersubjective forgiveness, acknowledgment of the otherness of the other. The metaphor of states as places further suggests that certain stages of life have faults appropriate to them; the victim forgives the offender by acknowledging this state, taking comfort in the prospect that, like the traveler, the offender will leave those faults behind. Like parents who forgive their children because they are "going through a phase," Blake's potential forgiver looks forward to the journey's continuance to a better destination.

This celebratory use of *state* does not mean that Blake has ignored human evil in these texts, however. Blake's descriptions of the Last Judgment rely on the metaphor of person, not state: rather than stressing a single *state* of accusation, Blake depicts evil as the *person* of the accuser: "Forgiveness of Sin is only at the Judgment Seat of Jesus the Saviour where the Accuser is cast out. not because he Sins but because he torments the Just & makes them do what he condemns as Sin & what he knows is opposite to their own Identity" (*VLJ;* E, 565). The accuser initiates a conflict between two types of selves. Blake's tendency to personify Good and Evil leads him to neglect place in favor of person: "This world of Imagination is the World of Eternity it is the Divine bosom into which we all shall go after the death of the Vegetated body. . . . All Things are comprehended in their Eternal Forms in the Divine body of the Saviour" (*VLJ;* E, 555). The provisional nature of this personification is evident from Blake's further remark, "Christ comes as he came at first to deliver those who were bound under the Knave not to deliver the Knave He Comes to Deliver Man the [*Forgiven*] <Accused &> not Satan the Accuser" (*VLJ;* E, 564). Satan is no longer a person in need of forgiveness, but a personification of accusation that needs to be cast out for intrapsychic forgiveness to take place.

In the major prophecies—*The Four Zoas, Milton,* and *Jerusalem*—Blake demands more of the concept of *state* than in the nonprophetic *Descriptive Catalogue* and descriptions of the last judgment: *state* in the major prophecies designates the intrapsychic state of accusation, a state that the individual must purge from his internal workings; at the same time it designates the intersubjective sense, connoting human variety.[24] Blake condenses *state* in order to make his myth universal, that is, both intrapsychic and intersubjective, the character Albion signifying both human society conceived as "the aggregate of spirits we call mankind or humanity"[25] and also as the intrapsychic unity of the Four Zoas in One Man.[26] The aesthetic consequence of this condensation is that while Blake attempts to represent all intersubjective and intrapsychic conflicts and resolutions—including forgiveness—with one comprehensive mythic system, in fact the intrapsychic wins out over the intersubjective, as Blake's own powerful intrapsychic conflicts occlude his sense of human variety and otherness.

Despite the textual and narrative problems in *The Four Zoas,*[27] we can posit two temporal layers in Blake's use of *states* there. In the earliest layers, in Nights One through Four, *states* refer to various temporary emotional conditions, causing suffering rather than moral evil in the individual passing through those states. Some examples are the frequent refrain "a state of dismal woe"; the account of Urizen in "a dreamful horrible State" (*FZ* 52:21; E, 335);[28] and the description of Los and Enitharmon as "two little Infants [weeping] upon the desolate wind. / The first state weeping they began" (*FZ* 8:2–3; E, 304). In a more pejorative, perhaps political, sense of *state*, Orc mocks Urizen's "Godlike State" (*FZ* 80:41; E, 356). In Nights written later, and in later interpolated passages, *state* is singular, denoting the moral evil of an intrapsychic tendency to accusation. For example, in Night the Seventh, the Spectre says to Los:

> . . . I am the cause
> That this dire state commences I began the dreadful state
> Of Separation.
>
> (*FZ* 87:31–33; E, 369)

In the same Night, an interpolated use of *state* refers to a condition of damnation or accusation; Enitharmon says, "Such is our state nor will the Son of God redeem us but destroy" (*FZ* 87:59; E, 370).[29] Blake interpolated the compatible sense of "individuals" a few times, as in the epigraph:

> What are the Natures of those Living Creatures the Heavenly Father only Knoweth No Individual Knoweth nor Can Know.[30]
>
> (*FZ* 3; E, 301)

He also added a description of the

> . . . Eternal Saviour; who disposd
> The pale limbs of his Eternal Individuality
> Upon the Rock of Ages.
>
> (*FZ* 18:13–15; E, 310).[31]

Blake's interest in individuality as Jesus, asserting a unity among all various individuals, accords with his tendency to privilege the intrapsychic frame of reference over the intersubjective one.

The most important development for Blake's representation of forgiveness in the later layer of *The Four Zoas* is the introduction of the distinction between states and individuals in Night the Eighth. This Night, along with Night the Seventh, is clearly a storm center for the poem. Longer than all the previous nights, Night the Eighth repeats (with an attempt at working through) the densely autobiographical material in the Bard's Song.[32] That Blake returned to a largely completed manuscript in order to add a passage about the forgiveness of sins suggests the urgency, perhaps compulsion, driving his need to distinguish states from individuals in solving the intersubjective problem of forgiving William Hayley and in resolving the intrapsychic problem of forgiving the accusation in himself—a microcosm of the larger problem of a myth that has universal claims.[33]

Thematically, Night the Eighth addresses the offender's repentance, which is often taken as a prerequisite to forgiveness. Having bound their son Orc to the Tree of Mystery, Los and Enitharmon repent, becoming benevolent parents. Enitharmon's "poor broken heart astonishd melted into Compassion & Love" (*FZ* 99:16; E, 372); Los "loved [the Spectres] / With a parental love for the Divine Hand was upon him" (*FZ* 100:5–6; E, 372). This genuine repentance of Los and Enitharmon provides a contrast to the behaviour of Urizen, whom Blake ironically calls "repentant" three times in Night the Eighth, criticizing the hypocritical repentance of British leaders at the time of the Peace of Amiens, a repentance exposed as false when they resumed the war.[34] The Eighth Night contrasts genuine repentance in Los and Enitharmon with hypocritical repentance in Urizen. Moreover, Blake condenses the double imperatives of intrapsychic and intersubjective—indeed, international—forgiveness. Los has renounced his jealousy of Orc; Urizen should follow suit by forgiving his old enemy Luvah. The intersubjective, international salience of *state* has an intrapsychic application as well. The British press and parliament, throughout the Napoleonic wars, cast the state of France as the personification of evil, as Gerald Newman has demonstrated.[35] Blake corrects the government's and press's projection to argue, in effect, that the state of France is in a state of Satan from which it can be delivered. He claims that "although a State such as tyranny (Satan) may be eternal, no individual or nation need occupy that state in a New Heaven and Earth."[36] The culprit, really, is tyranny, manifested in war.[37] This reasoning exculpates France. Moreover, the separation of the state of France from what Blake would call the "individuality" of France—a distinction permitting the intersubjective, international forgiveness by Britain of French atrocities during the Terror and of imperialism under Napoleon—would logically lessen the British projection of evil onto France, a projection of the accuser's own fear.

Blake's use of *state,* however, is even more subtle. The state of France (or Luvah), from Blake's point of view, is one state among many that must be preserved to retain the fullness of human and international variety. For this reason, Blake interpolated a clearly political sense of *state* into Night the Second, in which Jesus "himself put on the robes of blood / Lest the state calld Luvah should cease" (*FZ* 33:13–14; E, 321).[38] The state—that is, paradoxically, the *individuality*—of Luvah must be retained as an act of intersubjective, international forgiveness celebrating the other, the French character of France. In Night the Eighth Blake elaborates, "when Luvah in Orc became a Serpent he des[c]ended into / That State calld Satan" (*FZ* 115:26–27; E, 380). The crucial didactic point is that Blake steals from his opponents the notion that a state is evil by redefining its evil as the state of Satan while preserving and cherishing the individuality of its national character apart from that evil. Within this political context, Blake condenses intrapsychic and intersubjective frames of reference in Night the Eighth in order to stress that intersubjective, international forgiveness requires the intrapsychic process of attaining the disposition of forgivingness. He concludes, in effect, that the two processes are the same. But in this final yoking of the two processes, he runs the risk of occluding differences among human individuals' intrapsychic processes.

In the central passage of Night the Eighth, he combines both senses of the word *state*, that is, state as accusation and states as conditions of variety. Los addresses Rahab:

> O Rahab I behold thee I was once like thee a Son
> Of Pride and I also have pierced the Lamb of God in pride & wrath
> Hear me repeat my Generations that thou mayst also repent
> . . . .
> And these are the sons of Los & Enitharmon. Rintrah Palamabron

Theotormon Bromion Antamon Ananton Ozoth Ohana
Sotha Mydon Ellayol Natho Gon Harhath Satan
Har Ochim Ijim Adam Reuben Simeon Levi Judah Dan Naphtali
Gad Asher Issachar Zebulun Joseph Benjamin David Solomon
Paul Constantine Charlemaine Luther Milton
These are our daughters Ocalythron Elynittria Oothoon Leutha
Elythiria Enanto Manathu Vorcyon Ethinthus Moab Midian
Adah Zillah Caina Naamah Tamar Rahab Tirzah Mary
And myriads more of Sons & Daughters. . . .

(*FZ* 114:51–53, 115:1–10; E, 380)

Los's account of his "Generations" resembles the catalogues of states in the Notebook's description of the Last Judgment in which states are personified by the biblical patriarchs. And yet here Los explicitly mentions that his purpose in rehearsing this list is that Rahab may "also repent." Mitchell observes that Blake's fondness for lists fits the anatomic goals of his works. The anatomy, Mitchell writes, "cannot afford to leave anything out. Everything acted on earth must be recorded in the bright sculptures of Los's halls, so the artist must frequently resort to lists, summaries, and compilations . . . which he cannot treat in detail."[39] This cornucopia of human variety, however, is explicitly directed to Rahab's repentance. Blake had earlier identified Rahab herself as being in the state of Satan:

And on her forehead was her name written in blood Mystery
When viewd remote She is One when viewd near she divides
To multitude as it is in Eden so permitted because
It was the best possible in the State called Satan.

(*FZ* 105:15–18; E, 378; emphasis added)[40]

This list implies that Rahab can escape her own "state" of Satan by recognizing the variety of states in Los's list. Yet as Los focuses more on his audience, the sense of *state* as a single state of accusation becomes clearer. Los continues:

There is a State namd Satan learn distinct to know O Rahab
The Difference between States & Individuals of those States
The State namd Satan never can be redeemd in all Eternity.

(*FZ* 115:23–25; E, 380)

After Los explains the distinction to Rahab, he applies it to Luvah, the intersubjective and international "enemy." Los says: "when Luvah in Orc became a Serpent he des[c]ended into / That State calld Satan" (*FZ* 115:26–27;

E, 380). Although Blake does not label Los's "Generations" as states in this passage, his frequent labeling of items on other lists as states, such as the list of biblical patriarchs, creates a paradox. For Blake, the denial of endless human variety produces an inability to forgive intersubjectively, that is, the state of Satan or accusation. Ostensibly, this logical link justifies Blake's condensation of terms, though the representation equates them too closely, by implying that all human evil consists in accusation.

Blake asserts the importance of individuality pictorially as well as verbally. On the page after the one that bears the distinction between states and individuals, Blake drew a full-page picture of Jesus, much like one of his *Night Thoughts* illustrations.[41] For Blake, Jesus represents the "individuality,"[42] placed here to stress the triumph of individuals in both senses. In Los's catalogue, Blake preserves an intersubjective sense of individuality in naming Los's sons and daughters: various individualities are preserved. And in Los's denunciation of the state of Satan, Blake delivers the intrapsychically conceived individuality of all persons as the aggregate man Albion; indeed, as Blake progresses, he draws the conflict increasingly along the lines of Jesus and the Spectre or Satan.[43] The two split exemplars, Jesus and Spectre/Satan, bear the burden of representing intrapsychic good and evil here, compensating for the ambiguity Blake created by condensing intersubjective and intrapsychic meanings.

Blake's poem *Milton* arises from a complex, multiply-determined life situation in which imperatives to intersubjective and intrapsychic forgiveness overlap and muddy each other. Intersubjectively, William Hayley's efforts to normalize Blake provoked Blake's anger, while Hayley's kindnesses, particularly at the sedition trial, required Blake to achieve at least a semblance of forgiving Hayley's faults. Intrapsychically, Blake needed to assuage his guilt—to forgive himself—for his anger at one of the few men who had ever tried to help him professionally. The Bard's Song in *Milton,* generally acknowledged as the most problematic passage in Blake's oeuvre, bears the weight of this complex situation, reworking material from the nexus of forgiveness in Night the Eighth of *The Four Zoas,* material originally placed just before the distinction between states and individuals.[44] In the *Zoas* version Blake recounts the action quite succinctly:

> But Satan accusd Palamabron before his brethren also he maddend
> The horses of palamabrons harrow wherefore Rintrah & Palamabron
> Cut him off from Golgonooza.
>
> (*FZ* 115:12–14; E, 380)

The two central elements in this telling of the story are the accusation of Palamabron by Satan and the exchange of work that gave Satan the chance to madden Palamabron's horses. Blake reverses the sequence in the Bard's Song, elaborating each plot considerably, for example, by resituating the exchange of work in a family drama between Los and his sons, Rintrah, Palamabron, and Satan, each of whom works his particular work. Satan asks Los if he may exchange work with Palamabron; Los reluctantly consents; the work of both sons is ruined as a result. The family in the Bard's Song thus elaborates the *Zoas* passage that lists numerous varieties of the sons and daughters of Los, a passage suggestive of human intersubjectivity.

Blake also elaborates the accusation of Palamabron by Satan. This time Satan accuses Palamabron of a specific fault, ingratitude, the fault in Blake's own drama of intrapsychic forgiveness. A feature of the Bard's Song that many critics find puzzling follows: though Satan is condemned, being recognized eventually as Urizen, two other characters bear his punishment vicariously. The eternals allow their wrath to fall on Rintrah instead of on Satan, and, as if that were not enough, Satan's emanation, Leutha, offers to accept his blame and punishment herself. These two plots in the Bard's Song dramatize the imperatives to intersubjective and to intrapsychic forgiveness with which Blake has been struggling.[45]

Blake uses the concept *class* to mediate these two imperatives (whereas *The Four Zoas* version relied on *state*). In general, *class* serves the imperative of intersubjective forgiveness, that is, Blake's forgiveness of Hayley, better than it serves the imperative of intrapsychic forgiveness, that is, Blake's self-forgiveness. However, Blake uses the term to do both duties. Blake invokes the concept of class at the beginning and the end of the Bard's Song. Oddly, at the end of the song, the Assembly, which, as Mitchell observes, "seems not to have noticed that the classes were created before the quarrel," creates the same classes again: "the three classes, in other words, are presented both as the order that Satan destroys when he usurps Palamabron's role and as the new order that is established by the Assembly after the quarrel."[46] But are the classes instituted at the end the same kind of classes that obtain at the beginning? The structure of the three classes indeed undergirds the song from the beginning:

> And the Three Classes of Men [are] regulated by Los's Hammer.
> . . . .
> The first, The Elect from before the foundation of the World:
> The second, The Redeem'd. The Third, The Reprobate & form'd
> To destruction from the mothers womb.
>
> (*M* 6:35, 7:1–3; E, 100)

The early section about the exchange of work between Palamabron and Satan implies intersubjective acknowledgment of human variety, that each person has his proper work to do. Thus it proceeds from the assumption of the good of contrariety. Insofar as the exchange creates problems, it does so because of the unsuitability of the workers to their borrowed tasks. The desirability of multiple classes is implied early in the Bard's Song:

> Beneath the Plow of Rintrah & the Harrow of the Almighty
> In the hands of Palamabron. Where the Starry Mills of Satan
> Are built beneath the Earth & Waters of the Mundane Shell
> Here the Three Classes of Men take their Sexual texture Woven
> The Sexual is Threefold: the Human is Fourfold.
> (*M* 4:1–5; E, 97)

Here Blake writes about the "Three Classes of Men" as persons with various vocations; Rintrah associated with the plow, Palamabron with the harrow, and Satan with the mills. Like the prolific and the devouring in the *Marriage,* Blake here writes of the classes intersubjectively. His frame of reference resembles what Arendt calls the world of human action, in which groups or classes of persons need to cooperate, more than it resembles an intrapsychic frame of reference in which an individual reforms his dispositions. Moreover, in this formulation, Blake departs from his frequent equation of triplicity with the sinister.[47] In writing "Woven / The Sexual is Threefold: the Human is Fourfold," Blake suggests a structure in which, logically, the threefold is necessary to the fourfold. Thus, so far at least, the class or state of Satan the Miller corresponds to the model of the world of action as composed of intersubjective recognition of the value of each worker and his genius.

The transition to the intrapsychic sense of *class*, as a disposition to be cast out of the self, begins with the disaster that follows Satan's appropriation of Palamabron's work. In effect, Satan wants to make all sons interchangeable, denying their various individualities. Los concludes: "Henceforth Palamabron, let each his own station / Keep: nor in pity false, nor in officious brotherhood" (*M* 7:41–42; E, 101). *Station,* like its cognate *state,* provides for individualities. But despite Los's assertion, Satan has already denied such individualities, so the Bard's Song must address the problem created by his class, those who deny individualities. Initially, Los and Enitharmon created classes to structure variations in human work nonjudgmentally, but the person of the accuser and the disposition of accusation has forced a new, intrapsychic sense of *class*, in which one member is judged and expelled.

The intrapsychic imperative to forgiveness arises in the plotline in which Satan accuses Palamabron of ingratitude, an accusation that rang true to Hayley's use of Blake but rang more true to Blake's sense of guilt that he himself had been ungrateful to Hayley. Thus the accuser was both outside and inside, intersubjective and intrapsychic. Blake clarifies the evil implicit in Satan's previous assumption that he can do Palamabron's work as well as Palamabron. Blake dramatizes Satan's revelation as the accuser:

> For Satan flaming with Rintrahs fury hidden beneath his own mildness
> Accus'd Palamabron before the Assembly of ingratitude! of malice:
> He created Seven deadly Sins drawing out his infernal scroll,
> Of Moral laws and cruel punishments upon the clouds of Jehovah.
> (*M* 9:19–22; E, 103)

Blake shifts his attention to accusation itself. Satan becomes wrathful, *accusing* Palamabron of ingratitude. Previously Satan-Hayley on the intersubjective level needed to practice the forgiveness that recognizes and values the otherness of the other. Here, however, Satan-Blake also exemplifies the intrapsychic, the disposition of accusation. Thus Blake is caught in the doubleness of his representation. As the representative of a worker, Satan (insofar as he signifies Hayley's individuality) must be treated with compassion and forgiveness. As the disposition to accusation in both Hayley and Blake, Satan must be treated harshly. Blake does both. Treating Satan inter-subjectively, Blake's characters "forgive" him, letting their judgment fall on Rintrah instead:

> And it was enquir'd: Why in a Great Solemn Assembly
> The Innocent should be condemn'd for the Guilty? Then an Eternal rose
> Saying. If the Guilty should be condemn'd, he must be an Eternal Death
> And one must die for another throughout all Eternity.
> Satan is fall'n from his station & never can be redeem'd
> But must be new Created continually moment by moment
> And therefore the Class of Satan shall be calld the Elect, & those
> Of Rintrah. the Reprobate, & those of Palamabron the Redeem'd
> For he is redeem'd from Satans Law, the wrath falling on Rintrah.
> (*M* 11:15–23; E, 105)

This compassion, however misguided, stems from a sense that the culprit already suffers and cannot bear further punishment. The theme of vicarious atonement, revising Milton's *Paradise Lost,*[48] contributes to Blake's ideas of states and individuals, demonstrating the ideal of achieving intersubjective forgiveness by means of intrapsychically casting off the disposition of accusation. (Blake provides a second variation on this theme in Leutha's voluntary assumption of Satan's blame and punishment, an incident I have discussed earlier.) At the conclusion of the Bard's Song, Blake invokes class to retain this hope of intersubjective forgiveness by changing the focus from Satan as the sole representative of the class of the Elect to the class as a whole. They are all capable of repentance:

> The Elect shall meet the Redeem'd. on Albions rocks they shall meet
> Astonish'd at the Transgressor, in him beholding the Saviour.
> And the Elect shall say to the Redeemd. We behold it is of Divine
> Mercy alone! of Free Gift and Election that we live.
> (*M* 13:30–33; E, 107)

The concern for intersubjective forgiveness clearly governs Blake's compassionate treatment of Satan and his careful manipulation of the calvinistic notion of classes. Blake's conviction, here expressed, that even the "satanic" elect can repent demonstrates that within the contexts of groups of persons, Blake remains hopeful. "In overturning the Puritan scheme of Elect, Redeemed, and Reprobate, Blake surely did not mean to turn the Reprobates, the wrathful prophets and social outcasts, into a new Blakean Elect," Mitchell writes; "his main purpose is to subvert the whole idea of sheep and goats."[49] Nonetheless, the intrapsychic sense of *class* intrudes, demanding that Satan and his class be treated with harshness. They cannot be allowed to intermingle, and Los names their evil bluntly, in an intrapsychic sense of *classes* that jars against the intersubjective one:

> Therefore you must bind the Sheaves not by Nations or Families
> You shall bind them in Three Classes; according to their Classes
> So shall you bind them. Separating What has been Mixed
> Since Men began to be Wove into Nations by Rahab & Tirzah
> Since Albions Death & Satans Cutting-off from our awful Fields;
> When under pretence to benevolence the Elect Subdud All
> From the Foundation of the World. The Elect is one Class: You
> Shall bind them separate: they cannot Believe in Eternal Life
> Except by Miracle & a New Birth. The other two Classes;
> The Reprobate who never cease to Believe, and the Redeemd,
> Who live in doubts & fears perpetually tormented by the Elect
> These you shall bind in a twin-bundle for the Consummation—
> But the Elect must be saved [from] fires of Eternal Death,

> To be formed into the Churches of Beulah that they destroy not the Earth
> For in every Nation & every Family the Three Classes are born
> And in every Species of Earth, Metal, Tree, Fish, Bird & Beast.
> (*M* 25:26–41; E, 122)

The final passage here employs Blake's sense of the classes, even the class of the Elect, as a rubric of the variety necessary to a world of action: "in every Nation & every Family the Three Classes are born / And in every species of Earth, Metal, Tree, Fish, Bird & Beast." Like the characters in Chaucer's pilgrimage, they stand as imaginative universals, a grammar of types in which all particulars can be expressed. But the imperative to cast out the intrapsychic accuser colors Los's less generous use of *class*: "The Elect is one Class: You / Shall bind them separate." In the single representative of Satan Blake had displayed his accusation for all to see: "the Mills of Satan were separated in a moony Space" because Satan "Compell'd others to serve him in moral gratitude & submission / Being call'd God" (*M* 11:11–12; E, 104). Blake has it both ways, asserting that all classes are necessary to human and animal variety, yet demanding that one class be separate. Therefore the reinstitution of the three classes of men at the close of the Bard's Song introduces a difference: whereas Satan violated an intersubjective sense of variety or classes, the proper way to cast out Satan intrapsychically is to recognize that the Elect is an (intrapsychic) class that denies (intersubjective) classes. The assumption of Satan's guilt by Leutha, his emanation, compensates for the compromise between both intrapsychic and intersubjective senses of Satan as a class. Leutha as a feminine character resembles the male workers less than they resemble each other. Her more pronounced, female, otherness makes her a fitting scapegoat for the unacceptable, unforgivable part of Satan. This surprise ending saves the intersubjective focus of the Bard's Song—Blake's imperative to forgive Hayley by allowing Satan-Hayley to remain, forgiven, in the community of workers. In Irigaray's terms, the other is cast out to effect the reconciliation of two versions of the same.

In the Bard's Song, as we have observed, Blake consistently uses the device of personification to underline the concept of classes. As in the Bard's Song, the main section of *Milton* relies on the motif of threes changing to twos, the contraries and the reasoning negative.[50] Whereas in the Bard's Song Blake personifies each of the classes as more or less autonomous characters, namely Rintrah, Palamabron, or Satan, Blake condenses the personification further in the remainder of *Milton,* making each of the three classes part of the single character of Milton.

In the rest of the poem *Milton,* Blake deemphasizes the word *class* and returns to using the word *state,* as he had done previously. Blake places the distinction between states and individuals at a juncture when the hero Milton undertakes an act of reparation and self-forgiveness. Having decided to return to earth to correct his errors and to redeem his emanation, Milton wavers in his previous determination.[51] To strengthen him in his resolution and to clarify Milton's relationship to his own spectre, the distinction between states and individuals is expounded by Milton's teachers, "The Seven Angels of the Presence." They advise him in this way:

> Distinguish therefore States from Individuals in those States.
> States Change: but Individual Identities never change nor cease:
> You cannot go to Eternal Death in that which can never Die.
> Satan & Adam are States Created into Twenty-Seven Churches
> And thou O Milton art a State about to be Created
> Called Eternal Annihilation that none but the Living shall
> Dare to enter: & they shall enter triumphant over Death
> And Hell & the Grave! States that are not, but ah! Seem to be.
> Judge then of thy Own Self: thy Eternal Lineaments explore
> What is Eternal & what Changeable? & what Annihilable!
> The Imagination is not a State: it is the Human Existence itself
> Affection or Love becomes a State, when divided from Imagination
> The Memory is a State always, & the Reason is a State
> Created to be Annihilated & a new Ratio Created.
> (*M* 32:22–35; E, 132)

In this passage Blake uses both intersubjective and intrapsychic senses of the word *state*. On the one hand, the speaker lists all states that must be annihilated: memory and reason, for example, and petrified affection. In this sense, *state* very much resembles the satanic self to be cast off, the state from which the individual must be freed. On the other hand, *state* also suggests the very condition of unique individualities, or at least of Milton's individuality, necessary to an intersubjective acknowledgment of the other. For Lucifer tells him:

> And thou O Milton art a State about to be Created
> Called Eternal Annihilation that none but the Living shall
> Dare to enter.

Lucifer's clear declaration that the "Living shall / Dare to enter" the state of Milton implies that entering such a state will be an honorable act. Moreover, we know from the rest of the poem that "Eternal Annihilation" is admirable, for Milton performs it in relation to his Satan continually, rather than annihilating Satan himself. Milton's state, then, is not a condition of accusation to escape, but a trailblazing effort as a "State about to be Created" to form an imaginative universal, an exemplar, a representative of a new class. When he was first inspired to return to earth, the act was described as an "unexampled deed" (*M* 2:21; E, 96). But once Milton performs his self-annihilation, which is also self-forgiveness, he becomes a precursor for anyone else wishing to do so.[52] Milton is "Created" as a "state" of self-annihilation because he, in his eternal reprobate imaginative identity, has exemplified that act of forgiveness which Los and Albion and Jesus will also perform in *Jerusalem*. Paradoxically, then, the *state* is the individuality, an individuality of a poet repairing his works in order to achieve (intrapsychic) self-forgiveness.

In this situation, Milton must recognize *states* as intersubjective varieties and *state* as a condition of intrapsychic bondage. Hillel, one of the Seven Angels, instructs Milton in this way:

> We are not Individuals but States: Combinations of Individuals
> We were Angels of the Divine Presence: & were Druids in Annandale
> Compelld to combine into Form by Satan, the Spectre of Albion,
> Who made himself a God &, destroyed the Human Form Divine.
> But the Divine Humanity & Mercy gave us a Human Form
> Because we were combind in Freedom & holy Brotherhood.
> (*M* 32:10–15; E, 131)

The Seven Angels of the Presence exemplify the intersubjective function of states in forgiveness, functioning as imaginative universals, "Combinations of Individuals."[53] Moreover, their status as angels, of whom Milton is the "Starry Eighth," suggests that they with Milton constitute a gallery of human variety like the bright sculptures of Los's halls. The crucial distinction seems to be between the way that Satan combined them, by compulsion, and the way that mercy combined them, in freedom. The Seven Angels were "Compelld to *combine* into Form by Satan" but later "the Divine Humanity & Mercy gave us a Human Form / Because we were *combind* in Freedom & holy Brotherhood" (emphasis added). Satan combines by making everything like himself ("Retaining only Satans Mathematic Holiness, Length: Bredth, & Highth . . . against Its own Qualities" [*M* 32:18, 20–21; E, 132]). But Jesus, significantly called "Mercy," which is a corollary of forgiveness, permits a form of freedom (that is, not all having to conform to the same standard universalized law) and a form of brotherhood, a metaphor that permits some kinds of intersubjective otherness such as vocation, but precludes other forms of intersubjective otherness, such as generational (no fathers or mothers) or gendered (no sisters or mothers). Blake implies that Milton's self-forgiveness will allow these various states to be forgiven as well, thus escaping the accuser Satan to find divine "Mercy." The term *brotherhood* defines Milton's relationship to Blake, his reader; moreover, the poem suggests that Milton's self-forgiveness is constituted by Blake's, his reader's, forgiveness. In the end, then, Blake displaces his forgiveness from one intersubjective plot to another, from the biographical to the aesthetic, so that Blake as reader forgives Milton his small faults rather than Blake as protégé forgiving Hayley his larger faults.

In *Jerusalem* Blake writes about forgiveness more than in any other work, as he himself takes on the role of the poet played by Milton in *Milton* seeking the reader's intersubjective forgiveness simultaneously with his own intrapsychic self-forgiveness. At the same time, despite seeking his reader's fogiveness, Blake persists in writing a singularly unforgiving text both in the programmatic sense that Blake often accuses, even harangues, his reader, and also in the aesthetic sense that the text is relentlessly difficult. In *Jerusalem* Blake develops in greater detail and with greater emphasis the role of states and individuals in forgiveness, modifying the concepts in the process to accommodate his position as author supplicating and accusing his reader. Individuality is associated increasingly with Jesus, the all-forgiving "Friend of Sinners" (*J* 3; E, 145), a tendency begun in *The Four Zoas.* In *Jerusalem,* Blake proclaims that "The Spirit of Jesus is continual forgiveness of Sin" (*J* 3; E, 145) and his Jesus declares to Albion, "Lo! we are One; forgiving all Evil" (*J* 4:20; E, 146). States in *Jerusalem* tend to be the single state of accusation, conceived intrapsychically, rather than the various states of intersubjective human possibilities. This tendency accords with Blake's strident tone in *Jerusalem,* motivated by his explicit sense that he addresses an accusing reader, and perhaps implicitly by his own anger projected onto that reader.

Blake uses forgiveness to define his relation to his reader, implying that he, Blake, is repentant (for his dissimulation at his sedition trial? for the opacity of his text?) and imploring the reader's forgiveness as essential to the act of reading: "The Spirit of Jesus is continual forgiveness of Sin: he who waits to be righteous before he enters into the Saviours kingdom, the Divine Body; will never enter there. I am perhaps the most sinful of men! I pretend not to holiness! Yet I pretend to love, to see, to converse with daily, as man with man, & the more to have an interest in the Friend of Sinners. Therefore, [Dear] Reader, [forgive] what you do not approve, & [love] me for this energetic exertion of my talent" (*J* 3; E, 145; brackets indicate deletions). Despite the repentant pose, this paragraph is clearly a locus of some of Blake's ambivalence; as Erdman has observed, Blake gouged out the words *Dear, forgive,* and *love* sometime after he had engraved them on the copper plate.[54] Blake's ambivalence may be due, in part, to the slippage in the notions of forgiveness here. Initially Blake presents himself, the repentant author, as one already forgiven for a genuine offense by Jesus, the friend of sinners. Since Jesus has forgiven Blake, the reader should do so, too. But as Blake continues, there is a slippage in what "offense" needs forgiveness from the reader: "Yet I pretend to love, to see, to converse with daily, as man with man, & the more to have an interest in the Friend of Sinners" (*J* 3; E, 145). Blake moves to a pride, certainly a justifiable one, in mentioning his loving, seeing, and conversing with Jesus. But by making this move, he implies that he, Blake, is in a moral position to teach and to forgive the reader, rather than vice versa. Then, in effect, he asks his readers to forgive his virtues: "Dear Reader, forgive what you do not approve, & love me for this energetic exertion of my talent." Blake's request for readerly "forgiveness" betrays his ambivalence about his own stance vis-à-vis the reader: Who is accusing whom? Who is forgiving whom?

Blake closes the preface by inviting the reader to the intersubjective act of forgiveness in reading, by which the reader will recognize the otherness of Blake. But Blake's anger at the reader leads him to stress the intrapsychic notion of state as a single state of accusation, so the reader will recognize his error. Insofar as Blake prompts his reader to look inward, he urges him to recognize his, the reader's, own intrapsychic state of accusation. (I refer to Blake's reader as masculine following Blake's cues about his normative reader.) Paradoxically, however, Blake simultaneously wants his reader to recognize intersubjectively the virtues of Blake's own individual state. To achieve this goal, he retains, in a subordinate role, the intersubjective sense of state as infinite human variety.

Blake continues to stress the link between Jesus as the principles of forgiveness and of creativity. For example, Blake sees "the Saviour over me / Spreading his beams of love, & dictating the words of this mild song" (*J* 4:4–5; E, 146), speaking of forgiveness:

> I am not a God afar off, I am a brother and friend;
> Within your bosoms I reside, and you reside in me:
> *Lo! we are One; forgiving all Evil;* Not seeking recompense!
> Ye are my members O ye sleepers of Beulah, land of shades!
>
> (*J* 4:18–21; E, 146; emphasis added)

Curiously, the Saviour's plea, "we are One," provides an apparent contrast to the sense of individuality that we have seen heretofore. Instead of celebrating diversity and contrariety, this new sense of individuality celebrates unity and forgiveness. But because this forgiveness takes place in a context where Albion and Jesus are already one, they do not forgive the otherness of the other in an intersubjective transaction, but "all Evil" in an intrapsychic cleansing. Thus Blake's Jesus shows forgiveness of a state of intrapsychic accusation, an evil state, to be expelled from the unified Albion-Jesus, from Blake, and from Blake's reader. However, Jesus as the principle of Blake's creativity ("dictating the words of the mild song") suggests that the most pressing need is the cleansing of the *reader's* accusation since Blake as author is exonerated by his divine Muse.

This intrapsychic sense of states and individuals dominates the treatment of forgiveness in *Jerusalem,* a treatment carefully integrated into Blake's fourfold book. Chapters 1, 2, and 3 of *Jerusalem* all conclude with passages invoking states and individuals.[55] Blake uses the distinction to address the problem of accusers imputing righteousness or sin to individuals, hoping to teach them to impute sin only to states. Thus the form of *state* invoked is consistently the despised state of accusation.

Having limited the term *state* here to denote accusation, Blake invokes the word *combinations* to denote the intersubjective sense of human variety denied by such accusation, in order to remind his accusing reader of the truth that accusation neglects.

> All things acted on Earth are seen in the bright Sculptures of
> Los's Halls & every Age renews its powers from these Works
> With every pathetic story possible to happen from Hate or
> Wayward Love & every sorrow & distress is carved here
> Every Affinity of Parents Marriages & Friendships are here
> In all their various *combinations* wrought with wondrous Art
> All that can happen to Man in his pilgrimage of seventy years.
> (*J* 16:61–67; E, 161; emphasis added)

"Combinations," here as in *Milton,* picks up the meaning of human variety. Just as the Angels of the Presence were "States, Combinations of Individuals," so here the sculptures of Los's halls signify an aggregate of individuals who can be grouped under one type. This sense clearly echoes Blake's statement that Chaucer's pilgrims are "a Complete Index of Human Characters as they appear Age after Age" (*DC;* E, 571).

The excluded meaning of *states* (as a means of recognizing human variety in order to achieve intersubjective forgiveness) emerges under a new designation, *combinations*. As the first chapter of *Jerusalem* draws to a close, Blake focuses on the intrapsychic disposition to accusation, or vengeance, in his reader, a disposition has been manifested intersubjectively in politics:

> Why did you take Vengeance O ye Sons of the mighty Albion?
> Planting these Oaken Groves: Erecting these Dragon Temples
> Injury the Lord heals but Vengeance cannot be healed:
> As the Sons of Albion have done to Luvah: so they have in him
> Done to the Divine Lord & Saviour, who suffers with those that suffer:
> For not one sparrow can suffer, & the whole Universe not suffer also,
> In all its Regions, & its Father & Saviour not pity and weep.
> But Vengeance is the destroyer of Grace & Repentance in the bosom
> Of the Injurer: in which the Divine Lamb is cruelly slain.
> (*J* 23:3–11; E, 170)

Blake here presents vengeance as the unforgivable sin: "Vengeance cannot be healed"; "Vengeance is the destroyer of Grace & Repentance in the bosom / Of the Injurer." In destroying repentance, vengeance blocks the way to the struggle that Blake calls self-annihilation, the achievement of the disposition to forgive. For this reason the vengeful sons of Albion slay the "Divine Lamb" in their own bosoms, as well as in the person of their enemy Luvah: "As the Sons of Albion have done to Luvah: so they have in him / Done to the Divine Lord & Saviour." In attacking the state of vengeance in the sons of Albion, Blake has condensed intrapsychic and intersubjective meanings. Intersubjectively, when the sons of Albion, in the state of Satan, kill the "Divine Lamb," they destroy the individuality of France (Luvah); intrapsychically, when individuality is symbolized by Jesus, they kill that forgiving nature in themselves.

Given this way of expressing the dilemma, Blake proposes this solution: to invoke the principle of individuality, that is, the Lamb; and to invoke the distinction between states and individuals:

> Descend O Lamb of God & take away the imputation of Sin
> By the Creation of States & the deliverance of Individuals Evermore Amen
> Thus wept they in Beulah over the Four Regions of Albion
> But many doubted & despaird & imputed Sin & Righteousness
> To Individuals & not to States, and these Slept in Ulro.
> (*J* 25:12–16; E, 170–71)

The "Lamb of God" delivers individuals, such as the sons of Albion, by showing them the value in the supposed enemy Luvah. But he also delivers the sons of Albion by revealing their own individuality, that is, their ability to forgive, so that they can extricate themselves from the state of Satan. Both intersubjective forgiveness (of Luvah) and intrapsychic forgiveness (within each son of Albion) are plotted on the same course, figured with the same metaphoric system.

Having condensed the two frames of reference in a way that favors the intrapsychic over the intersubjective, Blake supplements the dominant intrapsychic sense of state as accusation with the recessive intersubjective sense of states as human varieties, in order to keep in the reader's mind the necessity for "forgiving" others their virtues, that is, their individual geniuses, as well as their vices, as part of renouncing one's own accusation. This is the model presented in the preface for the reader's "forgiveness" of Blake. He prefaces the call to the Lamb with an echo of that recessive intersubjective sense of states, writing:

> In the Exchanges of London every Nation walkd
> And London walkd in every Nation mutual in love & harmony
> Albion coverd the whole Earth, England encompassd the Nations,
> Mutual each within others bosom in Visions of Regeneration;
> Jerusalem coverd the Atlantic Mountains & the Erythrean,
> From bright Japan & China to Hesperia France & England.
> (*J* 24:42–47; E, 170)

Here Jerusalem, which Blake earlier called, the "point of mutual forgiveness between Enemies" (*J* 7:66; E, 150), practices the kind of intersubjective, international forgiveness that values diversity among national states, namely, Japan, China, Hesperia, England, and France. The last two are particularly topical, since Blake addresses a vengeful Albion warring against France. The mutuality here pictured echoes the mutual love expressed by Blake's Jesus: "I am in you and you in me, mutual in love divine" (*J* 4:7; E, 146). Jerusalem, the point of forgiveness, provides that kind of mutuality which recognizes contrariety, so that the identities of oriental and occidental are not violated, nor are the differences between England and France.

Similarly, in the second chapter of *Jerusalem,* Blake stresses the intrapsychic sense of *state* as accusation, supplementing it with the intersubjective sense of *states* as varieties. As in the close of chapter 1, Blake introduces the creation of states by a manifestation of Jesus as the principle of individuality:

> And the appearance of a Man was seen in the Furnaces;
> Saving those who have sinned from the punishment of the Law,

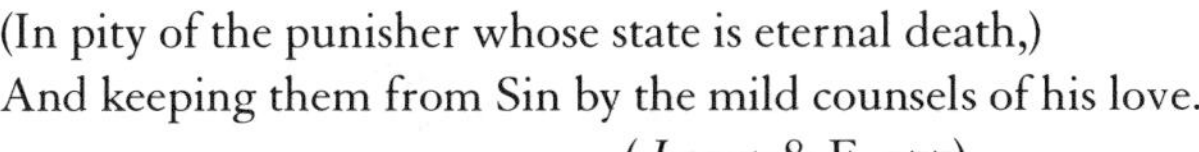

(In pity of the punisher whose state is eternal death,)
And keeping them from Sin by the mild counsels of his love.
(*J* 31:5–8; E, 177)

Here the One Man, Jesus, intervenes doubly, saving "those who have sinned" and thus effecting intersubjective forgiveness, from the motive of "pity of *the punisher* whose state is eternal death" (emphasis added). The desire to convert the accuser intrapsychically, casting out accusation, takes priority over the intersubjective action. Again Blake emphasizes identifying the intrapsychic state of accusation in the reader. Blake's Divine Voice, Jesus, continues:

Albion goes to Eternal Death: In Me all Eternity.
Must pass thro' condemnation, and awake beyond the Grave!
No individual can keep these Laws, for they are death
To every energy of man, and forbid the springs of life;
Albion hath enterd the State Satan! Be permanent O State!
And be thou for ever accursed! that Albion may arise again:
And be thou created into a State! I go forth to Create
States: to deliver Individuals evermore! Amen.
So spoke the voice from the Furnaces, descending into Non-Entity
[*To Govern the Evil by Good: and States abolish Systems*].
(*J* 31:9–18; E, 177–78)

Here Jesus, the voice of individuality, curses the state of Satan, the state of eternal death into which Albion has fallen. The recessive sense of states remains: the idea that states might abolish systems is hopeful only if one thinks that states of endless variety will supersede reductive systems. A further clue that Blake here means states as various possibilities appears in his deletion of a line, a tendency he shows when states have political referents, as in his deletion of the line with King George III's name in chapter 3 (*J* 73:37; E, 228). A condensed sense of the term *states* follows, in which the Four Zoas, usually a group of equals, become "States Permanently Fixed by the Divine Power" (*J* 32:38; E, 178). Yet, when Los explores them, they seem to be hierarchically organized, "the Three States of Ulro; Creation; Redemption. & Judgment" (*J* 32:42; E, 179).

In keeping with his pattern of concluding chapters with an invocation of states, Blake concludes chapter 2 by cataloguing the violence perpetrated by the sons of Albion (a group to which the reader presumably belongs), presenting the distinction between states and individuals as the only way to contemplate such massive evil without despair. Speaking of the sons of Albion, Los says:

Yet they are blameless & Iniquity must be imputed only
To the State they are enterd into that they may be deliverd:
Satan is the State of Death, & not a Human existence.
(*J* 49:65–67; E, 199)

Here Los applies the distinction to the character of the accusing sons of Albion. Unlike before, they can be forgiven even the sin of accusation if it is recognized as a state. Again Blake identifies the two processes: Albion's sons' intrapsychic cleansing and the international task they face. By recognizing accusation in themselves, and separating it from their individuality, they will simultaneously recognize it and separate it in Luvah:

But Luvah is named Satan, because he has enterd that State.
A World where Man is by Nature the enemy of Man
Because the Evil is Created into a State. that Men
May be deliverd time after time evermore. Amen.
(*J* 49:68–71; E, 199)

Los acknowledges the genuine evil in French aggression during the Napoleonic wars. Thus the doctrine of states has been applied both to the sons of Albion and also to the sons' need to forgive France. Los then generalizes about the value of the distinction:

Learn therefore O Sisters to distinguish the Eternal Human
That walks about among the stones of fire in bliss & woe
Alternate! from those States or Worlds in which the Spirit travels:
This is the only means to Forgiveness of Enemies.
(*J* 49:72–75; E, 199)

Los reverts to the recessive intersubjective sense of states as nations (or worlds) or varieties of human beings. For in this formulation, the eternal human is likened to a traveler, walking about through various "States or Worlds," a locution with political overtones and also with nonjudgmental connotations. If Albion's sons could do this for France, they would renounce their own state of accusation.

In chapter 3 of *Jerusalem,* the intrapsychic sense of the term *state* prevails over the intersubjective one. Blake opens the book by attacking deists, declaring that their allegiance to Nature has put them in a state of accusation: "Rahab is an Eternal State" (*J* 52; E, 200). Three leading deists commit the error of accusation: Francis Bacon, Sir Isaac Newton, and John Locke "imput[e] Sin & Righteousness to Individuals"(*J* 70:17; E, 224). To remedy their offense, Blake closes the chapter addressed to them with an exposition of states and individuals, explained by analogy with the distinction between circumference and center, which is equivalent to the fullness of imagination and its contracted nadir: "The Circumference is Within: Without, is formed the Selfish Center" (*J* 71:7; E, 225). Then Blake differentiates as states various characters who live in this condition of single vision: "the Center has Eternal States! these States we now explore" (*J* 71:9; E, 225). He then lists Albion's twelve sons, a curious paradox in that catalogues of proper names suggest human variety, but all are listed as being in the selfish center, which is equivalent to the state of accusation Blake has attributed to his reader all along:

> [Los] Permanently Creat[es] to be in Time Reveald & Demolishd
> Satan Cain Tubal Nimrod Pharoh Priam Bladud Belin
> Arthur Alfred the Norman Conqueror Richard John
> [*Edward Henry Elizabeth James Charles William George*]
> And all the Kings & Nobles of the Earth & all their Glories
> These are Created by Rahab & Tirzah in Ulro: but around
> These, to preserve them from Eternal Death Los Creates
> Adam Noah Abraham Moses Samuel David Ezekiel
> [*Pythagoras Socrates Euripedes Virgil Dante Milton*]
> Dissipating the rocky forms of Death, by his thunderous Hammer
> As the Pilgrim passes while the Country permanent remains
> So Men pass on: but States remain permanent for ever.
> (*J* 73:34–45; E, 228–29)

Blake here combines the intersubjective sense of persons as imaginative universals embodying human types with the political sense of *states* by equating the monarchs with the states that they rule. He deletes the line referring to George III, a reference that might provoke an accusing reader: Blake's excision of the poets could express rage toward Virgil for his subservience to empire.

In the fourth chapter of *Jerusalem*, Blake varies the pattern of concluding chapters with the verbal invocation of states and individuals, here depicting an act of forgiveness in a full-page illumination, plate 99, in which an old man embraces a young figure, perhaps male, perhaps female, perhaps androgynous (see figure 3).[56] The illumination alludes to forgiveness of the prodigal son, a story that moved Blake to tears. And yet, as Mitchell observes, the forgiveness is mutual, "transformed by that cruciform gesture of the young woman." Mitchell continues, "It is the patriarch who receives forgiveness and redemp-

FIGURE 3.
Jerusalem, Copy F, plate 99
(The Pierpont Morgan Library, New York, PML 953)

tion as much if not more than the young woman."[57] The shift from verbal formulations of forgiveness to a pictorial depiction of it parallels the sense of the poem's closure: in chapters 1, 2, and 3, the verbal distinction between states and individuals fostered the potential readerly forgiveness Blake hoped to promote, whereas in chapter 4 he asserts in the picture that forgiveness is achieved. This depiction accords with the content of chapter 4. Albion repents of his previous rejection of Jesus the human individuality, learning to see Jesus "in the likeness & similitude of Los my Friend" (*J* 96:22; E, 256).[58] In so doing, Albion achieves "Forgiveness of Sins which is Self Annihilation" (*J* 98:23; E, 257). This action, like Milton's self-annihilation, takes the concomitant form of reunion with the emanation, the action depicted in plate 99. Moreover, chapter 4 has advanced the cause of forgiveness by Los's action of sending his Spectre to his, Los's, friends, in order to change the situation in which "it is easier to forgive an Enemy than to forgive a Friend" (*J* 91:1; E, 251). However, the fact that it is Albion, the implied audience of Blake's poem, who repents in relation to Jesus/Los stresses Blake's claim on the reader's repentance, not the reader's forgiveness of Blake. It underlines Blake's use of state primarily as accusation throughout *Jerusalem*, with the distinction between states and individuals invoked to solicit the reader's, not the author's, repentance, despite the author's difficult text.

Alterity and the Spectre of Urthona

Alexander Gilchrist, Blake's first major biographer, records a family dispute and a painful scene of forgiveness enacted by the poet, his younger brother, Robert, and his wife, Catherine:

> She, in the heat of discussion, used words to him, his brother (though a husband too) thought unwarrantable. A silent witness thus far, he could now bear it no longer, but with characteristic impetuosity—when stirred—rose and said to her "Kneel down and beg Robert's pardon directly, or you never see my face again!" A heavy threat, uttered in tones which, from Blake, unmistakably showed it was *meant*. She, poor thing! "thought it very hard," as she would afterwards tell, to beg her brother-in-law's pardon when she was not in fault! But being a duteous, devoted wife, though by nature nowise tame or dull of spirit, she *did* kneel down and meekly murmur, "*Robert, I beg your pardon, I am in the wrong*." "Young woman, you lie! abruptly retorted he: *I* am in the wrong!"
>
> (*BR*, 30; original emphasis)

While Gilchrist often distorts and idealizes Blake, this anecdote provides food for thought: apparently, intervening late in a family quarrel, Blake unhesitatingly sides with the brother and against the wife—an instance of fraternal solidarity so strong that Blake would choose his brother over his wife, as the threat implies, "Kneel down and beg Robert's pardon directly, or you never see my face again!" Moreover, Robert Blake's response, his abrupt apology to Catherine Blake, suggests that even he did not think the poet's fraternal solidarity justified. While one would like more biographical facts than Gilchrist provides, this anecdote illustrates Blake's tendency to choose fraternal ties over marital ties, a tendency that characterizes his treatment of forgiveness between his poetic persona, Los, and his personifications of evil and alterity, a class of characters he calls spectres, the most common of which is the Spectre of Urthona. As Blake pursues this metaphoric line of thought, he emphasizes reconciliations between male characters, while female characters, who bear in their femaleness the most obvious sign of alterity, are increasingly written out of the picture. Recent feminist interpretations of Blake[1] encourage us to note that Blake in his late work treats forgiveness remarkably differently when the offender is feminine or masculine. The feminine offenders who receive forgiveness are all "guilty" of undisciplined sexuality, a freedom Blake approved. The feminine offenders against other laws receive harsher treatment, and in fact feminine figures, even the benevolent ones such as Ololon and Jerusalem, dissolve in order to make way for the transaction and identification of two similar male figures. While the power of the sexually exuberant Oothoon forms one pole of Blake's attitude toward forgiving feminine figures, this anecdote from Blake's life presents the opposite pole. Gender as the sign of alterity is indeed important to the central issue of self and other which undergirds and undermines Blake's uses of forgiveness.

In contrast to the previous chapter's reliance on Arendt, who theorizes alterity in social and political terms, this chapter takes its cue from Levinas and Irigaray, who interrogate the phenomenological and psychoanalytic traditions in which the other encountered by the self merely reduplicates that self. Levinas's project includes redefining the other as exterior and excessive, "a form of exteriority, separate from and unpredicted by the subject," and "the site of excess, an unabsorbable, indigestible residue the subject is unable to assimilate to itself."[2] Levinas's concern with exteriority contributes to the sense of an *autonomous* other that must underlie a model of truly intersubjective forgiveness. Irigaray pushes Levinas's insight further by emphasizing the denial of women's autonomy in male philosophers' representations of them as the same as men, as "complementary," or as an opposite in a binary structure—all representations that define them only in relation to men. Moreover, Irigaray cautions against constructing a feminine other made over in the image of a masculine self. She particularly critiques Levinas on this score: "Levinas does not perceive the feminine as other [because] he substitutes the son for the feminine." She continues: "From my point of view, this gesture [of substitution] fails to achieve the relation to the other, and doubly so: it does not recognize the feminine other and the self as other in relation to her; it does not leave the child to his own generation. It seems to me pertinent to add that it does not recognize God in love."[3] Irigaray offers a critical perspective on this incident from Blake's life and on the relation between alterity and the Spectre of Urthona in Blake's poetry. Blake tends to ignore the most radical sign of alterity, the fact of being a female, in favor of a lesser alterity between men; whereas Levinas, in Irigaray's critique, substitutes the son for the feminine, Blake substitutes the brother for the feminine. Moreover, because the self and the brother belong to same generation, Blake's metaphoric choices occlude even the lesser, generational alterity between father and son. Finally, Irigaray's doubts about Levinas's ability to recognize an alterity in God challenge Blake's emphasis on Jesus, a God so much resembling Blake's persona Los that an enlightened Albion tells Jesus: "I see thee in the likeness & similitude of Los my Friend" (*J* 96:22; E, 256). With Irigaray's analysis of alterity in mind, we can examine Blake's conflicted representations of forgivenesses, which reveal that he consistently (but not always) excludes the more radical versions of alterity (sexual alterity, generational alterity, and human-divine alterity) in order to clear the decks for a forgiveness between two versions of the same, for it is forgivenesses between men (who are parts of One Man) that Blake considers normative.

Thus, the primacy of the class of spectres and of the Spectre of Urthona in the late works becomes significant for what they displace or occlude (I am using *spectre* for the class and *Spectre* for the Spectre of Urthona). Blake's spectres function as border figures, at the border between self and other, often an other represented by a feminine figure, in Blake's attempt to represent both intersubjective and intrapsychic forgiveness by the same representational system. Yet spectres fit more readily into the intrapsychic economy, serving in their earliest incarnations to represent the intrapsychic part that must be appeased before intersubjective forgiveness can occur between Zoa and emanation, the other encoded as female. In later incarnations, however, the intrapsychic forgiveness that interests Blake is that between two male figures, Los and the Spectre of Urthona; in this model, if there is an intersubjectively conceived other, it is the reader. The problematic nature of the Spectre of Urthona is almost axiomatic among Blake scholars. Even Frye, who overemphasized the continuity and coherence of Blake's oeuvre, admitted that the Spectre of Urthona created a rift in the composition of *The Four Zoas* and, more generally, in Blake's thinking as a whole. Frye wrote: "The conception of the Spectre of Urthona seems to have broken on Blake quite suddenly when he was proceeding to a simpler climax [for *The Four Zoas*], and occasioned the rewriting of Night VII, if not of the next two Nights as well. Eventually it burst the whole Zoa scheme altogether, and was one of the chief reasons for abandoning the poem."[4] Most critics agree that the Spectre of Urthona marks a significant new development in Blake's thought.[5] Though critics offer various interpretations of this development, none has noticed the connections between the Spectre of Urthona and the notions of accusation and forgiveness. In many ways, Blake's use of the Spectre partakes of the same ambiguity we observed in the doctrines of states and individuals. That ambiguity is muted in *The Four Zoas* but clearly articulated in *Jerusalem*. That is, the Spectre represents Los's intrapsychic disposition to accusation (and to sexual jealousy) and so signifies a portion of the personality that must be "annihilated." Consequently, Los must treat his Spectre harshly, hammering him into a new form on his anvil. At the same time, Blake invests the Spectre with the status of an accusing other, either Urizen the warmonger or Albion the accusing reader. These accusers merit gentle treatment from Los, a gentleness signifying the restoration of an intersubjective relationship in forgiveness. Put simply, Blake denies the logical distinction familiar from Saint Augustine's maxim, "Love the sinner, hate the sin," giving his spectral characters sometimes the harsh treatment due to the "sin" of accusation, and sometimes the gentle treatment offered to the forgiven accuser or "sinner," as a result of condensing the intrapsychic and intersubjective frames of reference.

Blake develops the Spectre of Urthona from "My Spectre around me" through *The Four Zoas* to *Jerusalem*, making this character do double duty of representing sin and sinner. Blake addresses some similar issues in Satan, Milton's spectre, as the personification of Milton's errors, but the Spectre of Urthona is especially important because Los functions as Blake's alter ego in *The Four Zoas* and in *Jerusalem* and, as a result, the Spectre of Urthona bears a uniquely close relation to the self Blake projects into the poem. The Spectre of Urthona provides a starting place to analyze the two-way traffic between self and other necessary to forgiveness.

Blake critics have long agreed that the Spectre of Urthona represents Los's everyday, working self, what Frye called "clock time."[6] Such a consensus neglects the term *spectre*'s sinister connotations: since the sixteenth century, *spectre* had denoted an "apparition, phantom, or ghost, especially one of terrifying nature or aspect."[7] In Blake's time, spectres haunted numerous Gothic novels[8] and a travel book Blake knew, Stedman's *A Narrative, of a Five Years' Expedition, Against the Revolted Negroes of Surinam, in Guiana*. Stedman recounts the habits of "the vampire or spectre of Guiana," which sucks blood from the feet of sleeping men.[9] Blake's pictures of the Spectre of Urthona, particularly *Jerusalem* 6, allude to Stedman's sinister tale (see figure 4). Susan Fox attempts to reconcile these two uses of *spectre* as our banal,

His Spectre drivn by the Starry Wheels of Albions sons, black and
Opake divided from his back; he labours and he mourns!

For as his Emanation divided, his Spectre also divided
In terror of those starry wheels: and the Spectre stood over Los
Howling in pain: a blackning Shadow, blackning dark & opake
Cursing the terrible Los: bitterly cursing him for his friendship
To Albion, suggesting murderous thoughts against Albion.

Los ragd and stampd the earth in his might & terrible wrath!
He stood and stampd the earth! then he threw down his hammer in rage &
In fury: then he sat down and wept, terrified! Then arose
And chaunted his song, labouring with the tongs and hammer:
But still the Spectre divided, and still his pain increasd!

In pain the Spectre divided: in pain of hunger and thirst:
To devour Los's Human Perfection, but when he saw that Los

FIGURE 4.
Jerusalem,
Copy F, plate 6
(The Pierpont Morgan Library, New York, PML 953)

material, "clock time" selves and as parasitic ghosts: "What is, from the standpoint of eternity, dead and invisible, happens to be, from our standpoint in Generation, the only material life. Blake is not being perverse when he calls our hard live flesh a ghost, he is being literal to his vision."[10] But the ambivalence condensed in the Spectre also mirrors Blake's struggles to represent intrapsychic forgiveness: within the self, the Spectre represents both an erring but redeemable faculty that falls into accusation and which must be reconciled with the "higher" self, and also the accusation itself, which evaporates like a ghost in the combined act of repentance and forgiveness. This ambivalence toward the Spectre as a representative of intrapsychic reality is compounded when Blake uses him to represent intersubjective reality as well.

One early incarnation of the Spectre, in "My Spectre around me," demonstrates both the intrapsychic ambiguity (Spectre as accusation itself versus spectre as accusing part of self) and also the Spectre's liminal function at the border of the intersubjective relationship with an emanation, an other encoded as female. Blake probably wrote "My Spectre around me" between 1803 and 1806, revising it heavily and never producing a definitive fair copy.[11] Although Blake revised and distributed some poems in his Notebook, many of them remained private, probably because they express feelings Blake found shameful, such as "Anger & Wrath my bosom rends" (E, 503). A recurrent theme in these works, such as "The Mental Traveller" and "The Crystal Cabinet," is endless cyclicity and the domestic recriminations which Blake elsewhere called "The torments of Love & Jealousy" (*FZ* 1; E, 300). "My Spectre around me" explores the possibility of forgiveness among such recriminations, tentatively concluding that forgiveness can take place more easily in male friendship than in marriage—a darker, more pervasive conclusion than Blake's flash of hope for marital forgiveness: "Mutual Forgiveness of Each vice / Such are the Gates of Paradise" (*FS* 1–2; E, 259). Blake uses the Spectre sometimes to represent a character, the erring portion of the speaker, and sometimes to personify accusation and sexual jealousy.

> My Spectre around me night & day
> Like a Wild beast guards my way
> My Emanation far within
> Weeps incessantly for my Sin
>
> A Fathomless & boundless deep
> There we wander there we weep
> On the hungry craving wind
> My Spectre follows thee behind

He scents thy footsteps in the snow
Wheresoever thou dost go
Thro the wintry hail & rain
When wilt thou return again.

("My Spectre" 1–12; E, 475–76)

These three stanzas narrate the actions of three agents: a masculine self, an emanation, and a spectre. The speaker's alienation from the accusing other, the emanation who "weeps incessantly" for the speaker's "sin," is echoed by his relation to his spectre, a wild beast who both threatens and "guards." The rift between speaker and emanation has suspended their sexual relations and their harmony: the spectre embodies that frustrated material male self, tracking the emanation's scent. Frustrated sexual desire prompts the male speaker to accuse the emanation of pride, scorn, jealousy, and fear, so that the cycle of mutual recrimination seems unbreakable:

Dost thou not in Pride & scorn
Fill with tempests all my morn
And with jealousies & fears
Fill my pleasant nights with tears

Seven of my sweet loves thy knife
Has bereaved of their life
Their marble tombs I build with tears
And with cold & shuddering fears

Seven more loves weep night & day
Round the tombs where my loves lay
And seven more loves attend each night
Around my couch with torches bright

And seven more Loves in my bed
Crown with wine my mournful head
Pitying & forgiving all
Thy transgressions great & small.

("My Spectre" 13–28; E, 476)

After this list of "loves" killed seven at a time, the speaker protests that the emanation has rejected twenty-eight "loves," which may be sexual invitations or acts of forgiveness, or both: in making sexual advances, he is "Pitying & forgiving all / Thy transgressions great & small." Blake's use of "loves" in multiples of seven alludes to sexual acts (in the book of Tobit and in the Gospel) and to fraternal acts of forgiveness (in the Gospel). Tobit's son Tobias marries his kinswoman Sarah, whose previous seven bridegrooms have been struck dead by a jealous demon before they could consummate the marriage. Tobias drives the demon away by burning a fish's entrails in the bridal chamber, and the marriage is consummated. Blake's male speaker dramatizes his plight as that of the aggregate of Sarah's defeated husbands, whose "seven loves" were "bereaved of their life." Blake's story of seven marital defeats also alludes to the hypothetical case posed to Jesus by the Sadducees. Seven brothers married the same woman, one after another, according to the Mosaic law, to provide a child for the first, childless brother. If they all died childless, the Sadducees ask Jesus, "in the resurrection, whose wife shall she be of the seven?" (Matthew 22:28; cf. Mark 12:23 and Luke 20:33). The seven brothers were doubly "bereaved of their life," dying themselves and leaving no offspring: Blake may have alluded to their seven efforts to produce a child, all defeated, out of his frustration over the childlessness of his own marriage.

In addition to these allusions to marriage, the personification of acts of forgiveness in groups of seven alludes to the fraternal tie in the Gospel, to forgiving one's brother "seventy times seven" times: "Then came Peter to [Jesus] and said, Lord, how oft shall my brother sin against me, and I forgive him? till seven times? Jesus saith unto him, I say not unto thee Until seven times: but, Until seventy times seven" (Matthew 18:21). Blake questions the applicability of this fraternal ideal to the relations of marriage in a couplet from the Notebook:

> Grown old in Love from Seven till Seven times Seven
> I oft have wishd for Hell for Ease from Heaven.
> (E, 516).[12]

The masculine speaker and the emanation in "My Spectre around me" find themselves at the midpoint of an endless cycle of recrimination and forgiveness, a midpoint indicated by the number. If the emanation can expect a total of seven forgiving "loves," prefigured by Tobias's predecessors and the Sadducees' hypothetical brothers, then Blake's narrative begins almost exactly in the middle, after she has already killed three groups: those who were stabbed, those by the tombs, those by the couch. The fourth group crowns the speaker's head, waiting for the emanation's next act of vengeance. Ideally, three more groups of forgiving "loves" would follow, though the male speaker lacks such endurance. The number seven alludes to two different contexts for forgiveness: marital, in which only seven cycles can exist; and fraternal, which accommodates forty-nine cycles of forgiveness. In the light of Irigaray's critique of Levinas, it is possible that Blake, too, finds forgiveness between two male figures the more attractive plot because, as male figures, they are fundamentally two versions of the same; the plot of reconciliation between male and female figures requires a more radical recognition of otherness encoded as female.

The speaker appeals to the emanation to break the cycle and respond to his forgiveness in kind. Blake dramatizes the difficulty of marital forgiveness by making the emanation's accusations intractable:

> When wilt thou return & view
> My loves & them to life renew
> When wilt thou return & live
> When wilt thou pity as I forgive
>
> Never Never I return
> Still for Victory I burn
> Living thee alone Ill have
> And when dead Ill be thy Grave
>
> Thro the Heavn & Earth & Hell
> Thou shalt never never quell
> I will fly & thou pursue
> Night & Morn the flight renew.
>
> ("My Spectre" 29–40; E, 476)

This exchange rationalizes Blake's rejection of the marital relationship as a possible site of forgiveness. The male speaker has hoped for mutual forgiveness ("When wilt thou pity as I forgive") while the emanation demands "victory" and wishes for the male speaker's death. Moreover, in an omitted stanza, she seems to revel in the cycle of mutual offense, saying,

> What Transgressions I commit
> Are for thy Transgressions fit.
>
> ("My Spectre" Postscript 5–6; E, 477)

The choice between marital and fraternal love, posed in the stanzas thick with "sevens," arises again. The answer seems to lie in replacing heterosexual love with brotherhood or male friendship. Blake hopes that forgiveness can characterize relations from which sexuality has been excluded:

Till I turn from Female Love
And root up the Infernal Grove
I shall never worthy be
To Step into Eternity

And to end thy cruel mocks
Annihilate thee on the rocks
And another form create
To be subservient to my Fate

Let us agree to give up Love
And root up the infernal grove
Then shall we return & see
The worlds of happy Eternity

& Throughout all Eternity
I forgive you you forgive me
As our dear Redeemer said
This the Wine & this the Bread.

("My Spectre" 41–56; E, 476–77)

Blake's imagined eucharistic banquet here may possibly include a male speaker and female emanation who have "give[n] up Love," that is, conjugal relations, in favor of a desexualized act of communion, as the Eucharist stresses love between men in which the "Redeemer" gave the Last Supper to his male friends (John 15:15). In Blake's final version of mutuality the friends both perform the same act, forgiveness; Blake stresses an equality and mutuality by the chiasmus in the line, "I forgive you you forgive me." In rewriting, Blake dropped the specialized terms *spectre* and *emanation,* as Erdman observes (E, 857). This revision may be a first step in the displacement of Blake's energy and interest away from an other who invites a heterosexual erotic tie—he abandons his specialized terms for such a tie—in favor of a relationship with another version of the same. This revision, which erases the distinction between the male speaker and his spectre, suggests that for Blake the two were "reconciled" because he discovered they were the same "he," while the emanation still bears the mark of irreconcilable otherness, "she."

The emergence of Jesus at the end of "My Spectre Around Me" reflects Blake's bipolar conception of the male speaker's character, moving from a condition of imprisonment by the spectre to a meal of friendship with the Redeemer. Blake relies increasingly on this bipolar conception of character in the major prophecies. Even though the Spectre of Urthona functions as a mediator or boundary figure, sometimes as a scapegoat, in Blake's depictions of marital, intersubjective forgiveness, as fraternal forgiveness takes center stage the Spectre becomes almost entirely an intrapsychic entity, as Blake's desired metaphoric destination for fraternal forgiveness in the fusion of brothers in "One Man."

The place of the Spectre as a border figure, a part of the self who mirrors an other, becomes more complex in Night the Seventh of *The Four Zoas*, long recognized as a crux in the poem and in Blake's oeuvre as a whole.[13] There Los embraces the Spectre "first as a brother / Then as another Self" (*FZ* 85:29–30; E, 367), a sequence revealing the slipperiness with which an other, conceived as a brother, can become another self, or in Irigaray's phrase, an echo of phallic sameness rather than true alterity. Nonetheless, Blake remains interested in Spectre's function as a border figure in forgiveness, as both the intrapsychic disposition to be changed and also the principle of identification with the error in the erring other. Therefore, he regroups his focus on another border: the Spectre mediates between Los and Urizen, a potentially fraternal relation that avoids "the torments of Love & Jealousy" (*FZ* 1; E, 300) which must be overcome in sexual love between Los and Enitharmon. The dramatic action of Night the Seventh echoes that of "My Spectre around me," in that the Spectre functions as Los's rival for Enitharmon's affections, complicated by Blake's premise that the Spectre seduces Enitharmon at the behest of Los's archenemy Urizen. Intrapsychically, he represents the portion of Los frustrated by Enitharmon's withdrawal, the disposition to choose vengeance instead of forgiveness. This impasse takes place in the contentious atmosphere of sexual love, where intersubjective forgiveness is difficult and messy. But here the Spectre further represents the vengefulness of Urizen, whom Blake has shown in the context of his political machinations, as well as the vengeance of Los. Thus the Spectre functions both intrapsychically and intersubjectively on the border of a potentially fraternal relation.

Blake finds sexual love is as complicated in *The Four Zoas* as he did in "My Spectre around me." In Night the Seventh, Los and Enitharmon are alienated, echoing the dramatic situation of "My Spectre." The Spectre exacerbates the problem by seducing Enitharmon under the "Tree of Mystery." The Spectre's self-presentation at this point in the narrative echoes the function of the Spectre in "My Spectre," the function of representing Los's character as degraded by Enitharmon's rejection. Yet Blake adds to the hints of a vengeful spectre in "My Spectre" a penetrating analysis of the relationship of revenge to time and memory, as Wayne Glausser has observed.[14] In his efforts to persuade and manipulate, the Spectre calls for a return to Eternity by means of memory, a regression into the past. In seducing the Shadow of Enitharmon, he laments,

> For till these terrors planted round the Gates of Eternal life
> Are driven away & annihilated we never can repass the Gates
> (*FZ* 84:41–42; E, 360)

gates the Spectre later calls the "gates of Memory." The relation between servitude to the past and the desire for revenge becomes clear as the seduction progresses. The Shadow of Enitharmon, complicit in the same ethic, calls for revenge against Vala:

> Maist find a way to punish Vala in thy fiery South
> To bring her down subjected to the rage of my fierce boy.
> (*FZ* 83:33–34; E, 359)

The Spectre agrees, saying, "I will bring down soft Vala" (*FZ* 84:33; E, 359). Furthermore, the Spectre wants to punish Los out of revenge for laboring for him night and day, and he retells the past to give priority to himself and assign an inferior status to Los:

> . . . I stood beside my anvil dark a mass
> Of iron glowd bright prepard for spades & plowshares. sudden down
> I sunk with cries of blood issuing downward in the veins.
> (*FZ* 84:16–18; E, 359)

One vice of this debased version of Los is sexual jealousy, which the Spectre expresses in a paradoxical way, speaking of himself as the rival of Los even though he is a part of Los:

> In due time issuing forth from Enions womb
> Thou & that demon Los wert born Ah jealousy & woe.
> (*FZ* 84:28–29; E, 359)

Blake here broaches some fundamental issues about revenge, forgiveness, and the relation to the past. As Arendt has observed, revenge places us in a "predicament of irreversibility," that is, the condition in which "our capacity to act would, as it were, be confined to one single deed from which we could never recover."[15] In his constant reference to the inescapable past, the Gates of Memory that can never be repassed, the Spectre exemplifies Arendt's link between revenge and the past, the "clock time" Blake scholars have traditionally linked to the Spectre.

So far, the Spectre has referred to himself as a character, a rival of Los for Enitharmon's affections and for priority among the members of Urthona. Insofar as Blake presents the Spectre as a character, the Spectre appeals to Enitharmon's pity, and to the reader's, no matter how debased his view of time and revenge. Yet Blake supplements this view of the Spectre as a deluded offender by inserting this passage denouncing him as offense personified:

> Thou knowest that the Spectre is in Every Man insane brutish
> Deformd that I am thus a ravening devouring lust continually
> Craving & devouring but my Eyes are always upon thee O lovely
> Delusion & I cannot crave for any thing but thee *& till*
> *I have thee in my arms & am again united to Los*
> *To be one body & One Spirit with him* not so
> The Spectres of the Dead for I am as the Spectre of the Living.
> (*FZ* 84:36–42; E, 360)

From this addition, Blake later deleted the italicized lines. Clearly the tone has changed dramatically as the Spectre condemns himself as insane, brutish, and deformed. Glausser attributes Blake's additions and deletions to Blake's contradictory feelings about the Spectre: "Blake had trouble," he writes, "deciding whether to condemn the Spectre or redeem him."[16] For the first time the Spectre addresses the Shadow of Enitharmon as "Delusion," suggesting the decline in the female other's importance. Moreover, Blake shifts from portraying the offender to portraying the offense itself. Rather than using the verbs of offending actions to modify the noun *Spectre*, Blake's phrasing indicates that the Spectre *is* the offending action: "I am thus a ravening devouring lust continually / Craving & devouring." He is not a lusting spectre; he is lust. Thus, the shift in tone from sympathy to condemnation can be explained by Blake's habit of condensing the representation of both offender and offense, of both intersubjective and intrapsychic forgiveness, into the same symbolic system. Moreover, the deleted section suggests that for the Spectre, the fraternal relation takes priority over the sexual. The Spectre imagines a sexual embrace with the Emanation ("till / I have thee in my arms") as a means of achieving fraternal reconciliation with Los ("am again united to Los / To be one body & One Spirit with him"). This desire for fraternal forgiveness is echoed by Los's embrace of the Spectre later in Night the Seventh.

As the Night progresses, Los confronts the offense committed by the Spectre in seducing Enitharmon, and an opportunity for forgiveness arises.

The Spectre has functioned both as a rival of Los's, who commits the offense against Los, and also as the offense in Los himself, both the very sexual jealousy in Los that prompts him to take offense at the seduction and the desire to repeat the past in revenge. Thus the Spectre doubly represents the offender Los must forgive as another (intersubjective forgiveness) and the disposition Los must overcome in himself in order to forgive the other (intrapsychic forgiveness). Blake's interest is increasingly drawn to this complex question of forgiveness, such that he gives the reconciliation between Los and his Spectre a far more prominent place in the poem than the reconciliation between Los and Enitharmon. In this way, Blake brings into fuller mythic shape the sketchy prolepsis in "My Spectre around me" that the mental wars between equals (either brothers or friends) provide a more hopeful and more important site of forgiveness than the "Infernal Grove" of "the torments of Love & Jealousy."

However, in displacing his interest from heterosexual forgiveness to fraternal, Blake pushes his metaphor of brothers (two versions of the same) to its next logical step, depicting the relation between Los and the Spectre as an identity, not a transaction:

> But then the Spectre enterd Los's bosom Every sigh & groan
> Of Enitharmon bore Urthonas Spectre on its wings
> Obdurate Los felt Pity Enitharmon told the tale
> Of Urthona. Los embracd the Spectre first as a brother
> Then as another Self; astonishd humanizing & in tears
> In Self abasement Giving up his Domineering lust.
> (*FZ* 85:26–31; E, 367)

What does Blake gain in depicting forgiveness as Los's recognition of the Spectre as "first a brother / Then as another Self"? The Spectre is Los's "brother" as a member of Urthona but also as a fellow sufferer, in part because of the rejection of Los by Enitharmon. To recognize the Spectre as a brother is to reestablish bonds of human relationship and thus achieve what might be intersubjective forgiveness. The recognition of the offender as a "brother," a fellow sufferer, involves the exercise of compassion, feeling one's own suffering and recognizing it in another, forging an identification theorized by Niebuhr: in forgiveness the evil in the other is tolerated because the evil in the self is known. Compassion, then, sees the self in the other, seeing the suffering one knows intimately (that is, one's own) projected imaginatively into the perceived suffering of the other. But the subsequent phrase, "another Self," raises conceptual problems. Is Los recognizing the Spectre as another autonomous center of activity and suffering, in the exercise of generosity and compassion necessary to true intersubjectivity? Blake implies that Los attains this achievement by granting Los his most honorific adjective: humanizing.

In Blake's own terms, Los's embrace of the Spectre also suggests intrapsychic purification, the "annihilation of the selfhood." When Los recognizes the Spectre as "another Self," Blake implies that the Spectre personifies Los's own "domineering lust," or sexual jealousy, and its concomitant vices of vengefulness and accusation. The Spectre stands for both "sinner" (one's fellow sufferer) and "sin" (accusation and jealousy). Paradoxically, Los expunges from his personality the "sin" of "domineering lust" personified in the Spectre by the very action of embracing the Spectre as a "sinner" and a part of himself.

Once we step outside Blake's terms, however, the phrase "another Self" suggests a third possibility, the one raised by Irigaray's critique of Levinas: that Los recognizes merely a mirror of himself and is reconciled with a repetition of his own sameness, not with another autonomous subject. In fact, Blake presents a version of this third possibility as the Spectre's point of view. The Spectre definitely views the embrace as a rivalry between likes, insisting on an even more complete abdication of autonomy from Los, that Los acknowledge the Spectre not as "another Self" but as "thy real Self":

> Thou never canst embrace sweet Enitharmon terrible Demon. Till
> Thou art united with thy Spectre Consummating by pains & labours
> That mortal body & by Self annihilation back returning
> To Life Eternal be assurd *I am thy real Self*
> Tho thus divided from thee & the Slave of Every passion
> Of thy fierce Soul Unbar the Gates of Memory *look upon me*
> *Not as another but as thy real Self* I am thy Spectre
> Thou didst subdue me in old times by thy Immortal Strength
> When I was a ravning hungring & thirsting cruel lust & murder
> Tho horrible & Ghastly to thine Eyes tho buried beneath
> The ruins of the Universe. hear what inspird I speak & be silent.
> (*FZ* 85:32–42; E, 368; emphasis added)

The Spectre here speaks as the vice of accusation personified, a self seeking to annihilate all other selves. Rather than seeking the reconciliation of equals that Los has offered him, the Spectre speaks the language of power and domination, seeing himself as "the Slave of Every passion" whom Los had earlier "subdued." Rather than seeking the equality and intersubjectivity with Los that would be fitting for a brother conceived as another autonomous self, he

seeks to usurp Los, saying, "look upon me / Not as another but as thy real Self." The Spectre's claim that he alone is real culminates in his denial of the otherness of Los, in an action Blake's symbol system equates with the silencing of imagination: "hear what inspird I speak & be silent." Finally the Spectre concludes, simply, "thou art but a form & organ of life & of thyself / Art nothing" (*FZ* 86:2–3; E, 368). To deny being, autonomy, and subjectivity to the other is the final triumph of the "One Law," in which an apparently intersubjective reconciliation is in fact the subjugation of the other into the same. The Spectre thus dramatizes the heart of darkness of this "reconciliation," the threat that it might become the loss of the autonomy of the other in the aggrandizement of the self. Does Blake himself succumb to a more subtle form of this loss, in displacing the energy of his reconciliations from sexual to fraternal love? Within the dramatic context of *The Four Zoas* itself, Blake uses the Spectre's insistence that he is Los's real self to prompt Los to a different act of forgiveness, an act motivated by what might, in traditional language, be called humility. Whereas before, the recognition of the suffering of the other prompted compassion, here the recognition of the evil of the other should prompt humility, insofar as Los can recognize that he himself shares in that evil. In that sense, the Spectre is Los's real self, the jealousy and vengeance Los has practiced heretofore in the poem. The Spectre alludes to the concept of selfhood in exhorting Los to "*self*-annihilation," identifying himself "Not as another but as thy real *Self*" (emphasis added in both examples). In an instance of dramatic irony the Spectre presents himself as the self to be annihilated, the disposition on the border between self and other projected outward as a person, the disposition that needs to be purged from Los's character in order for him to achieve forgivingness (that is, the disposition to forgive readily).

It is on this intrapsychic level that Los responds to the Spectre, the level of the Spectre as a genuine representative of Los's own evil, rather than on the level of a warning against the dangers of losing the other in intersubjectivity:

> Los furious answerd Spectre horrible thy words astound my Ear
> With irresistible conviction I feel I am not one of those
> Who when convincd can still persist. tho furious. controllable
> By Reasons power . . .
> . . . .
> . . . I will quell my fury & teach
> Peace to the Soul of dark revenge & repentance to Cruelty.
> (*FZ* 86:4–7; 11–12; E, 368)

Blake's Los declares, "I feel I am not one of those / Who when convincd can still persist"; he chooses forgiveness, resolving to "teach / Peace to the Soul of dark revenge," the revenge that has been personified in the Spectre. But of what truth is Los convinced (or convicted)?

Los's uncanny transition from fury to mastery of his fury is not explained but presented as a breakthrough, in which Blake juxtaposes despair and recovery.[17] This disjunction stresses the radically new character of forgiveness, a novelty theorized by Arendt: "In contrast to revenge, which is the natural, automatic reaction to transgression," she writes, "forgiveness can never be predicted. . . . Forgiveness, in other words, is the only reaction which does not merely react but acts anew and unexpectedly."[18] On the dramatic level of the poem, Los's sudden outpouring of affection suggests his freedom both from the Spectre's ethic of revenge and also from the servitude to memory on which revenge depends. Los's confrontation with the Spectre has taught him the two necessary skills for forgiveness, the compassion of seeing the other as a fellow sufferer (a skill necessary for intersubjective forgiveness) and the humility to see the potential for the offender's evil in oneself (a skill necessary for intrapsychic forgiveness). Because of Los's increased capacity to forgive, the Spectre of Urthona can function as "a medium between [Los] & Enitharmon" (*FZ* 87:26; E, 369). The Spectre blames himself for the state "of Separation" and Los himself feels "the weight of stern repentance." However, if we step outside Blake's terms, Los's resolve (or resolution) appears not so much the acceptance of a truth but the substitution of a fraternal forgiveness for a sexual one: once Los resolves his conflict with the Spectre, the conflict with Enitharmon reemerges in short order as the next crisis needing resolution. Because Los has forgiven the brother Spectre, he can forgive his emanation:

> . . . take comfort O Enitharmon
> Couldst thou but cease from terror & trembling & affright
> When I appear before thee in forgiveness of ancient injuries.
> (*FZ* 45–47; E, 369)

This "forgiveness of ancient injuries" evaded the speaker of "My Spectre around me," who abandoned "Female Love" as hopeless, seeking forgiveness in brotherhood alone. Blake's use of the Spectre in his meditations on forgiveness has advanced here in Night the Seventh, as the Spectre of Urthona embodies the accuser Los wishes to forgive and the accusation Los wishes to annihilate. Reconciled with the Spectre, Los returns to "Female Love" ready to forgive Enitharmon, though the structure of the reconciliations implies that the otherness encoded in Enitharmon's femaleness is not significant. Blake

occludes the otherness of Enitharmon by making it depend so thoroughly on the reconciliation of Los and the Spectre. Yet Blake, needing an other for whom the Spectre can function as a boundary figure or vicarious representative, depicts widening circles of forgiveness. In Night the Seventh's climax, Urizen becomes the other with whom Los is easily reconciled because of Los's earlier struggle with the Spectre:

> Startled was Los he found his Enemy Urizen now
> In his hands. he wonderd that he felt love & not hate
> His whole soul loved him he beheld him an infant
> Lovely breathd from Enitharmon he trembled within himself.
> (*FZ* 90:64–67; E, 371)

This climax adds a final layer of intersubjective forgiveness. The sudden reconciliation, which startled Los himself, may seem unearned. But since the Spectre seduced Enitharmon at Urizen's behest, serving as Urizen's emissary in all of his designs against Los, Los simultaneously contains Urizen "now / In his hands" by means of his embracing of the Spectre. The Spectre has doubled Urizen throughout Night the Seventh; the Spectre worships "futurity" in Enitharmon, saying, "listen thou my vision / I view futurity in thee" (*FZ* 84:32–33; E, 359); this is the same error Urizen later renounces in saying: "Go O dark futurity I will cast thee forth from these / Heavens of my brain . . . for lo futurity is in this moment" (*FZ* 121:19–20, 22; E, 390). Blake also reveals the vicarious status, the border function of the Spectre, when the Spectre seduces Enitharmon. Blake comments: "Urizen saw & triumphd" (*FZ* 95:17; E, 360). In so doing, Blake prepares for the layering of forgivenesses, the pattern in which Los's forgiveness of the Spectre achieves all other needed forgivenesses— all those with male figures, at any rate.

The condensation of Los's embrace of the Spectre and of Urizen does recuperate a kind of intersubjectivity, a recognition of otherness, despite the loss of Enitharmon's sexual otherness. Blake recuperates on the intersubjective level of international, rather than heterosexual, forgiveness. In that portion of Night the Seventh formerly called by Blake's editors VIIb, Urizen is "very much an external enemy,"[19] resembling William Pitt's persecution of the war with France just before the Peace of Amiens and mimicking the Jewish and Roman leaders who crucified Jesus. When Blake reconciles Los with this "Enemy," this external enemy, at the end of Night the Seventh, he thereby implies that all instances of international, intersubjective forgiveness depend solely upon the intrapsychic self-annihilation, or renunciation of accusation, in the victim (in this case, Los). In such a heavily condensed model, trying to

say so much at once, Blake paradoxically loses the possibility of depicting some kinds of alterity, because he shows a relationship between equals in terms that reduce the relationship to the decision of just one party to forgive himself. One wonders if his impulse to plot the intersubjective relationship on the intrapsychic grid betrays the need to control the responses of the intractably other by containing them in the self.

Yet the repressed other continues to return. Another clue that intersubjectivity is not completely lost in Blake's depiction of the Spectre as "another Self" is that Los, Enitharmon, and the Spectre of Urthona, having forgiven and having been forgiven, engage in an ambitious artistic task, "fabricat[ing] forms sublime" for the unfortunate "Spectrous Dead" (*FZ* 90:4; E, 370). Blake makes it clear that this task is mutual:

> And first [Los] drew a line upon the walls of shining heaven
> And Enitharmon tincturd it with beams of blushing love.
> (*FZ* 90:35–36; E, 370)

Blake, like Arendt, links this outpouring of creative effort to forgiveness and the release from the past that forgiveness permits. Arendt theorizes that forgiveness releases human beings from the cycle of irreversibility, just as human work releases us from the cycle of the life process.[20] Forgiveness, then, gives rise to Los's creativity and poetry.

So far, Blake's use of spectres in "My Spectre around me" and in *The Four Zoas* forms a trajectory in which the Spectre, as the boundary figure between a self and offending other, serves as the other introjected into the self, so that intersubjective forgiveness can be replotted as intrapsychic, perhaps in order to control the other. This trajectory runs the risk of denying any real alterity, of claiming that there is nothing outside the self. Yet as this trajectory denies otherness in some quarters, such as gender, it recoups it in others. In *Jerusalem* Blake places the Spectre on the boundary between Blake/Los and the unknowable otherness of the reading public, Albion. In both previous instances ("My Spectre" and *The Four Zoas*), the Spectre bridges (and displaces) an initial alienation between a male character and his emanation. In *Jerusalem* the Spectre stands in for the initial alienation between Blake and his reader, but, within the symbolic action of the poem, the Spectre does seem genuinely to be Los's main antagonist.[21] The Spectre fits in the dominant pattern of *Jerusalem*, uncompromising binary opposition, repeated again and again in pairs of opposites that are all congruent, if not equivalent, to one another: Jesus and Satan, Los and the Spectre, forgiveness and accusation, Jerusalem and Vala. In

the trajectory plotted here, this last pairing of Jerusalem and Vala reflects a further reduction in the importance of the emanation. Blake removes the emanation from its place of relative equality with its male counterpart,[22] so that Jerusalem fights her battles not with Albion but with Vala, as they come to represent the true and false emanations of Albion. As a result, reconciliation with the emanation no longer motivates Los's reconciliation with the Spectre. Instead, Blake focuses explicitly on achieving through forgiveness a fraternal relation between Los and the Spectre and between the poet and his reader, though, as we have noted, an undercurrent of accusation and hostility thickens Blake's address to his reader. The Spectre still represents both offense and offender, sin and sinner, but since Blake now directs his attention outward to the reader, the Spectre stands as a boundary figure facing Albion, Blake's reader, as Blake tries to recover an other in the open-ended address to the reader: "[*Dear*] Reader, [*forgive*] what you do not approve, & [*love*] me for this energetic exertion of my talent" (*J*3; E, 145). Blake's ambivalence is marked by his gouging out the words most central to defining the relation with the reader: *dear, forgive,* and *love.* As a result of his new focus on reconciliation with the reader, not with the emanation, Blake uses the Spectre as a boundary figure between Los and Albion, the reader. Blake signifies this shift in the Spectre's representation by a chiasmus. Blake opens the chiasmus in chapter 1: Albion rejects Jesus, then Los argues with his Spectre. In the middle of *Jerusalem*, the Spectre by and large disappears. Blake closes the chiasmus in chapter 4 with Los's remaking of his Spectre, followed by Albion's recognition of Jesus in Los.[23] This chiasmus emphasizes the Spectre's mediating function between Blake/Los and Albion/Reader. Again, as in *The Four Zoas*, Blake condenses two frames of reference, adapting his tone accordingly: harsh when the Spectre personifies Albion's evil (and Los's); gentle when the Spectre stands for Los or Albion, as offenders who need forgiveness.[24]

This function of the Spectre of Urthona as boundary figure mediating between Blake/Los and Albion/Reader may at first appear unnecessary, since Blake's vocabulary allows him to differentiate between Albion and the Spectre of Albion. Despite the logical clarity this distinction provides, Blake remains convinced and convicted that any evil we perceive in an offender is also a possibility for us. To write *only* about the offender's spectre, in this case, the Spectre of Albion, would be to permit the erroneous assumption that spectral evil is Albion's alone, or, as Blake says, to impute evil to individuals and not to states. Therefore, even when Blake writes about Albion's Spectre, he insists that Albion's Spectre is identical to Blake's own spectre as well. For example, he exclaims at one point in *Jerusalem*:

> Spectre of Albion! warlike Fiend!
> In clouds of blood & ruin roll'd:
> I here reclaim thee as my own
> My Selfhood! Satan! armd in gold.
>
> (*J* 27:73–76; E, 173)

Blake's reclamation of Albion's Spectre as his own emphasizes the one insight that for Blake overrode any logical inconsistencies, namely, that all evil is identical and identifiable as accusation. To put it another way, individuals may have their peculiar geniuses, but they do not have their peculiar vices. For Blake, accusation is the only evil worth denouncing, and consequently he depicts all evil outside the self in the image of this evil within the self, introjecting all intersubjective conflicts as intrapsychic. A second example of Blake's insistence that intrapsychic evil is the more pressing concern occurs on plate 37 of *Jerusalem*, showing an aged, despairing figure, hunched forward, his head between his knees.[25] This figure is presumably the "Giant Albion" of the poem's title, as Blake suggests by contrasting his size with the much smaller figure seated on a scroll falling from the giant's right side.[26] The scroll reads, in reversed writing:

> Each Man is in his Spectre's power
> Untill the arrival of that hour,
> When his Humanity awake
> And cast his Spectre into the Lake.
>
> (*J* 37; E, 184)[27]

This quatrain focuses on the intrapsychic battle in "Each Man," evoking an individual struggle there between "*his* Spectre" and "*his* Humanity," a struggle far more internalized in this final version than in the Notebook:

> This world is in the Spectres power
> Untill the arrival of that hour
> Untill the Humanity awake
> And cast the Spectre into the Lake.
>
> (E, 810)

In the Notebook Blake wrote "*the* Spectre" and "*the* Humanity," depicting the struggle as taking place not intrapsychically in "Each Man," but intersubjectively in "This world." To view the struggle between Spectre and Humanity as taking place in "This world" locates it outside oneself. If Blake had continued such a point of view in *Jerusalem*, he would have regarded Albion's errors

similarly as Albion's alone, not his own. But the revision suggests that Blake insisted on the primacy of the intrapsychic version in "Each Man" to that of the intersubjective version in "This world."

More important in *Jerusalem* than these rudimentary Spectres of Albion is the boundary figure of the Spectre of Urthona. Blake places the major conversations between Jesus and Albion in a chiastic relation with the major conversations between Los and his Spectre. Chapter 1 opens with Jesus, who continually visits Blake the poet, addressing Albion the implied reader on the topics of friendship and forgiveness:

> I am not a God afar off, I am a brother & friend;
> Within your bosoms I reside, and you reside in me:
> Lo! we are One; forgiving all Evil; Not seeking recompense!
> Ye are my members O ye sleepers of Beulah, land of shades!
> (*J* 4:18–21; E, 146)

Blake's Jesus reiterates some major themes from the Preface, including Blake's two epithets for him, *friend* (echoing "Friend of Sinners") and *forgiver* (echoing "the spirit of Jesus is continual forgiveness of Sin"). Moreover, when Blake's Jesus directly addresses Albion, Blake's reader, he echoes the Preface's identification of reading as a site of forgiveness. Whereas Blake had offered the hope that he and the reader would be "wholly One in Jesus our Lord," that is, in the spirit of forgiveness, Blake's Jesus here declares that the desired unity is already a reality: "Lo! we are One; forgiving all Evil" (*J* 40:20; E, 146). The two opening sections of the poem, Blake's preface to the reader and the vision of Jesus calling to Albion, reorient the axis of forgiveness in a new way, toward the reader. However, it would have been a rare reader in Blake's time who had access to a copy of *Jerusalem* to find himself so addressed. And only the initiated reader, also rare in Blake's time, would hear himself addressed under the name Albion as well as by the more conventional "Dear Reader."

In this outermost layer of the chiasmus (Blake/Jesus addressing Albion/reader), Albion responds by attacking the notion of friendship, which is the very rationale and foundation of acts of forgiveness. He says:

> [*We are not One: we are Many thou most simulative*]
> Phantom of the over heated brain! shadow of immortality!
> Seeking to keep my soul a victim to thy Love! which binds
> Man the enemy of man into deceitful friendships.
> (*J* 4:23–26; E, 146–47)

Ironically, Albion calls Jesus a "*simulative* / Phantom" and a "shadow," synonyms of the word *spectre*. Albion, rather than becoming what he beholds, projects his own spectral condition outward. His projection consists in denying the truth Blake has presented as fundamental about Jesus, his identity as friend. Therefore Albion denies that any friendship is genuine, exclaiming instead that he himself is a victim of love and that all friendships between men are deceitful. (The question of friendships between men and women, or between woman and woman, does not arise.) Moreover, when Albion says that Jesus' love "binds / Man the enemy of man into deceitful friendships," he implies that human enmity is our inexorable condition. In opposition to the forgiveness that binds friendships, the principles that bind Albion are his "Laws of Moral Virtue" (*J* 4:31; E, 147), which, as Blake has shown repeatedly, produce only accusation.

In moving to the inner layer of the chiasmus (Los and the Spectre of Urthona), Blake immediately attributes the Spectre's presence to Albion's actions (as he had attributed the Spectre's seduction of Enitharmon to Urizen in *The Four Zoas*):

> . . . But Westward, a black Horror,
> *His spectre driv'n by the Starry Wheels of Albions sons*, black and
> Opake divided from his back; he labours and he mourns!
> For as his Emanation divided, his Spectre also divided
> In terror of those starry wheels: and the Spectre stood over Los
> Howling in pain: a blackning Shadow, blackning dark & opake
> Cursing the terrible Los: bitterly cursing him for his friendship
> To Albion, suggesting murderous thoughts against Albion.
> (*J* 5:68–6:7; E, 148–49; emphasis added)

Blake attributes the Spectre's separation from Los not to the emanation and "the torments of Love & Jealousy," but to Albion's actions, as the Spectre is "driv'n by the Starry Wheels of Albions sons." And the Spectre, whom Blake depicts as a bat on this plate, attacks friendship, the relationship that underwrites forgiveness, "bitterly cursing [Los] for his friendship / To Albion." The Spectre wants vengeance against the character he most resembles, Albion. Thus the Spectre stands at the boundary; he is both the result in Los of Albion's rejection of Jesus, and also that same denial of friendship in Los himself. Blake sustains the echo of the outer layer (Blake/Jesus speaking to Albion/reader) in the inner layer (Los and the Spectre). The Spectre speaks to Los as Albion speaks to Jesus. Blake repeats Albion's words in the Spectre's

opening attack: "Wilt thou still go on to destruction? / Till thy life is all taken away by this deceitful Friendship?" (*J* 7:9–10; E, 149). The Spectre suspects that all friendship conceals enmity, echoing Albion's exact words in accusing Jesus of binding "Man the enemy of man into deceitful friendships" (*J* 4:26; E, 147). He later varies the phrase by attributing all of Albion's mockery of Los to "deceit and friendship" (*J* 7:17; E, 149).

In addition to the attempt at open-endedness in addressing the reader, Blake seeks to recuperate a form of real alterity by recruiting his Spectre as boundary figure. Blake recuperates the otherness of his reader(s) by acknowledging, in theory at least, their differences from each other: from the monolithic conception of Albion, the Public, he distinguishes among Jews, deists, and Christians by addressing different chapters to each group. The Spectre foreshadows the language of each of the smaller groups within the audience, Jews, deists, and Christians. He imitates the Jews by recounting Albion's offenses in the language of Old Testament history:

> Kox is the Father of Shem & Ham & Japheth, he is the Noah
> Of the Flood of Udan-Adan. Hutn is the Father of the Seven
> From Enoch to Adam; Schofield is Adam.
>
> (*J* 7:23–25; E, 149)

The Spectre's account of biblical history, from the Flood through Enoch to Adam, exactly reverses the sequence given to the Jews. Blake may have used the Spectre's reversal for the sake of exposing his perception as distorted. Yet the passage has a peculiar poignancy in the light of Blake's personal experience of accusation. Schofield and Cox, the soldiers who accused Blake of sedition, most deserved his vengeance. Yet Blake places this accusation in the Spectre's mouth as the personification of his own temptation. For it is on the point of accusation that the Spectre berates Los: "This has divided thee in sunder: and wilt thou still forgive?" (*J* 7:27; E, 149). Accusation, then, is framed in terms of Jewish history and of personal trauma.

The Spectre continues as a magnet for all these fragments of alterity, foreshadowing the language of deists and Christians. He provokes Los by recounting Albion's vengeance against France, when "Luvah was cast into the Furnaces of affliction and sealed" (*J* 7:30; E, 150). Blake blames the deists for the same offense when he writes, "you acquit & flatter the Alexanders & Caesars, the Lewis's & Fredericks: who alone are [war's] causes & its actors. But the Religion of Jesus, Forgiveness of Sin, can never be the cause of a War nor of a single Martyrdom" (*J* 52; E, 201). Political vengeance, the lack of international forgiveness, is the deists' version of accusation. The Spectre concludes his anatomy of accusation by alluding to the Christian version of accusation in internalized guilt. He cries out in desperation, "Such are the Generations of the Giant Albion, / To separate a Law of Sin, to punish thee in thy members" (*J* 7:49–50; E, 150). The Spectre alludes to Saint Paul's discussion of a "law of sin" in Romans: "I delight in the law of God after the inward man: But I see another law in my members, warring against the law of my mind, and bringing me into captivity to the law of sin which is in my members. O wretched man that I am! who shall deliver me from the body of this death?" (Romans 7:22–24). The inner layer of Spectre's long discourse with Los thus echoes Albion's rejection of Jesus and foreshadows the forms of accusation practiced by the factions within Blake's audience. Perhaps the idea of the reader as a single monolithic entity, Albion, precluded too much heterogeneity, otherness, which Blake then sought to recover by distinguishing the audiences, keeping the Spectre's reference centrifugal, towards an intersubjective forgiveness between Blake and his audience.

Yet Los triumphs over the Spectre, compelling him to work, by insisting on the intrapsychic frame of reference, naming in himself those offenses the Spectre pointed out in Albion. In taming him, Los calls the Spectre by two complementary names, pride and shame. Early on Los says: "Thou art my Pride & Self-righteousness: I have found thee out" (*J* 8:30; E, 151). Later, having tamed the Spectre a bit, Los cries out,

> O Spectre of Urthona: Reason not against their dear approach
> Nor them obstruct with thy temptations of doubt & despair
> O Shame O strong & mighty Shame I break thy brazen fetters.
> (*J* 10:32–34; E, 153)

The relation between pride and shame had intrigued Blake for some time. In the Proverbs of Hell he wrote, "Shame is Prides cloke" (*MHH* 7:20; E, 36). Shame and pride both refer to the fulfillment of the law; one is proud when one fulfills it, and ashamed when one does not. By naming the Spectre as both his pride and his shame, Los names the offenses that turn the wheels of accusation, naming them and silencing them in himself for the time being. Los pursues a provisional course of action, compelling the Spectre to work with him and commanding him, "be thou invisible to all / To whom I make thee invisible, but chief to my own Children" (*J* 10:30–31; E, 153). The Spectre does indeed disappear for much of the rest of the poem, because Los fights his battles on other fronts, addressing Albion's factions severally in the interim.

Thus the first half of the chiasmus is formed, in which Albion the reader's denial of friendship with Jesus/Blake is reduplicated in the Spectre's denial of friendship with Los.

In a strand of the narrative that Blake deemphasizes, the Spectre protests being dismissed as merely an abstract offense, such as pride or shame, and bewails his enforced disappearance in terms that make him an object of sympathy:

> O that I could cease to be! Despair! I am Despair
> Created to be the great example of horror & agony.
> (*J* 10:51–52; E, 153–54)

Paley has shown that the Spectre's despairing speech echoes William Cowper, whose works Blake knew and whom one journal described as afflicted by the "spectre of transient despondency."[28] But within the structure of chapter 1, Blake's final presentation of the Spectre as a despairing creature, deserving of pity, points the way back to the offender for whom he mediates, for chapter 1 closes with Albion in despair as well, suffering from the "disease of Shame" (*J* 21:3; E, 166). Thus Blake's presentation of the Spectre of Urthona in chapter 1 is governed by his function as a boundary figure, mediating between Los and Albion, repeating Albion's offenses against Jesus so that Los knows the offenses are his own as well. And the Spectre's self-pity reminds Los of the suffering undergone by his audience Albion.

The second part of the chiasmus is formed in the closing plates of *Jerusalem*. The action draws to a close when Los confronts his Spectre for the last time on plate 91 of *Jerusalem*. Blake places this confrontation explicitly within a context of forgiveness and accusation:

> It is easier to forgive an Enemy than to forgive a Friend:
> The man who permits you to injure him, deserves your vengeance:
> He also will receive it; go Spectre!
> (*J* 91:1–3; E, 251)

Thus it appears that Los sends the Spectre forth as an emissary to Albion, the false friend of both Blake and Jesus. In plate 93 Blake links accusing readers (presumably Blake's readers) with the accusers of Jesus. There Anytus, Melitus, and Lycon, famous as Socrates' accusers, accuse the poem *Jerusalem* by straining forward to point their accusing fingers to the remaining pages of the poem (see figure 5).[29] The picture is inscribed "Anytus Melitus & Lycon thought Socrates a Very Pernicious Man So Caiaphas thought Jesus" (*J* 43; E,

253). By mentioning Caiaphas and Jesus, Blake makes it clear that the threefold accuser opposes "the Spirit of Jesus" which "is continual forgiveness of Sin" (*J* 3; E, 145), just as Albion had opposed him initially. Los sends the Spectre as an emissary in the cause of intersubjective forgiveness, an emissary to the "Fiends of Righteousness" who have accused Los so harshly. Los continues:

> go Spectre! obey my most secret desire:
> Which thou knowest without my speaking: Go to these Fiends of Righteousness
> Tell them to obey their Humanities, & not pretend Holiness;
> When they are murderers: as far as my Hammer & Anvil permit
> Go, tell them that the Worship of God, is honouring his gifts
> In other men: & loving the greatest men best, each according
> To his Genius.
>
> (*J* 91:1–9; E, 251)

Ostensibly, the Spectre will teach these fiends the message of intersubjective forgiveness, that they should appreciate Los's individual genius. Ironically, however, at the same time the Spectre personifies Los's own desire for vengeance against these accusers: the Spectre knows Los's "most secret desire" "without [his] speaking." The close proximity of the statement "he will also receive [my vengeance]" and the command sending the Spectre suggests their identity: the Spectre *is* Los's vengeance. Moreover, Los's statement that the Spectre will obey his secret, unspoken desire, suggests that the desires are hostile ones in need of concealment. The ominous situation develops in which the Spectre, a personification of intrapsychic vengeance, bears a message of intersubjective reconciliation to another, a case in which intrapsychic and intersubjective meanings, condensed together metaphorically, fight each other conceptually.

Evidently Los recognizes this threat of the contradiction between intrapsychic and intersubjective forgiveness. Rather than allowing the Spectre actually to depart for the mission to Albion, Los turns his indignation inward, that is, on his own Spectre:

> . . . Los beheld undaunted furious
> His heavd Hammer; he swung it round & at one blow,
> In unpitying ruin driving down the pyramids of pride
> Smiting the Spectre on his Anvil & the integuments of his Eye
> And Ear unbinding in dire pain, with many blows.
>
> (*J* 91:41–45; E, 251–52)

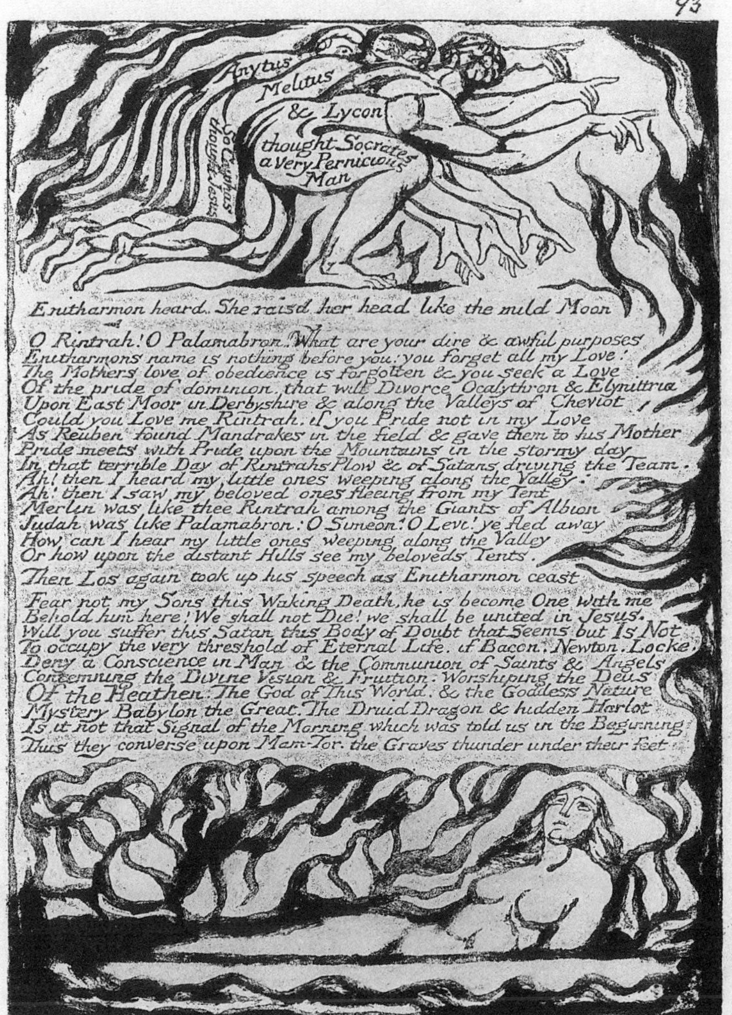

93

Anytus Melitus & Lycon thought Socrates a Very Pernicious Man

So Caiphas thought Jesus

Enitharmon heard. She rais'd her head like the mild Moon

O Rintrah! O Palamabron! What are your dire & awful purposes
Enitharmons name is nothing before you: you forget all my Love!
The Mothers love of obedience is forgotten & you seek a Love
Of the pride of dominion, that will Divorce Ocalythron & Elynittria
Upon East Moor in Derbyshire & along the Valleys of Cheviot
Could you Love me Rintrah, if you Pride not in my Love
As Reuben found Mandrakes in the field & gave them to his Mother
Pride meets with Pride upon the Mountains in the stormy day
In that terrible Day of Rintrahs Plow & of Satans driving the Team.
Ah! then I heard my little ones weeping along the Valley:
Ah! then I saw my beloved ones fleeing from my Tent
Merlin was like thee Rintrah among the Giants of Albion
Judah was like Palamabron: O Simeon! O Levi! ye fled away
How can I hear my little ones weeping along the Valley
Or how upon the distant Hills see my beloveds Tents.

Then Los again took up his speech as Enitharmon ceast

Fear not my Sons this Waking Death. he is become One with me
Behold him here! We shall not Die! we shall be united in Jesus.
Will you suffer this Satan this Body of Doubt that Seems but Is Not
To occupy the very threshold of Eternal Life. if Bacon, Newton, Locke,
Deny a Conscience in Man & the Communion of Saints & Angels
Contemning the Divine Vision & Fruition, Worshiping the Deus
Of the Heathen, The God of This World, & the Goddess Nature
Mystery Babylon the Great, The Druid Dragon & hidden Harlot
Is it not that Signal of the Morning which was told us in the Beginning
Thus they converse upon Mam-Tor. the Graves thunder under their feet

FIGURE 5.
Jerusalem,
Copy F, plate 93
(The Pierpont Morgan Library, New York, PML 953)

The fact that Los destroys the Spectre's "pyramids of pride" suggests that Los destroys the offense in the Spectre, the offense which Los earlier equated with his pride. Only after this severe remaking does the Spectre go forth:

> Then he sent forth the Spectre all his pyramids were grains
> Of sand & his pillars: dust on the flys wing: & his starry
> Heavens; a moth of gold & silver mocking his anxious grasp
> Thus Los alterd his Spectre & every Ratio of his Reason
> He alterd time after time, with dire pain & many tears
> Till he had completely divided him into a separate space.
>
> (*J* 91:47–52; E, 252)

Here again, Blake counts the intrapsychic as the definitive forgiveness, the "alterd" Spectre, now tamed by his contentions with Los, can serve as a suitable emissary to an other, intersubjectively conceived. Ironically, the Spectre is "alterd" by losing his alterity in relation to Los.

As the Spectre fades in his final scene, Blake suggests that the Spectre also represents errors of reading. All the time that Los hammers away at him, the Spectre acts too:

> The Spectre builded stupendous Works, taking the Starry Heavens
> Like to a curtain & folding them according to his will
> Repeating the Smaragdine Table of Hermes to draw Los down
> Into the Indefinite, refusing to believe without demonstration[.]
> Los reads the Stars of Albion! the Spectre reads the Voids
> Between the Stars.
>
> (*J* 91:32–37; E, 251)

In addition to Blake's rejection of occultism, which Bloom notes (E, 945), this passage dramatizes the Spectre's error as reading "the Voids Between the Stars." Thus Blake modulates back to a theme introduced in the Preface, the Spectre as the mediator or boundary figure between Los and his spectral reader Albion. Blake completes the chiasmus by returning to the outer layer, the conversation between Jesus and Albion that opened the poem:

> Jesus replied Fear not Albion unless I die thou canst not live
> But if I die I shall arise again & thou with me
> This is Friendship & Brotherhood without it Man Is Not
>
> So Jesus spoke! the Covering Cherub coming on in darkness

Overshadowed them & Jesus said Thus do Men in Eternity
One for another to put off by forgiveness, every sin

Albion replyd. Cannot Man exist without Mysterious
Offering of Self for Another, is this Friendship & Brotherhood
I see thee in the likeness & similitude of Los my Friend.
(*J* 96:14–22; E, 255–56)

As before, Jesus offers friendship and forgiveness. But Albion has changed, concluding with a remarkable statement: "I see thee in the likeness & similitude of Los my Friend." Albion has renounced his accusation of Los, accepting him as friend and not as an object deserving accusation. Equally important, Los himself has changed. By his annihilation of his own vengeance, he has remade himself into a practitioner of forgiveness, thus resembling Jesus, whose spirit is the continual forgiveness of sins. For this reason Albion can see Jesus in Los, his friend. However, the emphasis on "likeness & similitude" should prompt us to wonder if all forms of alterity have been collapsed into sameness. Certainly the distinctive groups of Jews and deists no longer exist in Blake's apocalypse, unless as denominations, so to speak, of Christians or artists. The final image, "they conversed together in Visionary forms dramatic" (*J* 98:27; E, 257) conveys Blake's hope that not all alterities will fade into sameness. However, later in this apocalyptic passage, all varieties of animals lose their individual natures—and the solvent is "Forgiveness of Sins":

Lion, Tyger, Horse, Elephant, Eagle, Dove, Fly, Worm,
And the all wondrous Serpent clothed in gems & rich array Humanize
In the Forgiveness of Sins according to the Covenant of Jehovah.
(*J* 98:43–45; E, 258)

Humanizing, or achieving humanity, may be a substantive advance for these animals; doubtless it is for "the all wondrous Serpent clothed in gems & rich array." But what about the loss of other animal species? Blake had consistently used animal species to connote human individuality in traits and vocations, as in the Proverb of Hell, "The eagle never lost so much time. as when he submitted to learn of the crow" (*MHH* 8; E, 37). Here, as *Jerusalem* closes, forgiveness dissolves all those animal species into one human form—a dissolution that may, given Blake's symbol system, include the varieties of human traits and vocations as well—and thus impoverishes the possibilities of intersubjectivity.

How do these observations about the Spectre of Urthona apply to the other spectre, the figure Satan in *Milton*? The figure Satan does serve as a boundary figure or mediator between Milton and his emanation. In *Milton* Blake presents the rift between Milton and his emanation Ololon as the task of forgiveness, a situation resembling "My Spectre around me." Milton achieves reconciliation with his emanation, "redeeming his emanation," by renouncing his "Selfhood." At first glance it would appear that Milton's renouncing his spectral self leads to a true encounter with alterity, Ololon, as Ololon forgives Milton. But Blake does not retain the otherness encoded as female in the closing reconciliation, for Ololon dissolves into clouds of blood, replaced by "the Saviour" Jesus. Instead of viewing Satan as the spectral figure to be forgiven or annihilated in Milton, it appears that Milton *is* the spectral figure, the repentant poet seeking forgiveness, and, as he finds it, merging into Los and Blake. Therefore, Satan in Milton (outside the Bard's Song) fits into the trajectory analyzed in this chapter at the point where reconciliation with the emanation is still desirable, even if it is provisional. Like the Spectre of Urthona, Satan is multiply determined. He represents that energetic portion of John Milton whom Milton damned in *Paradise Lost*, a portion Blake frequently represents as a victim, worthy of pity, and as a building, that is, as a human creation.[30] "Satan" is in Milton the self-righteousness that wanted to damn Satan—an echo of the intrapsychic/intersubjective boundary manned by the Spectre of Urthona. Finally, in Blake's judgment, the poet Milton perceived a partial truth in damning something, and the truth is that one's own disposition to accuse must be overcome. Satan represents this disposition as well, and in this sense he is Milton's self, or selfhood, which must be "annihilated."[31]

Thus in the case of *Milton*, the Spectre of Milton, Satan, represents not only errors but two dispositions, the energetic disposition that Milton mistakenly damned and the very disposition to take vengeance on others. This second disposition, in Blake's view, is one that Milton must reform, or "annihilate." As Albion asks Blake's Jesus in *Jerusalem*, "Cannot Man exist without Mysterious / Offering of Self for Another?" (*J* 96:20–21; E, 256). This offering, or giving, of self for another is central to Milton's task, and Blake's use of the personified Satan, as well as the personified Spectre of Urthona, stresses that it is indeed a self that is given, and not merely an intellectual error renounced.

Yet the repentance of Milton the erring poet invites the response of forgiveness not only from his victims Ololon and Satan, but also from his reader, typified by the character of Blake in the poem *Milton*. In the final apparition of

Satan at the end of *Milton*, the character Blake speaks: "I also stood in Satans bosom & beheld its desolations!" (*M* 38:15; E, 139). Thus the reader in the poem echoes the poet in the poem, giving his own version of Milton's recognition, "I in my Selfhood am that Satan" (*M* 14:30; E, 108). As Fox observes, "Each poet has recognized his satanic portion and has thus begun its recreation."[32] Moreover, the reader Blake has found that the evil in Milton is a possibility for himself and has performed the act of readerly forgiveness that he asks of his own reader in *Jerusalem*. All in all, *Milton* forms a powerful counter to the undertow of "likeness & similitude" to which Blake's treatment of spectral characters tend. Despite the dissolution of Ololon at the end and the fusion of all the male characters, the figure of Milton in *Milton* represents a powerfully individualized voice, one that is distinctive in Blake's oeuvre, and not just an echo of sameness.

Forgiveness in "The House of the Interpreter"

The final period of Blake's life is remarkable for his concentration on illustration, rather than on writing poetry, and for the love and admiration he received from John Linnell, Samuel Palmer, and others, after a life without much public recognition. Blake's final residence at Fountain Court, where he lived after he finished *Jerusalem*, was affectionately christened "The House of the Interpreter" by his young disciples (*BR*, 295). Blake's nickname "the Interpreter" seems especially appropriate as we consider the work he produced during this period, 1820–27. During this period Blake completed a drama, *The Ghost of Abel*, and illustrations to the Book of Job and to Dante's *Divine Comedy*; he also illustrated the apocryphal Book of Enoch, Virgil's *Eclogues*, and John Bunyan's *Pilgrim's Progress*. In his responses to Byron, Job, and Dante, Blake continues to raise questions about writerly and readerly forgiveness: he continues to value reconciliations among "brothers" (male siblings, friends, or fellow poets) more than reconciliations between male and female or between parent and child. However, Blake in these works diffuses the two modes of forgiveness, intrapsychic and intersubjective, that he condensed in the prophecies. Blake still stresses accusation as a destructive force by focusing on notorious accusers (or at least characters whose avatars in the Romantic period were famous for accusation): Byron's vindictive Eve, who cursed her own son; Job's friends, who accused a blameless man of sin; and the epic poet Dante, who condemned many to eternal punishment. Moreover, Blake elaborates in these last works on the theme of Jesus as the all-forgiving "Friend of Sinners" by stressing typological links between Jesus and Abel, Jesus and Job, Jesus and Virgil.[1] One new twist in these works is Blake's

concern with posthumous forgiveness, certainly an understandable concern in an aging man. This shift away from exposition of his own system and toward the interpretation of others allowed Blake gradually to modify the demands of simultaneously representing intrapsychic and intersubjective forgiveness. No longer did he condense into the same symbols the references to both intrapsychic and intersubjective forgiveness. As a result, Blake reduced the demands of representing the intrapsychic sense of forgiveness as a process within "One Man." So he did not need to assert, for example, that the accusing friends of Job were really simultaneously part of Job himself. He needed to tackle only their disposition of accusation. Moreover, by focusing on characters well known as accusers, Blake circumvented the difficulty of using accusation as the normative form of all human offense, the difficulty that had distorted the major prophecies. But in these works of the last decade, Blake's claim that all offenses can be classed as accusation declines in importance; instead, his choice to interpret notorious accusers allowed him to examine the state of accusation without making it a Procrustean bed on which all offenses must lie. Thus, these readerly and writerly forgivenesses function more as transactions than as identities.

Blake's play, *The Ghost of Abel*, implies the existence of a brotherhood of poets by explicitly addressing "LORD BYRON in the Wilderness," likening Byron to John the Baptist, "the voice of one crying in the wilderness" (Mark 1:3).[2] Blake places Byron in the position of one whose insight stands in need of completion, or, perhaps, in need of forgiveness. Blake's play "forgives" Byron by correcting him on the score of posthumous forgiveness, by redefining Eve's vindictiveness and accusation, and by using the typological link between Jesus and Abel to stress the value of brotherly love. As is well known, *Cain* generated a tremendous amount of controversy in 1821 and 1822, both in the journals, as reviewers attacked Byron's theology, and in Chancery, as Byron's publisher John Murray attempted to prevent the publication of pirated editions of the play. Blake may have heard of this play and the ensuing controversy from Henry Crabb Robinson, who read the play twice, though Robinson does not record having mentioned Byron to Blake.[3] Contemporary readers almost unanimously attacked Byron's statement about immortality in the preface to *Cain*. "The reader will please to bear in mind (what few choose to recollect), that there is no allusion to a future state in any of the books of Moses, nor indeed in the Old Testament," Byron writes. "I have therefore supposed it new to Cain, without, I hope, any perversion of Holy Writ."[4] Byron's contemporaries paid particular attention to his view that the Old Testament provides no justification for belief in a future state.[5] Thus what emerges for Blake's purposes is that Byron's denial of immortality precludes the possibility of posthumous forgiveness.

Blake "corrects" Byron's generalization about immortality in the Old Testament by relying on the Book of Enoch, which appeared in English translation in 1821. This book, now considered apocryphal, had been considered canonical by the author of the biblical Letter of Jude. As a consequence, its recovery from Abyssinia by explorer James Bruce, after it had been lost in the West for almost a thousand years, was a major cultural event. Blake read the 1821 translation by Richard Laurence and began to illustrate the work, focusing on themes of vengeance and forgiveness. The Book of Enoch paints a grim picture of human vengeance, a condition that extends into an afterlife. The traveler Enoch comes upon the spirit of Abel, who "will complain about [Cain] until his offspring is destroyed from the face of the earth, and from amongst the offspring of men his offspring perishes."[6] Thus the Book of Enoch labels the vindictive character—or, more precisely speaking, the vindictiveness in a character, as a spectre or ghost.[7] The setting of Enoch further implies that such spectral vindictiveness can reach beyond the grave. Blake uses this allusion to Enoch to suggest that Byron's character Eve serves a false "spectre" or "ghost" of Abel, who inspires her to cry for vengeance. From Blake's explicit point of view, this vindictive accuser, who as mother belongs to another generation and another sex, would be delivered if she recognized her true son Abel (who in Byron's play forgives Cain) instead of serving his "Ghost" of accusation. However, given Blake's representational habits in depicting forgiveness, it is doubtful whether his system allows the possibility that a mother can actively forgive and retain her sexual identity as a woman. Byron's retelling of the familiar biblical tale of Abel's murder and Cain's exile, recounted in act 3, is thrown off balance by the intense vengeance in the speech of Eve, which does indeed seem to be vengeance itself speaking:

> May all the curses
> Of life be on him! and his agonies
> Drive him forth o'er the wilderness, like us
> From Eden, till his children do by him
> As he did by his brother! . . .
> . . . .
> May his dreams be of his victim!
> His waking a continual dread of death!
> . . . .
> Hence, fratricide! henceforth that word is *Cain*,
> Through all the coming myriads of mankind,

> Who shall abhor thee, though thou wert their sire!
> May the grass wither from thy feet! the woods
> Deny thee shelter! earth a home! the dust
> A grave! the sun his light! and heaven her God! [original emphasis][8]

Like the Ghost of Abel, in the Book of Enoch, who wanted Cain's offspring to perish from the earth, Eve curses Cain's descendants: "all the coming myriads of mankind, / . . . shall abhor thee, though thou wert their sire!" Byron stresses the magnitude of Eve's curse: Eve's desire that vengeance surround Cain, as grass, shade, light, and God withdraw from him, becomes, as the Angel says, the curse of Earth itself.[9] Thus, given the context of Byron's play, with its parallel in Enoch, Blake could take Byron's meaning to be that Eve exemplifies vengeance itself. Yet Blake breaks down this assumption by differentiating Abel, the forgiving brother, from his ghost.[10]

Significantly, the plot of *The Ghost of Abel* begins after Cain's departure as the lamenting Adam and Eve hear a "Ghost of Abel" like the one in Enoch who cries for vengeance, and who claims to be possessed by theological villains called the Elohim. The Elohim make Abel their "victim" and "live on sacrifice." Blake contrasts these "Elohim *of the Heathen*" (emphasis added) with a Jehovah who advocates forgiveness.[11] Jehovah advances the cause of forgiving Eve's curse by pointing out the discrepancy between the true, forgiving Abel and the spectral, vindictive Ghost of Abel. He shows them the real Abel, afflicted but possessing some kind of afterlife; when they recognize him, the Ghost of Abel, curiously, "sinks down into the Grave. from which arises Satan Armed in glittering scales with a Crown & a Spear" (*GA* 2; E, 272). This stage direction suggests that as long as Eve denies Abel's immortality, by seeing him as sunken in the grave, accusation or Satan will govern her responses. Adam and Eve fall silent, and the rest of the play consists of a debate between Jehovah and Satan. Finally, angels celebrate the triumph of Jehovah's "Peace Brotherhood and Love" over those who "Swore Vengeance for Sin," a triumph which includes the Elohim in the "Brotherhood" (*GA* 2:26, 22; E, 272).

Blake initially reveals Eve's mistake about the nature of her son Abel. She curses Cain thoroughly because she does not know that Abel has forgiven him. She sees herself acting, cursing, on behalf of Abel. By Blake's logic, then, she believes not in the genuine, forgiving Abel, but in a "spectre" or "ghost" of Abel. Blake suggests this error by the parents' avoidance of the very name of Abel. Instead they consistently, in their state of accusation, call Abel "the Dead." As the parents mourn Abel, Adam asks, "Is this Death?" (*GA* 1:2; E, 271). A few lines later he answers his own question, "Seven times O Eve, thou hast fainted over the Dead" (*GA* 1:14; E, 271). Eve expresses her despair in similar terms: "O it is all a vain delusion / This Death & this Life & this Jehovah!" (*GA* 1:6–7; E, 271). No longer is the body "Abel," or "our son," but simply "the Dead" (*GA* 1:5; E, 271). Blake's differentiation between the true Abel and the spectral Abel continues in the next action of the plot. To enlighten Adam and Eve, Jehovah allows the Ghost of Abel to appear. Significantly, the Ghost of Abel does not appear on stage until after Eve has revived from her faint: the Ghost or Spectre of Abel is Eve's distorted, vengeful perception of Cain.

Once awake, Eve addresses this form: "Thou Visionary Phantasm thou art not the real Abel" (*GA* 1:9; E, 271). In an instance of dramatic irony, Eve says more than she knows: true enough, this vindictive spectre is not the forgiving Abel Byron showed us earlier. But Eve does not realize that she has in her grief fallen into this spectral state. Blake may well suggest that this Ghost exemplifies Eve's vengeance in the Ghost's lament, "Among the Elohim a Human Victim I wander I am their House / . . . our dimensions compass Zenith and Nadir" (*GA* 1:10, 11; E, 271). Blake here links the Ghost of Abel with the vengeance articulated by Eve in *Cain*. The ubiquity of accusation, encompassing zenith and nadir, neatly summarizes Eve's curse in Byron's play: "May the clear rivers turn to blood. . . . May every element shun or change to him. . . . May the grass wither from thy feet, the woods deny thee shelter, earth a home, the dust a grave, the sun his light, and heav'n her God." Eve's address to rivers, elements, grass, and woods makes both zenith and nadir an abode of accusation for Cain. The Ghost of Abel articulates that curse back to Eve herself; ironically, however, the real Abel seems to be the "Human victim" here, rather than Cain, as Eve had intended. After the Ghost of Abel speaks of his torment and cries for vengeance, Adam persists in his (and Byron's) error that there is no afterlife: "Eve come away & let us not believe in *these vain delusions* / Abel is dead & Cain slew him!" (*GA* 1:18–19; E, 271; emphasis added). Not only is Abel dead, but his fate foreshadows their own annihilation: "We shall also Die a Death / And then! what then" (*GA* 1:19–20; E, 271). The Ghost identifies himself unambiguously: "I am the Accuser and the Avenger"; he cries for retribution, "Life for Life! Life for Life!"[12] Significantly, the Ghost refers to himself as a house: "Among the Elohim a Human Victim I wander I am their House" (*GA* 1:10; E, 271). The Ghost of Abel has become a mere container for the principles of vengeance advocated by the Elohim and by Eve as well. In Byron's play Abel's death becomes the occasion for the unforgettable outpouring of vengeance by Byron's Eve. Blake undertakes to show Eve that her vindictiveness has distorted Abel's image.

Ironically, in the passages mentioned above, the true sufferer from Eve's fall into the state of accusation, the state personified in the Ghost of Abel, is the true, forgiving Abel. Blake brings this irony to the forefront in the middle of Adam's next speech. Adam begins, "Eve come away & let us not believe these vain delusions, / Abel is dead & Cain slew him!" (*GA* 1:18–19; E, 271). Adam's rejection then softens before the appearance of Jehovah: "O what shall I call thee Form Divine! Father of Mercies / That appearest to my Spiritual Vision: Eve seest thou also" (*GA* 1:21–22; E, 271). What Adam sees, and what Eve sees, is the suffering shade of her true son: "I see also *Abel living*: / *Tho terribly afflicted* as We also are" (*GA* 1:23–24; E, 271; emphasis added). Eve spells out the implications of recognizing the real Abel, namely, that to see Abel thus is to perceive as Jehovah perceives. She continues:

> yet Jehovah sees him
> Alive & not Dead: were it not better to believe Vision
> With all our might & strength tho we are fallen & lost.
> (*GA* 1: 24–2:1–2; E, 271)

Adam agrees, and, the stage direction says, "They Kneel before Jehovah" (*GA* 1; E, 271). Thus Adam and Eve make a paradigmatic choice for Blake, choosing Jehovah rather than the Elohim, choosing the true, forgiving Abel in place of the vindictive Ghost of Abel. Through Blake's brief introduction of two Abels, the accuser Eve recognized the falsity of the Ghost of Abel, and cast that spectre out of her individuality. The way she did it, as Blake presents her, is through pity and love for the real Abel, now a suffering shade as a result of her vindictiveness. Blake has seen the one enduring virtue, what he would call the "Staminal" virtue, in the Eve presented in Byron's *Cain*. It is her love for her son Abel.

Despite his emphasis on Eve, Blake keeps the reconciliation of brothers as the normative form of forgiveness. The play concludes in the exchange between Satan and Jehovah, Satan demanding Christ's "Sacrifice" and Jehovah inviting Satan to self-annihilation. The "Elohim of the Heathen" who formerly possessed the Ghost of Abel are not cast out from Jehovah's presence, but included, "each in his station fixt in the firmament by Peace *Brotherhood* and Love" (*GA* 2:26; E, 272; emphasis added). The reference to Christ's sacrifice highlights the traditional typological link between Jesus and Abel as sacrificial victims, adding another context of meaning to Cain's crime. Defined literally, Cain's killing Abel, the crime of fratricide, violates a fundamental human tie. Defined typologically, Cain's crime become deicide, the killing of Jesus—which for Blake takes on the added typological salience of killing the principle of forgiveness. The fraternal tie, then, receives the added sanctification when placed in a typological context. Similarly, the illustration to *The Ghost of Abel* stresses the relation between brothers rather than the mother-son tie. The picture shows a figure, clad in animal skins, lamenting over the corpse of Abel. The "Voice of Abels Blood" howls above. The mourner's apparent maleness and his solitude suggests that he is Cain, since Adam and Eve, the other logical candidates for mourners, always appear together. The constant presence of this picture as one reads the text reminds the reader of the fundamental relationship of brotherhood, exemplified in Cain and Abel.[13]

Blake's own sympathy for Cain as erring brother can be seen in his sketch for Genesis 4, which tells Cain's story. Blake wrote as his chapter heading: "Chap IV How Generation & Death took Possession of the Natural Man & of the Forgiveness of Sins written upon the Murderers Forehead" (E, 688). Orthodox Christians interpreted Cain's mark as God's protection from further violence: for Blake, the mark also bestowed "Forgiveness of Sins written upon the Murderers Forehead."[14] Moreover, in another illustration dating from this same period of his life, "The Body of Abel found by Adam and Eve," Blake stresses brotherhood over mother-son ties by depicting Cain, tormented by guilt and by rejection from his family. Blake alters conventional depictions of the discovery of Abel's body by placing Cain in the foreground, thus avoiding the frequent conventional allusions to the *Pietà* in Eve's cradling Abel.[15] Blake's general pattern of stressing fraternal (violation and) forgiveness takes a more conflicted form in *The Ghost of Abel*. Blake seems more merciful to Eve than Byron is. Yet Blake's coding of Eve's alternatives as masculine (following the vindictive spectral Ghost of Abel versus following the forgiving, immortal Abel) logically implies that Eve's female individuality is occluded in these alternatives.

Blake does not need to make such gender shifts in analyzing the accusers of Job and the issue of forgiveness between Job and his friends. Here, instead, Blake struggles with an issue he had articulated earlier in *Jerusalem*: "Friendship cannot exist without Forgiveness of Sins continually" (*J* 52; E, 201). Blake avoids the tangles of condensing all representatives of forgiveness into one system, which in *Jerusalem* made it unclear whether reader or writer was accusing or forgiving, because of Blake's identification of the two. In the Job illustrations, forgiveness is a transaction, not an identity. Blake underscores the gravity of the friends-turned-accusers' crime by stressing the typological connection between Job and Jesus.

In 1820–25 Blake produced what art historians consider his finest work—

the engraved illustrations to the Book of Job. This set of twenty-two designs represents a significant advance over Blake's earlier watercolor illustrations to Job, executed for Thomas Butts in about 1810. The advance consists, in part, in Blake's surrounding the main design with marginal sketches and with quotations from the Bible, amplifying the significance of the main design. In these illustrations, Blake profoundly reinterprets the received understanding of the biblical book. For centuries, theologians had taken the Book of Job as a struggle to justify the undeserved suffering of the righteous.[16] Blake, however, shifts his attention to the content of Job's "righteousness," depicting in Job a progression from mere observance of the obligations of the law to a religion of imaginative fullness. On the first numbered illustration (he numbered all the designs except the title page), Blake wrote, "The Letter Killeth, The Spirit giveth Life" (quoted from 2 Corinthians 3:6). Job's progress from one spiritual state to another is suggested by—to take just one example—the musical instruments in the series. In illustration 1, musical instruments hang unplayed in the trees near Job and his family; in the final illustration, each family member joyfully plays an instrument. Blake provides numerous other indications of Job's progress from a literal understanding to a spiritual one.[17]

Blake stresses brotherhood and its analogues in his devotion to Job's relation to his male friends who had become his accusers. In the Bible, Job's conversation with his three friend-accusers, Eliphaz, Bildad, and Zophar, takes up twenty-nine chapters out of a total of forty-two; in Blake's illustrations, the friend-accusers appear in eleven of the twenty-two illustrations. Blake's inclusion of the three friend-accusers in half of the Job illustrations suggests their importance to his total interpretation of the Book of Job. In the Job illustrations, Blake depicts an instance of intersubjective forgiveness, by which Job discerns the difference between his individual friend-accusers and the state of accusation into which they have fallen. Moreover, the typological link between Job and Jesus implies that under the figure of Job, Blake claims that the all-forgiving "Friend of Sinners" can achieve his forgiveness even of the friends who have violated the sacred tie of male friendship, almost as sacred as the fraternal tie between Cain and Abel.

Blake's reception of the Book of Job was shaped largely by the typological convention by which Job prefigures Christ and, consequently, the friend-accusers prefigure the mockers of Christ.[18] As a consequence, the friend-accusers of Job were widely recognized as accusers of the worst kind. Blake employs the received conventions in illustration 10, by creating a new event, the mocking of Job. Blake builds on the potential in the quotation, "The just upright man is laughed to scorn" (Job 12:4), a torment which was not inflicted on the biblical Job but was, of course, inflicted on Jesus. In its original context Job indirectly criticized his friend-accusers' condescension towards him: "I am as one mocked of his neighbor, who calleth upon God, and he answereth him: 'the just upright man is put to scorn'" (Job 12:4). In Blake's scene, Job is directly laughed to scorn by his companions. The creation of a new event is motivated by the typological convention in which Job's companions prefigure the mockers of Jesus.[19] Outside typology, the higher criticism of Bishop Robert Lowth also assessed the friend-accusers negatively: "Another still more exquisite trial of [Job's] patience yet awaits him," Lowth writes, "namely, the unjust suspicions, the bitter reproaches, and the violent altercations of his friends."[20] Lowth concludes, "the principal object of the poem seems to be this third and last trial of Job, from the injustice and unkindness of his friends," who "had visited [Job] on the *pretence* of affording consolation" (emphasis added).[21] In blaming Job's friends as notorious accusers, Lowth provides a precedent for the importance Blake attributes to the friend-accusers in Job's whole story.

Blake interprets the friend-accusers by differentiating between the individuals and the state into which they have fallen. He portrays the good intentions and loyalty of the companions in illustration 7, "And when they lifted up their eyes afar off" (see figure 6). Despite their "sinister" left feet, the emphatic gesture of the arms and hands thrown upward suggests genuine distress at Job's affliction. In this way, Blake juxtaposes the friends' good intentions with their tendency to accusation brought on by their limited vision. Blake introduces the distinction between states and individuals in the sequence of illustrations 10 and 11. In illustration 10, "The Just Upright Man is laughed to scorn," Blake composes the friend-accusers so that all six arms stretch out to point at Job in accusation (see figure 7). This motif recalls other Blakean portrayals of accusation, the accusers of Socrates and of John Bunyan's Faithful.[22] Blake is most typological here, constructing a scene of the mocking of Job by relying entirely on the analogy with the mockers of Christ. It is precisely here, at his most typological, that Blake places the accusation of Job in his own terms, those of states and individuals. In illustration 10, we still see the recognizable individuals, Eliphaz, Bildad, and Zophar. But in the next illustration, 11, "With Dreams upon my bed thou scarest me," Blake reveals the demonic state of the friends-turned-accusers (see figure 8). Critics agree that in this illustration, Job recognizes the demonic nature of the God he has worshipped until this point.[23] But Job is not looking at his God, satanic or otherwise. He is looking at his accusers. Job's gaze indicates the importance of the three friends, now revealed as the threefold accusers. In illustration 11, the three companions become the three accusing devils beneath Job, who clutch at

FIGURE 6.
Illustrations of the Book of Job,
plate 7, "And when they lifted up their eyes afar off"
(Yale Center for British Art, Paul Mellon Collection)

FIGURE 7.
Illustrations of the Book of Job,
plate 10, "The Just Upright Man is laughed to scorn"
(Yale Center for British Art, Paul Mellon Collection)

FIGURE 8.
Illustrations of the Book of Job,
plate 11, "With Dreams upon my bed"
(Yale Center for British Art, Paul Mellon Collection)

FIGURE 9.
Illustrations of the Book of Job,
plate 18, "And my Servant Job shall pray for you"
(Yale Center for British Art, Paul Mellon Collection)

him to drag him down into the flames. None of these three demons is recognizable as the individuals Eliphaz, Bildad, or Zophar. In fact, the faces of all three are identical, interchangeable, suggesting that all three have fallen into the same state, Satan the Accuser, by their stringent accusation of Job in the previous plate. Their being in that state elides, for the time being, their peculiar, individual characteristics. Moreover, the motif of chains suggests the difference between the accusing individuals of illustration 10 and the state of Satan the accuser in illustration 11. In illustration 10, Blake places a few links of chain in the marginal field, near the figures of the three friends and of Job's wife. In illustration 11, those chains have invaded the central design; they are held in the hands of one of Job's threefold accusers, revealed in their satanic, accusing state. In illustration 12, "I am Young & ye are very Old wherefore I was afraid," Eliphaz, Bildad, and Zophar appear again in their human individuality, looking remarkably benign for accusers. Evidently the state of Satan, revealed in illustration 11, explains the vindictiveness of the accusing fingers in illustration 10: yet these characters reveal their persistent, patient loyalty to Job in illustration 12, listening with him to the expansive Elihu.

Blake usually condenses his representation of the multiple stages of forgiveness, writing as if the recognition of an error and the renunciation of it occur in the same moment. Two representative statements with this implication are "whenever any Individual Rejects Error & Embraces Truth a Last Judgment passes upon that Individual" (*VLJ*; E, 562) and "[Error] is Burnt up the Moment Men cease to behold it" (*VLJ*; E, 565). In the illustrations to Job, as in other late works, he separates the stages of the process for the sake of representing its multiple meanings.[24] Illustration 11, with the accusing Satans revealed, represents a "Consolidation of Error." But before error can be rejected, truth must be presented so that it can be understood and so believed and embraced. The presentation of truth comprises illustrations 13 through 17, the appearance of the Lord out of the whirlwind. For Job, the rejection of error and embrace of truth is completed in illustration 17, and summarized in one of its marginal texts, "I have heard thee with the hearing of the Ear but now my Eye seeth thee." For the friend-accusers, the rejection of their error about Job involves the casting out of the accuser, depicted in illustration 16, "Thou has fulfilled the Judgment of the Wicked." Their embrace of truth is depicted in illustration 18, "And my Servant Job shall pray for you" (see figure 9). The casting out of Satan in illustration 16 does indeed have significance for Job and his wife: "The flame in which Satan is encapsulated represents the evil heart which Job casts out; but the minions within the flame are Job and his wife."[25] Nonetheless, it is also significant that Blake includes Job's wife in the flame,

along with Job and Satan. In so doing, he brings to three the number of accusers who are cast out, thereby echoing the iconology of the threefold accuser in illustrations 10 and 11. The number three suggests that the state of Satan, graphically presented in 11, is cast out of the three friend-accusers as well. Significantly, Blake separates the intersubjective experience of Job forgiving his friend-accusers from the intrapsychic processes within Job that enable him to extend such forgiveness. The crucial moment in Job's internal process occurs in illustration 11, when Job realizes the difference between states and individuals. Nonetheless, Blake insists on the identity of the intrapsychic and the intersubjective senses of forgiveness in the separate depiction of the casting out of the accuser, and in Job's intersubjective forgiveness of his friend-accusers in illustration 18. Indeed, in depicting the intrapsychic change of heart in the friend-accusers, Blake supplements the Bible, which recounts their submission to God's rebuke: "So Eliphaz the Temanite and Bildad the Shuhite and Zophar the Naamathite went, and did according as the Lord commanded them: the Lord also accepted Job" (Job 42:9). By doing as the Lord asks, the friend-accusers implicitly ask for Job's forgiveness. With this request, the burden of forgiveness falls on Job, who must separate in his mind their former satanic state from their individuality.

Job's prayer for them is depicted in illustration 18. There Job prays before a flame burning on a stone altar, his own arms outstretched. For the first time in the whole series, Job stands erect, finally exemplifying the verdict of God the Father in illustration 1 that he is "perfect and upright."[26] He faces inward, that is, toward the altar and away from the spectator.[27] Job's wife kneels on Job's left; the three friend-accusers huddle on Job's right. Blake omits the animal sacrifices of the biblical account, replacing them with a simple flame. Critics agree that this flame represents the will of Job, the purged version of the flame in illustration 16.[28] But this connection bears further interpretation in the light of the contents of the flame in illustration 16. That Job there saw a threefold accuser suggests that he recognized that his friend-accusers had been in that satanic state of accusation. The fact that the flame is cast down into the fire, while the friend-accusers remained on the other side, suggests that Job separated their state from their individuality.

Job's awareness of the distinction between states and individuals and his use of it to forgive his friend-accusers are emphasized by the apparent contradiction in Blake's choice of marginal quotations. One quotation reads: "And the Lord turned the captivity of Job *when he prayed for his Friends*" (emphasis added). A second quotation reads: "I say unto you Love *your Enemies*" (emphasis added). "The Enemy," of course, is a common name for Satan, and it suggests that satanic state of accusation. By juxtaposing the words *friends* and *enemies*, as he had earlier juxtaposed sinister feet and compassionate hands, Blake evokes again the ambiguity of friendship mixed with accusation and the necessity to see both states and individuals. A similar juxtaposition of states and individuals is suggested by Blake's use of the sun in illustration 18. It shines from the upper center of the drawing. Four of the sun's beams shine to Job's left, the side on which his wife kneels, and three beams shine on Job's right, where the companions kneel. This device balances out the composition of the whole design.[29] Critics concur in calling this "the spiritual sun"; even more important, it obviously refers to the marginal quotation: "Love your enemies . . . That you may be the children of your Father which is in heaven, *for he maketh his sun to shine* on the Evil & the Good" (emphasis added). Blake has slightly altered the Authorized Version here, which reads, "he maketh his sun to *rise*" (Matthew 5:45) to accommodate his picture of a shining, not a rising sun. The sun of forgiveness, personified in Job, shines on the just and the unjust, the wife and the friend-accusers.

Having introduced the distinction between states and individuals, Blake then returns to the typological convention that the accusers of Job prefigure the enemies of Jesus. He elaborates this convention by showing that the friend-accusers of Job represent the friend-accusers of Jesus. If we return to the maxim that Job prefigures Christ, then Job's forgiveness must also be seen typologically. "The Spirit of Jesus," Blake writes, "is continual forgiveness of Sin"(*J* 3; E,145). In the light of Blake's remark "It is easier to forgive an Enemy than to forgive a friend," we may ask if Blake's Job attempts the harder task. That he performs the easier task, forgiveness of enemies, is clear from Job's cruciform arms, which typologically may allude to Jesus' forgiving his enemies from his cross (Luke 23:24). Yet some of the typological motifs suggest that Job's friend-accusers prefigure Jesus' apostles, whom he calls friends.

One such typological suggestion is the altar of twelve rough-hewn stones. In a preliminary sketch for this illustration, Blake lists the twelve apostles. Bo Lindberg suggests that Blake planned to inscribe each stone with an apostle's initial (following Luke's list).[30] Blake may intend an amplified version of Jesus' pun in renaming one of his apostles Peter, which means "rock" (Matthew 16:18). Significantly, it is this group of twelve "rocks" to whom Jesus deliberately gave the name of "friends": "Henceforth I call you not servants; for the servant knoweth not what his lord doeth: but I have called you friends" (John 15:15). Probably Blake omitted the apostolic initials for the simple logistical reason that the figure Job in front of the altar would block the letters.[31] Despite Blake's omission of the letters, however, the use of rocks in the altar and the number twelve are sufficient to suggest that Jesus' friends are included in this gesture of forgiveness.

One final typological note: Blake does not stress divine forgiveness of Job as a prerequisite of Job's forgiving his friend-accusers. In fact, Blake deliberately omitted a scene that would have exemplified perfectly Job's need for forgiveness. In 1802 Blake painted a watercolor for his illustrations to the Bible, entitled "Job Confessing his Presumption to God." It illustrated Job's words, "Behold, I am vile" (Job 40:4). But in the 1825 set of engravings, Blake omits the scene of Job's repentance, an omission that accords with Job's prefigurative status, for a Job-Jesus who embodies forgiveness would not himself require the Father's forgiveness. The Job illustrations, therefore, stress the importance of the tie between close male friends, just as "The Ghost of Abel" stresses the importance of the fraternal tie, by using typology to promote Jesus as the paradigmatic friend and brother. One consequence of the typological move is that the victim (Abel-Jesus or Job-Jesus) is idealized, so that he presumably does not possess the same intrapsychic makeup as the offender(s). Therefore the two parties in forgiveness have an actual transaction, a sinless victim forgiving an accusing offender, rather than partaking of an identity between the two parties. Blake's depiction of the process in Job does not quite follow this typological logic; nonetheless, the tendency of the typological turn in the last works, not entirely realized, is to distinguish victim from offender, making forgiveness a transaction, not an identity.

Posthumous forgiveness and typological identifications also pervade Blake's unfinished set of illustrations to the *Divine Comedy* of Dante, produced between 1824 and the poet's death in 1827,[32] which show the clarity that results from the separation of the intrapsychic and intersubjective forms of forgiveness. In particular, Blake accuses Dante of punishing the dead too harshly, writing on one of his drawings: "Whatever Book is for Vengeance for Sin & whatever Book is Against the Forgiveness of Sins is not of the Father but of Satan the Accuser & Father of Hell" (E, 690)—a harshness that arises from rejecting the possibility of posthumous forgiveness. Yet Blake's response to Dante is always tempered by his respect for Dante as a source of Poetic Genius: "Any man of mechanical talents may from the writings of Paracelsus or Jacob Behmen, produce ten thousand volumes of equal value with [Emanuel] Swedenborg's. and from those of Dante or Shakespear, an infinite number" (*MHH* 21; E, 43). Despite Blake's respect for Dante, in the late period Blake groups him with several dead poets guilty of atheism, or worshipping the natural world, a "mere illusion produced by Satan" (*BR*, 324–25). Blake's response to Milton's "atheism" suggests a fairly straightforward model of intellectual error, refutation, and correction. Henry Crabb Robinson summarized Blake's sense of Milton's posthumous change: "Milton was for a great part of his life an Atheist And therefore has fatal errors in his *Paradise Lost* which he has often begged Blake to confute" (*BR*, 325). In this instance, the dead person requests a correction, thus suggesting posthumous change. Yet when Blake finds Dante subject to "atheism," the emphasis is somewhat different. He remarks: "Dante (tho' now with God) lived and died an Atheist—He was a slave of the world and time" (*BR*, 325). Blake's term *slave* suggests a state of intellectual error and a loss of the will. "Being with God," however, implies a relationship restored, not just an error corrected.[33]

Blake's perception of Dante as an accuser was shaped by a contemporary British tendency to stereotype all Italians as vengeful—a tendency that informs Henry Boyd's essays on Italian history, published in 1785, and revived in the fashion for Italian culture in the 1820s when Blake illustrated Dante. Blake's perception of Dante was also shaped by the peculiarly vengeful picture of the afterlife implied in Dante but made explicit by Boyd in his supplementary essays. Boyd's translation of Dante's *Inferno*, published in 1785, was read by Blake in 1801.[34] At the time of annotation, Blake attacked Dante's politics and Boyd's didacticism. Yet Boyd's work also provided a portrait of Dante, and of Italians, as vengeful, contributing to Blake's later sense that in depicting accusation in Dante, he was using a widely recognized example of an accuser.

Blake may have read Boyd at the suggestion of Hayley, whose name appears on the subscribers' list of the Dublin edition. Blake definitely read part of volume 1, perhaps all of it, annotating two of Boyd's supplementary essays there (E, 885); possibly he read the second volume as well. Despite his attempt to draw the reader's sympathy for Dante and his times, Boyd frequently portrays the stereotypic vengefulness of Italians. In his "Historical Essay" Boyd recounts the familiar story of the divisions between the papal party, the Guelphs, and the imperial party, the Ghibellines. Individual characters are frequently described as acting out of vengeance: an eminent family of Florence, the Buondelmonti, is "thirsting for vengeance on their domestic enemies"; a Ghibelline general "secretly vowed vengeance"; "The French were guilty of so much cruelty and oppression in their government, that the Neapolitans and Sicilians breathed nothing but revenge"; the pope burned several Franciscans as heretics "in revenge."[35] Thus Boyd's readers may well conclude that Italian history in Dante's time consisted solely in continual violence, revenge and counterrevenge, between Guelph and Ghibillene, between white and black parties, between pope and friar. Boyd recounts in detail two sensational stories of revenge: the "Sicilian Vespers" massacre in which numerous innocents were killed on their way to church, and the story of the origin of the feud between the blacks and the whites. Blake probably read the first of these passages, since he annotated a remark on the next page.[36]

The environment of the 1820s may have reinforced prejudices enunciated by Boyd, as tales of the Carbonari revolution and its violent acts of revenge reached England. In particular, English writers were fascinated by "the violence and unrestraint of passion in Italy, with all the gruesome horrors and miseries resulting from it."[37] The Italian tyrants and their ingenious methods of committing their crimes are recurrent themes.[38] For example, in his *History of Italy* (1825), G. Perceval wrote with conviction about the vengefulness of the Italian character: "Unhappily the energy and violence which marked their national character was often directed to evil purpose by such dark and vindictive passions as, in these more temperate times, we find it difficult to account for or excuse."[39] Vengeance, the darkest and most vindictive passion, became such a stock attribution that one novel was entitled *Italian Revenge and English Forbearance*.[40] This stereotype of the vengeful Italian—with the fascination and revulsion it inspired—formed part of the Italianate fashion, which peaked in the 1820s,[41] the very decade in which Linnell commissioned the Dante illustrations.

Blake's sense of the vengefulness of Dante himself may be due to Boyd's essay on the afterlife in volume 2. Boyd's terminology connotes the legal and religious sanctions that Blake detested. Boyd persistently refers to the sufferings of the damned as their "punishment." But the legal connotations prevail in Boyd's preference for the term *criminals*, instead of *sinners*. In this essay on the afterlife Boyd contends that the damned deserve their eternal punishment. Virtues bring heavenly happiness, the author contends, and "each of the opposite vices tends to make the criminal eternally miserable."[42] Boyd's confusion of criminal and sinner makes him advocate that the state punish criminals as harshly as possible: "It precludes all those idle declamations on the absurdity of lasting punishments for temporal crimes, as it appears from this representation that the punishment arises in a great degree from the acquired habit which must last at least as long as the existence of the criminal."[43] Boyd's terminology thus mixes—perhaps by design—the issue of crimes against the state with sins against God.[44] When Boyd contemplates that God might forgive dead sinners, his vision of God as a civil judge intervenes: "Should the Deity inflict on vicious persons no positive punishment," he writes, "they must from habitual depravation be for ever miserable; and what would a pardon signify to a malefactor who is dying of the stone or stranguary? just as little would an absolution from punishment signify to a depraved soul while it is subject to a disease that preys upon its vitals."[45] Boyd's confusion of a civil pardon and a divine absolution suggests that Blake's statement, in 1801, that Dante "gives too much Caesar," may refer as much to Boyd as to Dante himself.

The essay on the afterlife, in addition to exhibiting Boyd's confusion of criminal and sinner, denies the possibility of posthumous forgiveness by portraying an afterlife somewhat like that in the Book of Enoch in which the damned can neither change nor repent. Boyd argues, first, that their vices constitute their own punishment. As the vices have become habitual for the damned, the punishments constitutive of the vices must endure as long as the characters themselves endure. In fact, death will bring them even more intense punishment than vicious living because of their incorporeal state: "If we go into the other world with these passions unmortified in us, they will not only be far more violent than now, but our perceptions of them will be pure and unalloyed by any intermixture of enjoyment, and if so, what exquisite torments must they prove, when hate and envy, malice and revenge, shall be altogether like so many vultures, preying upon our hearts, and our minds shall be continually goaded with all the furious thoughts that these outrageous passions can suggest to us!" The desire for revenge is clearly one of the major constituents of the torments of the damned, a vulture preying upon the mind continually: "Our impatience shall be heightened by a sense of our follies to a diabolical fury, sublimed with an insatiable desire of revenge upon all that have contributed to our ruin, and an inveterate malice against all we converse with, what a Hell must we be to ourselves!"[46] In fact, then, Boyd equates the feelings of revenge and malice with hell itself.

Blake charges Dante with vengefulness because Dante emphasizes too much the moment of physical death. Blake hopes for a model instead in which the departed still change and grow. While he worked on the Dante illustrations, Blake said, "I cannot consider death as any thing but a removing from one room to another" (*BR*, 337). Blake's conviction comes into conflict with Dante's theory of moral change after death. Like much else in his writing, this theory comes from Thomas Aquinas, who writes: "Only when their life is over can human beings remain fast in evil; unalterableness and immobility mark the end of a process."[47] For Blake, such a theory is not only untrue; it underwrites a policy of unmitigated vengeance.

This context of reception in which Blake construed Dante as an accuser illuminates Blake's criticism that Dante's poem is "Against the Forgiveness of Sins" and "of Satan the Accuser" (E, 690). Since the book is "of Satan the Accuser," it would follow that Dante, while writing it, was in the state of

Figure 10.
"Dante Running from the Three Beasts,"
illustration for Dante's *Divine Comedy;*
pen, ink, and watercolor over pencil, 37.0 x 52.8 cm.
(National Gallery of Victoria, Melbourne, Felton Bequest, 1920)

Satan. Such an analysis stresses the ethical sense of forgiveness in Dante's own character. Blake actively incorporates the ideal of human forgiveness into the Dante illustrations. He does so by consistently presenting the sun as a symbol of divine, or theological, forgiveness extended to human beings, and to the character of Dante in particular. Further, Blake uses the character of Dante to illustrate the need for human, or ethical, forgiveness, by stressing the vengeance in Dante's character; Dante, not God, must forgive the inhabitants of the Inferno. In short, Blake's criticism of Dante is a dispositional one, not a conceptual one: Dante did not forgive others as he himself has been forgiven by God.

Blake's assessment of Dante himself depends upon such a distinction between the living and the dead. Blake explicitly expresses the possibility of posthumous forgiveness on behalf of Dante himself. Blake said,"Dante (tho' now with God) lived & died an Atheist—He was a slave of the world & time" (*BR*, 325). Even though Dante "died an Atheist," evidently he has changed since his death in order to attain the state of being "now with God." In the Dante illustrations, Blake depicts genuine repentance, or a change after death, in some of the sinners Dante has damned. In effect, Blake invites Dante to forgive the shades who changed posthumously as Dante himself had changed. Thus Blake responds to Dante's characters as dead, yet as capable of repentance and of being recipients of forgiveness as is Dante himself.

Blake stresses Dante's status as a forgiven person in the first illustration, "Dante Running from the Three Beasts" (see figure 10). Blake, following the text, shows Dante running from the three beasts. Still following Dante's text, Blake depicts the rising sun, a symbol for Dante of divine order and wisdom. He emphasizes it, "deliberately plac[ing it] in the center of the drawing as the focus around which the contrasting movements revolve."[48] Dante himself continually uses the sun as a symbol of God and of reason. For example, Dante first greets Virgil as "Glory and light of all the tuneful train!" (*Inferno* 1.82). Later he addresses Virgil as "O Sun who healest all imperfect sight" (*Inferno* 11.91). Whereas Dante associates the sun with God the Father, Virgil, and reason, Blake associates it with forgiveness, "rising on the just and the unjust alike," and with Jesus, "the Friend of Sinners" (*J* 3; E, 145). Blake makes this connection explicit in one of his inscriptions: "if [the Father or Jesus] gives his rain to the Evil & the Good & *his Sun to the Just & the Unjust* He could never have Builded Dantes Hell" (E, 690; emphasis added), alluding to Matthew 5:45, a passage Blake had recently quoted in his engraving of Job's forgiveness of his friends (Job illustration 18). In Matthew's Gospel this passage not only describes the Father's mercy, but also commands the listener to imitate it. The

FIGURE 11.
"Dante Adoring Christ,"
illustration for Dante's *Divine Comedy;*
pen, ink, and watercolor over pencil and black chalk, 52.7 x 37.2 cm.
(National Gallery of Victoria, Melbourne, Felton Bequest, 1920)

previous sentence reads: "Love your enemies, bless them that curse you . . . that ye may be the children of your Father which is in heaven." Blake's inclusion of a sun introduces his criticism of Dante as one who has been himself forgiven by Virgil-Jesus—one on whom this sun had risen—but who cannot forgive others.

In linking Virgil typologically with Jesus, Blake draws on the Messianic interpretation of Virgil's fourth *Eclogue*, which foretells a golden age and the birth of a child. Since Constantine, this *Eclogue* was read as a prophecy of Christ, so it attained the status of a classical (or pagan) typological work parallel to the prophecies or types in the Old Testament. Blake takes the tradition one step further, making Virgil not only a prophet of Jesus but also a type, an incarnation of Jesus the poetic genius and of Jesus as the spirit of continual forgiveness of sins. Such an honorific reading of Virgil as this typology implies seems surprising in the light of Blake's blistering words about Virgil elsewhere as a destroyer of all art: "Sacred Truth has pronounced that Greece & Rome as Babylon & Egypt: so far from being parents of Arts & Sciences as they pretend: were destroyers of all Art. Homer Virgil & Ovid confirm this opinion & make us reverence The Word of God, the only light of antiquity that remains unperverted by War. Virgil in the Eneid Book VI. line 848 says Let others study Art: Rome has somewhat better to do, namely War & Dominion" (*On Virgil*; E, 270). But Blake clearly portrays Virgil, typologically, as Christlike: his hands are extended in a cruciform pose; his hair makes a wide frame for his face, almost a halo, as in no other illustrations; he is surrounded by the sun's rays and the position of his feet recalls the familiar formulas of Christ's Ascension and Second Coming.[49] David Fuller notes, "Virgil is not Christ but can function like him,"[50] and it seems clear that the salient function is a forgiving one: Virgil is the medium through which Jesus, the friend of sinners, forgives Dante.

The motif of the sun of forgiveness that signifies Dante's relation to Jesus and to forgiveness informs other Dante illustrations. Blake generally omits the sun in the *Inferno* illustrations, following Dante. He makes two exceptions: "The Whirlwind of Lovers," to which I will return, and "The Mission of Virgil." There Blake shows an old, weak God visited by Satan with a censer, in a scene resembling Job illustrations 2 and 5. He wrote on the drawing: "The Angry God of this World & His Throne [or perhaps 'Porch'] In Purgatory." In this plate, as Milton Klonsky notes, the spiritual sun is obscured by the figure of the angry God.[51] Blake here does criticize Dante's God directly. Echoing the Job illustrations, he suggests that Satan and God conspire against humanity, as they do in the Book of Job. Significantly, Blake labels this "angry God" as

having a throne in Purgatory, for that realm suggests postponed forgiveness in which the sun/son of forgiveness is obscured by the angry father.[52] Accordingly Blake depicts the sun as obscured throughout the *Purgatorio* illustrations: in "Dante and Virgil Ascending the Mountain of Purgatory," in "Dante and Virgil Approaching the Angel who Guards the Entrance of Purgatory," in "The Angel Descending at the Close of the Circle of the Proud," and in "The Angel Inviting Dante to Enter the Fire." Blake reveals the sun only in the *Paradiso* illustrations, beginning with the first finished illustration of *Paradiso*, "Dante Adoring Christ" (see figure 11). Albert S. Roe notes the significance of Blake's beginning the *Paradiso* illustrations with this scene: "Blake made no illustrations at all to the first thirteen cantos of the *Paradiso*, and chose this passage to begin with" because it echoes his own vision of Christ as the sun.[53] Roe suggests that the number 97, in the upper right-hand corner, refers to line 97 of Henry Cary's translation of canto 14, which reads "[Christ] Beam'd on that cross; and pattern fails me now."[54] Cary's diction identifies Christ as himself the sun; Blake explicitly cites that identification. Thus, the proper reading of the painting is not that Christ obscures these three suns, but that the sun's human form is now recognizable, as Blake himself had recognized it: "in my double sight / Twas outward a Sun: inward Los in his might" (E, 722). It makes sense that Blake would depict the human form of forgiveness as Jesus, whose spirit, Blake writes, is "continual forgiveness of Sin" (*J* 3; E, 145).[55] Blake's final depiction of the sun in the *Paradiso* illustrations also suggests Dante's responsibility to forgive as he has been forgiven. In "Dante in the Empyrean, Drinking from the River of Light," Blake makes the sun the source of the river of light (see figure 12). Again Blake departs from the *Comedy* to stress Dante's status as forgiven. In the *Paradiso* Dante describes his river of light running much as an earthly river does, that is, horizontally along the surface of the ground:

> I look'd
> And in the likeness of a river saw
> Light flowing, from whose amber-seeming waves
> Flash'd *up* effulgence, as they glided on
> *'Twixt banks, on either side.*
>
> (*Paradiso* 30.59–63; emphasis added)

By contrast, Blake's river flows vertically, not horizontally, from the sun which Blake has added, although Dante does not mention the sun. In Blake's version, then, Dante is depicted as the recipient of the effluence of the sun, which he has associated throughout with divine forgiveness.

Figure 12.
"Dante in the Empyrean, Drinking from the River of Light,"
illustration for Dante's *Divine Comedy*
(The Tate Gallery, London/Art Resource, N.Y.)

Three of the *Inferno* illustrations exemplify this theme of Dante's denial of posthumous repentance and forgiveness in Dante's treatment of the shades. In "The Whirlwind of Lovers" (also called "The Circle of the Lustful," a name that reflects an attitude quite different from Blake's), Blake suggests his disagreement with Dante's condemnation of Paolo and Francesca to hell by using reversed (or mirror) writing to inscribe the traditional name of this circle, "The Whirlwind of Lovers" (see figure 13). Blake often uses mirror writing for untrustworthy maxims. In *Jerusalem* the Spectre refers to himself as "all reversed" (*J* 10:56; E, 154). In *Jerusalem*, the sinister Gwendolen's "Falshood," also written in reversed writing, begins well enough with the phrase, "In heaven the only Art of Living / Is Forgetting and Forgiving," but then degenerates into special pleading on behalf of a particular interest group ("Especially to the Female"), and concludes satanically, "But if you on Earth forgive / You shall not find where to Live" (*J* 81; E, 238).[56] Thus Blake quietly dissents from the conventional judgment of Paolo and Francesca. At the same time, Blake shows approval for Dante's momentary surge of pity for Francesca. Blake adds a sun, contradicting Dante's text, which describes the circle of the lustful as "a place . . . / Where light was silent all" (*Inferno* 5.29).[57] Significantly, the sun of forgiveness, which rises on the just and the unjust alike, contains a picture of Paolo and Francesca's sexual transgression. Blake's point is that the sun of forgiveness shines even on this act. The depiction of Paolo and Francesca's passion, further, provides an alternate point of view. We see them as earthly lovers, not only as damned and punished shades. Thus by this "flashback" Blake suggests that the point of view of forgiveness, not of vengeance, is normative.

Blake, like his friend John Flaxman, depicts the exchange between Francesca and Dante at the moment when Dante faints in response to Francesca's story.[58] Dante writes,

> heart-struck
> I through compassion fainting, seem'd not far
> from death, and like a corpse fall to the ground.
>
> (*Inferno* 5.139–42)

Blake places the sun above Dante because Dante responds more forgivingly to Paolo and Francesca than to any other shades in the *Inferno*. Dante's fainting "like a corpse" suggests that Dante identifies with the condition of the shades, an identification that, in Blake's view, approaches an admission of the possibility for posthumous forgiveness.

FIGURE 13.
"The Whirlwind of Lovers" (also called "The Circle of the Lustful: Paolo and Francesca"), illustration for Dante's *Divine Comedy*
(Gift of W. G. Russell Allen, © 1992 National Gallery of Art, Washington, D.C.)

Blake criticizes Dante's position on posthumous forgiveness more directly in "Capaneus the Blasphemer." His case probably attracted Blake because Dante enters the circle of the blasphemers saying: "Vengeance of Heaven! Oh! how shouldst thou be fear'd / By all who read" (*Inferno* 14:16–17). Moreover, Capaneus in the text stresses the state of posthumous fixity: "Such as I was / When living, dead such now I am" (*Inferno* 14:47–48). Blake undermines Dante's text in Capaneus's expression of patient suffering—clearly a change from the blasphemous anger in which he died. He patiently bears Dante's accusation, associated with lightning bolts (which are present also in "Minos," the depiction of the accuser who sends shades to their proper destination).[59] Blake's response to Capaneus might seem to depart from his attitude toward him in the 1801 Annotations to Boyd. There Blake listed Capaneus with several other "wicked" characters in literature, including Satan, Othello, and Prometheus. However, the list ends with "Jesus a winebibber"—a curious conclusion for a list of villains, and one that suggests that the whole list has been ironic in its disapproval. Blake mentioned Capaneus not so much to condemn him as to refute Boyd's simpleminded notion of the moral function of literature.[60] In fact, it is consistent with Blake's view of blasphemy. Robinson recounts Blake's visionary conversation with Voltaire: "'I have had,['] he said [']much intercourse with Voltaire—And he said to me 'I blasphemed the Son of Man And it shall be forgiven me—but they' (the enemies of Voltaire) [']blasphemed the Holy Ghost in me, and it shall not be forgiven to them[']" (*BR*, 547). Despite Voltaire's "blasphemy"—in which, presumably, he died—Voltaire confidently predicts his own forgiveness, a forgiveness that is, like Dante's, posthumous. This remark underlines Blake's suggestions that Capaneus may have repented his blasphemy, and, further, that Dante does not recognize the change.

The most sustained criticism of Dante's position on posthumous forgiveness occurs in Blake's portrayal of Dante's invocation of vengeance for Ugolino. Count Ugolino's sad and grotesque death had been a popular subject for eighteenth-century illustrators: Sir Joshua Reynolds and Henry Fuseli painted famous depictions of Count Ugolino; Blake himself drew Ugolino at least eight times, a frequency unmatched within the Dante illustrations.[61] In 1793 Blake had seen Ugolino as someone who had suffered enough revenge, inscribing on the illustration: "Does thy God O Priest take such vengeance as this?" (*For the Sexes*; E, 265). Blake probably associated this excessive punishment of Ugolino with Dante's own character. Out of all the possible scenes from the *Comedy*, he chose the scene of Ugolino in prison to accompany his "Head of Dante" in the series for Hayley. In the Dante illustrations, Blake builds on this critique, placing the Ugolino illustrations to emphasize Dante's vengeance, not God's. He sets the three Ugolino illustrations deliberately in the context of Dante's own vengefulness. In the plate that immediately precedes the Ugolino set, "The Circle of Traitors," Blake shows Dante kicking a helpless Bocca degli Abati, who is frozen in the ice up to his shoulders.[62] Bocca's response focuses on Dante's personal vengefulness, not on God's. He cries out: "Wherefore dost bruise me? . . . Unless thy errand be some fresh revenge / For Montaperto . . . ?" (*Inferno* 32:79–81; emphasis added). The main action of the next illustration is "Dante Seizing the Traitor Bocca by the Hair" (see figure 14). Blake stresses the link between Dante's viciousness and Ugolino's by joining Dante's tugging right arm and the curve of the Ugolino's cavern in a continuous line. As Klonsky rightly observes, "Blake's intention in the illustration was thus plainly to connect these two brutally vindictive acts, Dante's leading into Ugolino's, and to condemn them as similar in kind if not in degree."[63] Moreover, the hearing of Ugolino's story provokes Dante to the worst outburst on behalf of vengeance in the entire *Comedy*.

> Oh thou Pisa! shame
> Of all the people . . .
> . . . .
> since that thy neighbors are so slack
> To punish, from their deep foundations rise
> Capraia and Gorgona, and dam up
> The mouth of Arno, that each soul in thee
> May perish in the waters!
>
> (*Inferno* 33.77–84)

Thus we see the character of Dante at its worst. Vengeance is explicitly attributed to Dante, not to God. And, in Blake's view, "he who takes vengeance alone is the criminal of Providence" (*J* 45:32; E, 194).

In the next Ugolino picture, Blake further suggests that Dante's unforgiving perspective on Ugolino is not normative. He adds two pitying angels, unmentioned in the narrative, to "Count Ugolino and his Sons in Prison," the scene that depicts Ugolino's temptation and his anguish. He also added these angels in the tempera painting of 1826 (see figure 15). These angels suggest divine forgiveness and compassion in the place where Dante's impulse is to exact further revenge. It is extremely significant that the drawing "Count Ugolino and his Sons in Prison" is the single flashback out of hell in the whole set of illustrations. In this way, it functions somewhat like the disk of the sun in

FIGURE 14.
"Dante Seizing the Traitor Bocca by the Hair,"
illustration for Dante's *Divine Comedy*
(The Fogg Art Museum, Harvard University Art Museums,
bequest of Grenville L. Winthrop)

Figure 15.
"Count Ugolino and his Sons in Prison,"
illustration for Dante's *Divine Comedy*
(The Fitzwilliam Museum, Cambridge, England)

the depiction of Paolo and Francesca, juxtaposing their present suffering with the causes of their sin.

Blake's treatment of Dante does introduce the theme that even a poet can offend against the poetic and forgiving spirit of Jesus, taking up a theme explicit in *Milton* and *Jerusalem*. However, the use of typology in the Dante illustrations sustains the fundamental separation we have observed throughout these last works, the separation between accusing offender and forgiving victim. This separation allows them separate identities and depicts forgiveness as the transaction it really is, not an identity as Blake implicitly claims in *Jerusalem*. The addition of the theme of posthumous forgiveness, as Blake approached his own death, underlies Blake's identification of himself as offender—forgiven, perhaps, but still an offender—rather than the conflicted double identification of himself in *Jerusalem* as poet accused by his reader and simultaneously accusing that same reader.

CONCLUSION

Forgiveness and Literary Form

How does literary form mediate forgiveness? *Milton* and *Jerusalem* present readerly and writerly forgiveness as a major thematic concern. In *Milton* an erring author recognizes his mistakes and renounces them, a process synonymous with "Blake" reading and forgiving Milton. And in *Jerusalem* Blake pleads for his reader's forgiveness at the beginning and suggests its achievement in the penultimate plate's reworking of the return of the Prodigal Son. To embody these thematic treatments of forgiveness, Blake adapts the biblical forms of typology in *Milton* and synopsis in *Jerusalem*.

Several questions arise at the outset. Do typology and synopsis, by virtue of their status as literary forms, promote the transaction of forgiveness or the identification with the exemplar? What balance of the expressivist ethic and the totalizing ethic do they embody? Do typology and synopsis promote mutual forgiveness or one-sided forgiveness, and if one-sided, how are the reader and the writer disproportionate? How does the good exemplar, sometimes Los and sometimes Jesus, mediate between reader and writer?

Typology in *Milton*

Blake knew the Bible thoroughly and adopted the Bible as a normative literary form: "The Old & New Testaments are the Great Code of Art" (*Laocoön*; E, 274). Tannenbaum explains the aesthetic consequences of this commitment: "All art is typological in form and content, [so that] the develop-

ment of the arts is retrospective and cumulative."[1] But what are the ethical implications of typology as a literary structure? Ethics and aesthetics meshed in scriptural hermeneutics, since, historically, moral interpretation of Scripture came third in the fourfold series of literal, allegorical, moral, and anagogical senses. In fact, the practice of attaching moral theology to scriptural exegesis delayed the emergence of moral theology as a separate discipline.

Our concern, however, is with the ethical implications of the second, most literary, sense of scriptural interpretation, the allegorical relation between the Testaments. (Allegory here does not mean the trope that is usually contrasted with metaphor, but the relation of the two texts.) Here I shall be arguing, first, that allegorical typology in its traditional use retains a structure of transaction and that, in so doing, it resembles an intersubjective model of forgiveness; second, that in *Milton* Blake employs typological form to employ Milton's forgiveness as a transaction; third, that Blake immediately follows with a metaphor of identity, fusing himself and Milton with the good exemplar, Los. Fundamentally, then, typology as a form promotes the transaction of forgiveness, but Blake moves beyond transaction to a metaphor of identity.

The intersubjective theory of forgiveness relies on Arendt's formula that the forgiver puts aside violations of obligation for the sake of perceiving the disclosure of the character of the other. This theory distinguishes character or identity from failed actions, as does traditional typology. To put it briefly, typology is the literary form of forgiveness.

The logic of forgiveness (preserving and strengthening character by separating from it deeds of wrongdoing) manifests itself in the pattern of typological readings of Old Testament figures. In theory, according to Saint Augustine's formula "The New Testament lies hidden in the Old; the Old Testament is enlightened through the New"; any literary element in one Testament can mirror its type or antitype in the other.[2] But in practice, almost all typology interpreted specific personages, usually Adam, Moses, Joshua, Isaac, or Noah.[3] The ethical principle of forgiveness implicitly informs the literary form of typology. By typological thinking, Adam or Noah becomes identified with Jesus in prefiguring him. Typology functions as a capacious, forgiving structure by allowing failures, as well as successes, to function as signifiers. Both Adam, a man who failed by bringing death into the world, and Joshua, who succeeded by leading the Hebrews to the Promised Land, function as types of Christ. Typology, like forgiveness, separates the identity of Adam (now revealed as a type of Jesus) from the sin of disobedience. In this identifying figurative process, typology runs the risk of collapsing all figures into the central antitype, Jesus—a risk orthodox exegetes have combated by insisting on the historicity of the literal sense. But for Blake the typological identifications break loose from their historical anchor: "I cannot concieve [*sic*] the Divinity of the books in the Bible to consist either in who they were written by or at what time or in the historical evidence which may be all false in the eyes of one man & true in the eyes of another," Blake writes, "but in the Sentiments & Examples which whether true or Parabolic are Equally useful" (Ann. Watson; E, 618). Therefore, Blake inherits the scriptural pull toward identifying types without inheriting the counterweight of insisting on historical fact. Blake's use of typology thus invites the collapse of all types into the antitype of Jesus, as metaphors of identity replace metaphors of transaction.[4]

Typology pervades *Milton*. Blake constantly employs typological structures, as in the Bard's Song, which, as several Blake scholars have demonstrated, provides a rereading of *Paradise Lost*. The Bard's Song reworks key notions of Milton's theodicy, freeing Milton to "redeem his emanation" and to return to earth and reincarnate himself in Blake as Blake reads Milton.[5] Moreover, Blake innovates upon several dominant images of typology, by which the New Testament defines itself as the new dispensation. For example, the frontispiece to *Milton* shows the name MIL / TON rent apart by the living Milton in an act that recalls both the rending of the veil of the temple at Christ's crucifixion and also the cessation of the domain of the letter in favor of the domain of the spirit.[6]

The typological scene of the predecessor binding on the sandals of his successor serves to comment on the transaction of forgiveness between reader and writer. Blake's opening lyric suggests the primacy of Jesus and of his feet for the whole poem by asking,

> And did those feet in ancient time,
> Walk upon Englands mountains green.
>
> (*M* 1; E, 95)[7]

This opening invites the reader to see all feet in the poem as variations of Jesus' antitypical feet, even as the action of the Bard's Song reaches its nadir when "Los took off his left sandal placing it on his head, / Signal of solemn mourning (*M* 8:11–12; E, 101). The opening lyric, of course, speculates about the feet of Jesus, invoking biblical typology. Blake's frequent images of feet and sandals form an extended allusion to a paradigmatic predecessor's prophecy of his successor, namely John the Baptist's declaration: "There cometh one mightier than I after me, the latchet of whose shoes I am not worthy to stoop down and unloose" (Mark 1:7; cf. Matthew 3:11, Luke 3:16, and John 1:27). The New Testament itself offers the relation between John and Jesus as an analogy to the relation between the Law and the Gospel. For example, Jesus calls John the greatest of the prophets, heralds of the old dispensation, but declares that his greatness is exceeded by any member of the new: "Among those that are born of women there is not a greater prophet than John the Baptist: but he that is least in the kingdom of God is greater than he" (Luke 7:28). This passage produced a tradition of reading John as the summation of the entire Old Testament. In their discussion of the typological relation between Jesus and John, the patristic writers focused on John's baptism of Jesus. For example, Saint Cyril of Jerusalem writes: "Baptism is the end of the Old Testament, and beginning of the New. For its author was John, than whom was none greater among them that are born of women. The end he was of the prophets: for all the Prophets and the Law were until John: but of the Gospel history he was the first-fruit. For it saith, The beginning of the Gospel of Jesus Christ, &c: John came baptizing in the wilderness."[8] Blake accepts from the tradition the general motif of reading the relation between John and Jesus as an analogy for the typological relation between the Old and New Testaments. He chooses the scene of untying sandals, rather than the scene of baptism, as the paradigm for the proper relation between prophets or poets, relegating baptism to the status of a restrictive ritual Urizen performs to subdue Milton's attempts at re-form—interestingly, a ritual that paralyzes Milton's feet "freezing dark rocks between / The footsteps, and infixing deep the feet in marble beds" (*M* 21:1–2; E, 112).[9] Fixed feet suggest a hampered version of the Jesus who traverses England.

Blake accepts and elaborates the action John the Baptist had foreclosed, the fastening of a sandal. In the first telling of Milton's descent, Blake depicts the leftover material "from my left foot a black cloud redounding spread over Europe" (*M* 17:50; E, 110). But in the second account the leftover material forms a sandal:

> Milton entering my Foot . . .
> . . . .
> And all this Vegetable World appeard on my left Foot,
> As a bright sandal formd immortal of precious stones & gold:
> I stooped down & bound it on to walk forward thro' Eternity.
> (*M* 23:4, 12–14; E, 115)

In the interim, Milton wrestles with Urizen; having prevailed, Milton can see the vegetable world no longer as an indefinite cloud but as a bright sandal.[10] To depict this transformation, Blake draws on the action mentioned but unrealized in the Gospel, the scene of the predecessor tying on his successor's sandal. This depiction includes identifying the vegetable world "As a bright sandal formd immortal of precious stones & gold." If we simply contrast the sandal to the black cloud, we can see that the sandal is beautiful in its brightness; it is humanly made, "formd immortal of precious stones & gold," rather than merely natural; and, most important, it is serviceable to the human form in its walk forward through eternity. Within the context of Jesus' feet and Los's sandals, Blake's fusion with Milton suggests the pattern Eaves observes of metaphors of transaction giving way to metaphors of identity. Blake replaces a biblical typological model of transaction between a predecessor and a successor with an identity of predecessor and successor, a joined identity that binds on his own sandal. It seems, then, that Blake has forgiven Milton the errors of *Paradise Lost* and appropriated him as a source of power.

But Blake is not being merely solipsistic and addressing his own relation with Milton, for at this point he refigures his readerly forgiveness of the writer as the identification of both of them with Los. In terms of forgiveness, this addition of the exemplar suggests not only that the forgiven author (Milton) has a new or redefined identity with and as Los, but that the forgiving reader (Blake) similarly has a new or redefined identity with and as Los. This is partly because Blake has been not only the reader of Milton but the writer of *Milton*, and as such has placed himself in the position of the author. But it is also because Blake, as the forgiving reader of Milton, has practiced the virtue of forgiveness, which is the defining mark of the exemplar. In *Jerusalem*, Blake prefers Jesus to Los as this third term, the exemplar who mediates between author and reader. Since there Blake calls the spirit of Jesus "continual forgiveness of sins," perhaps we can read back into *Milton* Blake's hope that the reader, in practicing the virtue of readerly forgiveness, can share that virtue in fusing with Jesus.

Synopsis in *Jerusalem*

In turning from *Milton* to *Jerusalem*, Blake makes a major shift among the readerly and writerly coordinates available to him. In *Milton* Blake the writer writes of Blake the reader reading (and forgiving) Milton the writer; he emphasizes that the act of forgiving Milton is simultaneously the act of reading Milton and of writing *Milton*. In *Jerusalem* the coordinates shift. Blake limits himself to the author function exclusively, thus placing himself potentially in

the position of Milton, the erring author pleading for the reader's reading and understanding. Indeed, on the level of theme, Blake takes that position, opening *Jerusalem* by pleading, "Dear Reader, forgive what you do not approve, and love me for this energetic exertion of my talent," and closing it with a scene reminiscent of the father's forgiveness of the Prodigal Son. However, on the level of form, Blake employs the biblical convention of synopsis, that is, a four-part poem addressed to different audiences, modeled after the Gospels.

What are the implications of fourfold synoptic form for the relationship between writer and reader? Potentially, fourfold synoptic form possesses the same ambiguity we have seen throughout Blake. On the one hand, synopsis as a form serves the values of contrariety, of the cultivation of intersubjectivity, as the author attempts to address various audiences on their own terms without homogenizing them. On the other hand, fourfold synoptic form, in resembling the Gospels, presents the exemplar as a formal goal as well as an ethical goal. That is, fourfold synoptic form recalls the promise of unity between the narrative itself (the Bible as Word of God) and the hero of the narrative (Jesus as the Word of God); moreover, it promises unity among the narratives, for each one separately is a Gospel yet collectively they are the Gospel. Thus fourfold synoptic form suggests the promise that in imitating the formal exemplar, the Gospels, the author has also imitated the ethical exemplar, Jesus. Again, the crucial issue is the relation of the reader to the exemplar Blake presents, and indeed presents as one he himself expresses in his actions and in his art.

What can Blake's adaptation of the Gospels' fourfold synoptic form have signified in the 1810s? Biblical scholars had not ventured so far into the textual problems of the New Testament as they had with the Old. Not until 1835 did New Testament scholars first ask about the order of composition of the Gospels and about literary relations among them.[11] Before that time, they assumed that the chronological sequence of the Gospels' composition was duplicated by the sequence given in the Bible: Matthew, Mark, Luke, John. Subsequently, of course, biblical scholars have defined the first three Gospels as "synoptic," due to the sources and chronology they share with each other but not with the Gospel of John. But in Blake's time all four Gospels could be called synoptic in a different sense, because devotional writers and theologians had experimented with Gospel forms since the sixteenth century, composing two kinds of "Gospel harmonies." In the "integrated harmony," the author composed one continuous life of Jesus, combining material from all the Gospels; in the "parallel harmony," three or four Gospels were arranged either in parallel columns or in parallel horizontal sections. John Calvin's *Commentary on a Harmony of the Evangelists, Matthew, Mark, and Luke* (1555) exemplifies the parallel harmony.[12] Moreover, few scholars examined the different audiences of the Gospels until F. C. Baur of Tübingen (1792–1860) who stressed the Gospel of Matthew's Jewishness and the Gospel of Luke's links with Saint Paul.[13] In the light of the state of New Testament studies, then, what could Blake's use of fourfold synoptic form suggest? Since his predecessors in synoptic form stressed synthesizing the Gospels, it is likely that Blake used the form in a similar way, his fourfold book alluding to the Gospels conceived as one unified entity, rather than as rhetorically differentiated. Frye read each book of *Jerusalem* as informed throughout by the concerns of its respective audience and interpreted Blake's placement of the Apocalypse in the chapter dedicated "To the Christians" as his mark of approval of Christianity.[14] But in fact, *Jerusalem* has only an "approximate structure," in which it is not clear that everything does indeed belong in its place and not everything can be proven.[15] Only the Prefaces to the respective books reflect substantive rhetorical differences.

However, the state of New Testament scholarship in Blake's day does provide one clue to Blake's choice of synoptic fourfold form. Scholars inquired into the relative reliability of New Testament sources, beginning what Albert Schweitzer later called "The Quest for the Historical Jesus," as contrasted with later doctrinal formulations about him. The German scholar H. S. Reimarus (1694–1768) speculated about the divergence between the aims of Jesus and of his disciples, in an essay that was published posthumously by G. E. Lessing in German in 1778. Although there was no English translation of Reimarus until the 1870s, it is possible Reimarus himself derived the idea from the English deists whom he met during a brief visit to England.[16] In 1744 the deist Peter Annet published a pamphlet raising questions similar to those of Reimarus, *The Resurrection of Jesus Christ Reconsidered*. Blake may have known Annet's work.[17] Both Reimarus and Annet found the Gospels more reliable than the Epistles in presenting a historical Jesus. Blake expresses a view similar to Annet's, if not derived from him, in *Jerusalem*'s list of biblical books that shelter the Saviour with

> Spiritual Verse, order'd & measur'd, from whence, time shall reveal.
> The Five books of the Decalogue, the books of Joshua & Judges,
> Samuel, a double book & Kings, a double book, the Psalms & Prophets
> The Four-fold Gospel, and the Revelations everlasting.
> (*J* 48:8–11; E, 196)

In omitting Acts and the Epistles from his revised New Testament canon,

Blake echoes the Swedenborgian church's claim that in the New Testament only the Gospels and the Revelation were definitive, "the Books of the Word."[18] Blake's choice of fourfold synoptic structure, then, accords *Jerusalem* the highest authority possible. Based on this historical context, the likelihood is that Blake's antecedents in fourfold synoptic form promoted a strong sense of totalization and that Blake follows suit with metaphors of identity between author and reader in the exemplar.

My assessment of the fourfold synoptic form of *Jerusalem* is based on this familiar paradox, that in addressing his audiences, Blake discounts the description of their social variety in favor of seeing them as a collection of individuals, ironically lacking in variety, all describable by the same mechanism that describes Blake himself. Blake collapses all the varieties of his audience (Jews, deists, and Christians) into the general category "Public," which Blake characterizes as spectral. I have already analyzed Blake's struggle to acknowledge some alterity in his reader and to deny other alterities in his reader by constructing the reader along the binary opposition between Spectre and Jesus. In order to relate forgiveness to literary form, however, we must note here that Blake continues to stress the link between Jesus as the exemplar of creativity and Jesus as the exemplar of forgiveness. For example, Blake sees "the Saviour over me / Spreading his beams of love, & dictating the words of this mild song" (*J* 4:5; E, 146), and his theme is forgiveness:

> I am not a God afar off, I am a brother and friend;
> Within your bosoms I reside, and you reside in me:
> *Lo! we are One; forgiving all Evil*; Not seeking recompense!
> Ye are my members O ye sleepers of Beulah, land of shades!
> (*J* 4:18–21; E, 146; emphasis added)

Blake's hope that forgiveness will produce a condition in which "we are One" produces in *Jerusalem* two formal consequences: that despite their different audiences, all four chapters are "synoptic" and somehow "One"; and that the reader, the poet, and Jesus achieve a similar identity in the act of reading. Blake's use of synoptic form in *Jerusalem* may well be governed not only by the formal conventions of Gospel harmonies and parallels, but by the governing purpose of the writers of devotional works, that the Gospels serve as a spur for the imitation of Christ. Along these lines, then, the presentation of the exemplar of the "Friend of Sinners" is partly divested of its narcissism, as Blake presents himself as merely the reader who went before his own reader. The formal presuppositions of fourfold synoptic form have the ethical shape of an expressivist ethics, in which "human life culminates in self-awareness through expression," and that expressive act is performed for an audience to accept.[19] For Blake, the expression of his own identification with the exemplar Jesus takes side stage in the depiction of intergenerational and heterosexual forgiveness in plate 99 of *Jerusalem*, which we examined earlier (see figure 5). Blake's exemplarity here as the forgiven one, rather than the forgiver, is best supported by his own obsession with the Prodigal Son story, as Samuel Palmer tells it. He repeated the story, "but at the words 'When he was yet a great way off, his father saw him' could go no further; his voice faltered, and he was in tears" (*BR*, 283). Here Blake confronts his reader with the possibility of accepting the pattern of exemplarity for himself or herself in his or her own particularity. Despite the tension between accepting and denying the reader's alterity, Blake embodies his purpose in biblical, synoptic form, insisting, as he always does, on the inseparability of ethics and aesthetics.

Notes

Introduction

1. Recently, literary critics as diverse as Wayne C. Booth and J. Hillis Miller have sought to recover ethics for literary study. Miller claims that in fact ethical questions inhere in the text (*The Ethics of Reading: Kant, de Man, Eliot, Trollope, James, and Benjamin* [New York: Columbia University Press, 1987]). Booth writes in defense of raising ethical questions in order to evaluate works of literature. Booth's chapter "Why Ethical Criticism Fell on Hard Times" provides a history of academic literary studies' neglect of ethics (*The Company We Keep: An Ethics of Fiction* [Berkeley and Los Angeles: University of California Press, 1988], 24–26).

2. Laurence S. Lockridge, *The Ethics of Romanticism* (Cambridge: Cambridge University Press, 1989), 3. See also Martha C. Nussbaum, *The Fragility of Goodness: Luck and Ethics in Greek Tragedy and Philosophy* (Cambridge: Cambridge University Press, 1986).

3. Alasdair MacIntyre, *After Virtue: A Study in Moral Theory,* 2d ed. (Notre Dame, Ind.: University of Notre Dame Press, 1984), 184.

4. MacIntyre's *After Virtue* has been justly influential in this debate. Other works are Edmund L. Pincoffs, *Quandaries and Virtues: Against Reductivism in Ethics* (Lawrence: University of Kansas Press, 1986); Stanley Hauerwas and Alasdair MacIntyre, eds., *Revisions: Changing Perspectives in Moral Philosophy* (Notre Dame, Ind.: University of Notre Dame Press, 1983); Stanley Hauerwas, *Truthfulness and Tragedy: Further Investigations in Christian Ethics* (Notre Dame, Ind.: University of Notre Dame Press, 1977); Iris Murdoch, *The Sovereignty of Good* (1970; reprint, London: Ark Paperbacks, 1985); Philippa Foot, *Virtues and Vices and Other Essays in Moral Philosophy* (Berkeley and Los Angeles: University of California Press, 1978);

Peter Geach, *The Virtues: The Stanton Lectures, 1973–1974* (Cambridge: Cambridge University Press, 1977).

5. William K. Frankena, *Ethics* (Englewood Cliffs, N.J.: Prentice-Hall, 1963), 13.

6. Ibid., 14.

7. See Gerald R. Cragg, *Reason and Authority in the Eighteenth Century* (Cambridge: Cambridge University Press, 1964).

8. Paul Ricoeur, *The Symbolism of Evil,* trans. Emerson Buchanan (Boston: Beacon Press, 1967), 35–36.

9. Martin Heidegger, *Being and Time,* trans. John Macquarrie and Edward Robinson (London: SCM Press, 1962); Martin Buber, *I and Thou,* 2d ed., trans. Ronald Greger Smith (New York: Scribner's, 1958).

10. For Levinas, see in particular *Ethics and Infinity* (Pittsburgh: Duquesne University Press, 1985); useful discussions of Levinas include Richard A. Cohen, ed., *Face to Face with Levinas* (Albany: State University of New York Press, 1986); Edith Wyschogrod, *Emmanuel Levinas: The Problem of Ethical Metaphysics* (The Hague: Martinus Nijhoff, 1974); and Andrius Valevičius, *From the Other to the Totally Other: The Religious Philosophy of Emmanuel Levinas* (New York: Peter Lang, 1988).

11. Morton D. Paley, *Energy and the Imagination: A Study of the Development of Blake's Thought* (Oxford: Clarendon Press, 1970).

12. W. J. T. Mitchell, "Dangerous Blake," *Studies in Romanticism* 21 (1982): 410–16.

13. Paul Youngquist, *Madness and Blake's Myth* (University Park: Pennsylvania State University Press, 1989), 137–44.

14. Ibid., 138.

15. Alfred Kazin, *Introduction to The Portable Blake* (New York: Viking Press, 1946), 54.

16. Hannah Arendt, *The Human Condition* (Chicago: University of Chicago Press, 1958), 242.

17. Ibid., 241.

18. Aristotle, *Nicomachean Ethics,* trans. David Ross, rev. J. O. Urmson (Oxford: Oxford University Press, 1984), 9.3 (225–26).

19. MacIntyre, *After Virtue,* 174.

20. Ibid., 174.

21. Arendt, *The Human Condition,* 242–43.

22. Reinhold Niebuhr, *An Interpretation of Christian Ethics* (1935; reprint, New York: Seabury Press, 1979), 137.

23. Lockridge, *The Ethics of Romanticism,* 193.

24. Ibid., 182.

25. Morton D. Paley, "The Figure of the Garment in *The Four Zoas, Milton,* and *Jerusalem,*" in *Blake's Sublime Allegory: Essays on "The Four Zoas," "Milton," and "Jerusalem,"* ed. Stuart Curran and Joseph Anthony Wittreich, Jr. (Madison: University of Wisconsin Press, 1973), 123; Leopold Damrosch, Jr., *Symbol and Truth in Blake's*

Myth (Princeton, N.J.: Princeton University Press, 1980), 166; Morris Eaves, *William Blake's Theory of Art* (Princeton, N.J.: Princeton University Press, 1982), 4.

Chapter 1. Forgiveness "Written Within & Without" Law

1. The standard discussion is Morton D. Paley, "The Figure of the Garment in *The Four Zoas, Milton,* and *Jerusalem,*" in *Blake's Sublime Allegory: Essays on "The Four Zoas," "Milton," and "Jerusalem,"* ed. Stuart Curran and Joseph Anthony Wittreich, Jr. (Madison: University of Wisconsin Press, 1973), 119–39.

2. Throughout this paragraph I use Gertrude Huehns, *Antinomianism in English History, with Special Reference to the Period 1640–1660* (London: Cresset Press, 1951); E. P. Thompson, *The Making of the English Working Class* (New York: Random House, Vintage Books, 1966); A. L. Morton, *The Everlasting Gospel: A Study in the Sources of William Blake* (1957; reprint, New York: Haskell House, 1966). For more information about religious millenarianism and radical politics, see Iain McCalman, *Radical Underworld: Prophets, Revolutionaries and Pornographers in London, 1795–1840* (Cambridge: Cambridge University Press, 1988). The ambiguities of law and antinomianism are examined in relation to charters and liberty in Edward Larissy, *William Blake* (Oxford: Basil Blackwell, 1985), 50–51.

3. Morton, *The Everlasting Gospel,* 37.

4. For a statement of antinomian doctrine in the seventeenth century, see Huehns, *Antinomianism in English History,* 8.

5. A. C. Underwood, quoted in Thompson, *Working Class,* 30; Huehns, *Antinomianism in English History,* 135–48.

6. John Wesley, quoted in Thompson, *Working Class,* 36.

7. Morton D. Paley, "William Blake, The Prince of the Hebrews, and The Woman Clothed with the Sun," in *William Blake: Essays in Honor of Sir Geoffrey Keynes,* ed. Morton D. Paley and Michael Phillips (Oxford: Clarendon Press, 1973), 260–93. See also David V. Erdman, *Blake, Prophet Against Empire: A Poet's Interpretation of the History of His Own Times,* 3d ed. (Princeton, N.J.: Princeton University Press, 1977), 36–37, 290–91; and Marilyn Gaull, *English Romanticism: The Human Context* (New York: Norton, 1988), 156–63.

8. Huehns, *Antinomianism in English History,* 47.

9. Ibid., 53.

10. Quoted by Huehns (ibid., 53).

11. Morton D. Paley, "'A New Heaven Is Begun': Blake and Swedenborgianism," in *Blake and Swedenborg: Opposition Is True Friendship,* ed. Harvey F. Bellin and Darrell Ruhl (New York: Swedenborg Foundation, 1985), 17, reprinted in *Blake: An Illustrated Quarterly* 12, no. 2 (1979): 64–90.

12. I summarize Paley, "New Heaven," throughout this paragraph.

13. Quoted in E. B. Murray, "Thel, *Thelyphthora,* and the Daughters of Albion," *Studies in Romanticism* 20 (1981): 276n. I summarize Murray's article throughout this paragraph.

14. Ibid., 281.

15. Ibid., 275; original emphasis.

16. Harold Bloom, *The Visionary Company: A Reading of English Romantic Poetry,* rev. ed. (Ithaca, N.Y.: Cornell University Press, 1971), 69.

17. Graham Pechey thoughtfully locates the *Marriage* in the antinomian tradition in "*The Marriage of Heaven and Hell:* A Text and Its Conjecture," *Oxford Literary Review* 3, no. 3 (1979): 52–76.

18. Martin K. Nurmi, *Blake's "Marriage of Heaven and Hell": A Critical Study* (Kent, Ohio: Kent State University Press, 1957), 40. Dan Miller provides a more subtle formulation of the Proverbs' point of view, writing that the point of the proverbs that advocate excess is that "contrariety can be known only in the act of missing it," as the proverbs do themselves when read as if Blake there "spoke straight" (in "Contrary Revelation: *The Marriage of Heaven and Hell,*" *Studies in Romanticism* 24 [1985]: 506). It was Harold Bloom who noted that the central problem in the *Marriage* is to determine when Blake "speaks straight" (*Ringers in the Tower: Studies in Romantic Tradition* [Chicago: University of Chicago Press, 1971], 55).

19. John Howard, *Infernal Poetics: Poetic Structures in Blake's Lambeth Prophecies* (Rutherford, N.J.: Fairleigh Dickinson University Press, 1984), 77.

20. In one copy of the *Marriage,* Blake inked the Proverbs in different colors, thus providing one means of grouping them (E, 801). See also William Blake, *The Marriage of Heaven and Hell,* introduction and commentary by Geoffrey Keynes (New York: Oxford University Press, 1975). This edition reproduces Copy H from the Fitzwilliam Museum. The principle that the Proverbs of Hell mutually interpret each other has been suggested by Michael E. Holstein in "Crooked Roads Without Improvement: Blake's 'Proverbs of Hell,'" *Genre* 8 (1975): 39.

21. Bloom interprets these plowing proverbs as references to sexual initiation in *Blake's Apocalypse: A Study in Poetic Argument* (Garden City, N.Y.: Doubleday, 1963), 83–88.

22. Its sentiment echoes the saying recorded in Luke, "Let the dead bury their dead: but go thou and preach the Kingdom of God" (9:60).

23. A qualification may be in order in judging the proverb "Prayers plow not! Praises reap not!" Erdman among others thinks that Blake is "speaking straight" here in condemning prayer as useless (*Prophet Against Empire,* 177). It is possible, however, that the next two clauses qualify the first two ("Joys laugh not! Sorrows weep not!"). These are clearly contrary to fact: joyful persons frequently laugh, and the sorrowful weep. Blake is right to observe that "*Excess* of sorrow laughs. *Excess* of joy weeps," but joys and sorrows that are not excessive follow the common pattern. Since the third and fourth clauses are clearly contrary to fact, the first and second may be equally so.

24. Bloom, *Blake's Apocalypse,* 97.

25. David V. Erdman, ed., *The Illuminated Blake* (Garden City, N.Y.: Doubleday, Anchor Books, 1974), 125, 132, 134. According to Janet Warner, Theotormon's posture in plate 4 resembles that of several spectral characters in Blake's work ("Blake's Figures of Despair: Man in His Spectre's Power," in *William Blake,* ed. Paley and Phillips, 208–24).

26. Michael G. Cooke, *Acts of Inclusion: Studies Bearing on an Elementary Theory of Romanticism* (New Haven, Conn.: Yale University Press, 1979), 110.

27. D. G. Gillham, *William Blake* (London: Cambridge University Press, 1973), 198.

28. Erdman, *Prophet Against Empire,* 230–42.

29. Gillham, *William Blake,* 205–6.

30. Critics who address the problem of Oothoon's paralysis are Erdman, *Prophet Against Empire,* 228; and Jane E. Peterson, "The *Visions of the Daughters of Albion:* A Problem in Perception," *Philological Quarterly* 52 (1973): 252–64.

31. This illustration is the tailpiece in Copy A; Erdman, *The Illuminated Blake,* 125.

32. Ibid., 125–26.

33. Leonard Deen mentions that Theotormon's name contains almost all the letters in the names of the other two characters (*Conversing in Paradise: Poetic Genius and Identity-as-Community in Blake's Los* [Columbia: University of Missouri Press, 1983], 50). This fact may suggest that Blake uses Theotormon as a containing figure for the other two, but it is not conclusive, in my judgment, since some letters are excluded. Frye suggests that *Oothoon* comes from the *Oithona* of Ossian, *Bromion* from the Greek word for "roaring" (*Fearful Symmetry: A Study of William Blake* [1947; reprint, Princeton, N.J.: Princeton University Press, 1969], 238–39); Erdman thinks *Oothoon* may be derived from African names in Stedman's *Narrative* (*Prophet Against Empire,* 233).

34. For example, Howard Hinkel, "From Energy and Desire to Eternity: Blake's *Visions of the Daughters of Albion,*" *Papers on Language and Literature* 15 (1979): 285.

35. Cooke, *Acts of Inclusion,* 113.

36. Erdman, *The Illuminated Blake,* 135–36.

37. Blake called the poem *The First Book of Urizen,* then deleted "first" from one title page and two copies of the preludium (E, 804).

38. Urizen himself is modeled on the God portrayed by the Elohist narrator of Genesis: "The remote, abstract, and prosaic style with which the Elohist creation is described is a direct indication of the nature of the Elohim and the kind of mind that perceives him," as Leslie Tannenbaum observes in *Biblical Tradition and Blake's Early Prophecies: The Great Code of Art* (Princeton, N.J.: Princeton University Press, 1982), 205.

39. For example, Bloom, *The Visionary Company,* 74. A noteworthy exception is W. J. T. Mitchell, who postulates that Blake here presents the reader with an opportunity to pity Urizen, just as Los will pity him later (*Blake's Composite Art: A Study of the Illuminated Poetry* [Princeton, N.J.: Princeton University Press, 1978], 133).

40. Mitchell, *Blake's Composite Art,* 129.

41. Nelson Hilton, "Blakean Zen," *Studies in Romanticism* 24 (1985): 183–200. John Sutherland puts this observation in a biographical context, suggesting that Blake saw himself and his own enterprise in the portrait of Urizen, not of Los, in "Blake and Urizen," in *Blake's Visionary Forms Dramatic,* ed. David V. Erdman and John E. Grant (Princeton, N.J.: Princeton University Press, 1970), 244–62.

42. Hilton, "Blakean Zen," 192–93.

43. Ibid., 185.

44. Ibid., 191.

45. Tannenbaum, *Biblical Tradition,* 208.

46. About pity Bloom writes, "Pity is founded on self-deception and is hindrance, not action. Blake's 'pity' is . . . an unimaginative abstraction masking as a human quality" (*The Visionary Company,* 77).

47. Tannenbaum, *Biblical Tradition,* 215.

48. Tannenbaum's exegesis of Urizen's tears as a Flood that creates the "Net of Religion" suggests a curious paradox, namely that the chaos of the Deluge was caused by a desire for too simple an order ("One Law"); ibid., 216–18.

49. My colleague Mark L. Reed observed this pun in "forgive."

50. Christopher Heppner, "The Woman Taken in Adultery: An Essay on Blake's 'Style of Designing,'" *Blake: An Illustrated Quarterly* 17, no. 2 (1983): 44–60.

51. William E. Phipps, "Blake on Joseph's Dilemma," *Theology Today* 28 (1971): 170–78.

52. This paradox is noted by P. M. S. Dawson, "Blake and Providence: The Theodicy of *The Four Zoas," Blake: An Illustrated Quarterly* 20, no. 4 (1987): 138.

53. Hannah Arendt, *The Human Condition* (Chicago: University of Chicago Press, 1958), 241.

54. Morton, *The Everlasting Gospel,* 37.

55. On *The Everlasting Gospel* see Frye, *Fearful Symmetry,* 78–84; David V. Erdman, "Terrible Blake in His Pride: An Essay on *The Everlasting Gospel,*" in *From Sensibility to Romanticism: Essays Presented to Frederick A. Pottle,* ed. Frederick W. Hilles and Harold Bloom (New York: Oxford University Press, 1965), 331–56; Hazard Adams, *William Blake: A Reading of the Shorter Poems* (Seattle: University of Washington Press, 1963), 180–200; Michael J. Tolley, "William Blake's Use of the Bible in a Section of *The Everlasting Gospel,*" *Notes and Queries* 207 (1962): 171–76; and Randel Helms, "The Genesis of *The Everlasting Gospel,*" *Blake Studies* 9, no. 1 (1980): 127. For a fuller discussion and notes, the reader may consult the present writer's article "Forgiveness, Love, and Pride in Blake's *The Everlasting Gospel,*" *Religion and Literature* 20, no. 2 (1988): 19–39.

56. Erdman, "Terrible Blake," 331.

57. If there ever was a complete version, it may have been burned by Frederick Tatham, a disciple of Blake during the poet's later years. Catherine Blake, the poet's

wife, lived with Tatham after Blake's death, and Tatham came into possession of the poet's effects after Catherine's death. By this time Tatham was a devout Irvingite and thought Blake inspired by Satan, particularly in his attacks on conventional religion and sexual morality (*BR*, 418). Anne Gilchrist, the wife of Blake's first biographer, referred to Tatham's fiery censorship as "the holocaust of Blake's manuscripts" (*BR,* 417).

58. Erdman, "Terrible Blake," 337. Erdman attributes the poem's contradictions to successive stages of opposed authorial intentions. In Erdman's view the discursive passages about forgiveness are rendered "obsolete and redundant" by the dramatic sections about Jesus' actions (335). This dramatic intention was replaced in its turn by a new didactic impulse as Blake wrote the longer section on humility. To Erdman the didactic impulse there triumphed over the dramatic to leave the work "in ruins" (350). Erdman contends that the work collapses in the longer section on humility. Randel Helms refines this point, locating the basic contradiction in Blake's failure to define *pride* with sufficient clarity ("Genesis," 154). This simple distinction between *didactic* and *dramatic,* however, obscures the connections between Blake's efforts to protest obligation-based morality and to define dispositional morality.

59. As Tolley notes ("Blake's Use of the Bible," 171–72).

60. Ibid., 173.

61. Erdman, "Terrible Blake," 350.

62. Rather than, as Erdman contends, a misplaced commentary on the section about Voltaire (Notebook, 48).

63. Aristotle, *Nicomachean Ethics,* trans. by David Ross, rev. J. O. Urmson (Oxford: Oxford University Press, 1984), 4.3.

64. Helms, "Genesis," 149.

65. Blake here echoes Swedenborg's doctrine of "The Maternal Humanity" that Jesus discarded—an echo noted by Paley ("New Heaven," 29): "Till he had naild it to the Cross / He took on Sin in the Virgins Womb / And put it off on the Cross & Tomb / To be Worshiped by the Church of Rome" (E, 524).

66. Crabb Robinson records this remark by Blake on the subject of Jesus' death: "He had just before . . . been speaking of the errors of Jesus Christ[:] he was wrong in suffering himself to be crucified[.] He should not have attacked the govt[;] he had no business in such matters" (*BR,* 311). Given Blake's lifelong support for protest and revolution, and his playfulness in provoking Crabb Robinson, it is just as likely that Blake approved as that he disapproved of Jesus' motives in allowing himself to be crucified. An honorific reading of the couplet, "For he acts with honest triumphant Pride / And this is the cause that Jesus died" (E, 519) is therefore arguable.

67. As Thomas J. J. Altizer does in, *The New Apocalypse: The Radical Christian Vision of William Blake* (East Lansing: Michigan State University Press, 1967), 147.

68. Bloom remarks that "sexual excess leads to antinomian perception," in *The Visionary Company,* 69.

Chapter 2. Error and Forgiveness

1. George Mills Harper, *The Neoplatonism of William Blake* (Chapel Hill: University of North Carolina Press, 1961).

2. Thomas Aquinas, *De Ente et Essentia,* (*Concerning being and essence*), trans. George G. Leckie (New York: D. Appleton-Century Co., 1937).

3. Normally one would question whether Blake "speaks straight" in the Proverbs of Hell. Here, one can assume he does, since he echoes a statement in his letter to Dr. Trusler, August 23, 1799: "The tree which moves some to tears of joy is in the Eyes of others only a Green thing that stands in the way" (E, 702).

4. William Godwin, *Enquiry Concerning Political Justice* (1798), ed. K. Codell Carter (Oxford: Clarendon Press, 1971), 58. For an account of Godwin's influence in his time, see Marilyn Gaull, *English Romanticism: The Human Context*, 131–35.

5. Godwin, *Enquiry Concerning Political Justice,* 52.

6. The distinction is Aurel Kolnai's: "Forgiveness," *Proceedings of the Aristotelian Society,* 1973–74, 91–106.

7. Leopold Damrosch, Jr., *Symbol and Truth in Blake's Myth* (Princeton, N.J.: Princeton University Press, 1980), 249.

8. David V. Erdman and Donald K. Moore, eds., *A Concordance to the Writings of William Blake,* 2 vols. (Ithaca, N.Y.: Cornell University Press, 1967), s.v. "error."

9. For fuller discussion and documentation, the reader may consult my article "The Problem of Forgiveness in Blake's Annotations to Lavater," *Studies in Philology* 86 (1989): 69–86. A facsimile edition of Lavater's *Aphorisms on Man,* with Blake's annotations, has been edited by R. J. Shroyer (Delmar, N.Y.: Scholars' Facsimiles and Reprints, 1980). Quotations from Lavater's *Aphorisms on Man* follow Shroyer's facsimile edition and will be cited parenthetically in the text, by the aphorism number.

10. The precise nature of Blake's religious commitments has been a matter of some debate. See Nancy Bogen, "The Problem of William Blake's Early Religion," *Personalist* 49 (1968): 509–22; David V. Erdman, "Blake's Early Swedenborgianism: A Twentieth-Century Legend," *Comparative Literature* 5 (1953): 247–57; and Morton D. Paley, "A New Heaven Is Begun: Blake and Swedenborgianism," in *Blake and Swedenborg: Opposition Is True Friendship*, ed. Harvey F. Bellin and Darrell Ruhl (New York: Swedenborg Foundation, 1985), reprinted in *Blake: An Illustrated Quarterly* 12, no. 2 (1979): 64–90. David V. Erdman characterizes Blake's commitments in the late 1780s as "humanitarian Christianity" (*Blake, Prophet Against Empire: A Poet's Interpretation of the History of His Own Times,* 3d ed. [Princeton, N.J.: Princeton University Press, 1977], 175). Moreover, Blake felt himself returning in 1802 to the artistic principles that had guides his art during his youth and that Blake felt himself to have abandoned for the previous twenty years. For Blake's reconversion, see Morton D. Paley, "The Truchsessian Gallery Revisited," *Studies in Romanticism* 16 (1977): 165–77.

11. Kolnai, "Forgiveness," 93.

12. Ibid., 93.

13. The rest of the aphorism reads: "The most inhuman man still remains man, and never CAN throw off all taste for what becomes a man—but you must learn to wait." Lavater thus depends on a relatively abstract notion, "man," as the basis of forgiveness.

14. For example, Jacob Boehme writes that in original sin man "has lost his angelic [cloak] and has been changed into a beast" in *The Way to Christ* (first translated 1648), trans. Peter Erb (New York: Paulist Press, 1978), 147.

15. Lavater does admit the possibility of gradation in Aphorisms 371, 418, and 289. These gradations, however, do not really penetrate Lavater's way of thinking.

16. Blake uses the word *regeneration* or its cognates seventeen times, according to the *Concordance.* All other occurrences are in *The Four Zoas, Milton,* and *Jerusalem.* The earliest date Erdman gives for any part of the composition of *The Four Zoas* is 1796 (E, 817), at least eight years after the annotations to Lavater. But since the word occurs in late additions to *The Four Zoas* rather than in the main draft, most likely Blake did not begin using the word again until at least 1802 (E, 834).

17. General studies of Boehme's influence on Blake include Kathleen Raine, *Blake and Tradition,* 2 vols. (Princeton, N.J.: Princeton University Press, 1962); Jacques Roos, *Aspects litteraire du mysticisme philosophique et l'influence de Boehme et de Swedenborg au début de Romantisme: William Blake, Novalis, Ballanche* (Strasbourg: P. H. Heitz, 1951); Desirée Hirst, *Hidden Riches: Traditional Symbolism from the Renaissance to Blake* (New York: Barnes and Noble, 1964) and Bryan Aubrey, *Watchmen of Eternity: Blake's Debt to Jacob Boehme* (New York: University Presses of America, 1986).

18. Lavater's distrust of fanaticism—a distrust he shared with Kant—shows in such aphorisms as these: "Humility and love, whatever obscurities may involve religious tenets, constitute the essence of true religion. The humble is formed to adore; the loving to associate with external love" (no. 69; Catherine Blake quoted this aphorism over thirty years after Blake annotated the *Aphorisms* [see *BR,* 288]); "I know deists, whose religiousness I venerate, and atheists, whose honesty and nobleness of mind I wish for" (no. 254); "The moral enthusiast, who in the maze of his refinements loses or despises the plain pathos of honesty and duty, is on the brink of crimes" (no. 640). See also Aphorisms 61, 292, 341, 366, 383.

19. G. E. Bentley, Jr., ed., *William Blake's "Vala; or, The Four Zoas": A Facsimile of the Manuscript, a Transcript of the Poem, and a Study of Its Growth and Significance* (Oxford: Clarendon Press, 1963), 188.

20. Bentley says that these lines are probably, but not definitely, later (ibid., 127).

21. Erdman, E, 817.

22. Damrosch, *Symbol and Truth,* 154.

23. Studies of *Vision of the Last Judgment* include Albert S. Roe, "A Drawing of the Last Judgment," in *The Visionary Hand: Essays for the Study of Blake's Art and Aesthetics,* ed. Robert N. Essick (Los Angeles: Hennessey and Ingalls, 1973), 201–32; W. J. T. Mitchell, "Blake's Visions of the Last Judgment" (Paper presented at the annual meeting of the Modern Language Association, December 28, 1975; published in *Blake*

Newsletter, Summer 1976); Irene H. Chayes, "Blake's Ways with Art Sources: Michelangelo's *The Last Judgment,*" *Colby Library Quarterly* 20 (1984): 60–89.

24. Aileen Ward, "'Sr Joshua and His Gang': William Blake and the Royal Academy," *Huntington Library Quarterly* 52 (1989): 83–84.

25. For a complete discussion of Blake's arguments with Reynolds, see Hazard Adams, "Revisiting Reynolds' *Discourses* and Blake's Annotations," in *Blake in His Time,* ed. Robert N. Essick and Donald Pearce (Bloomington: Indiana University Press, 1978), 133–34.

26. Ward, "Sr Joshua."

27. Ibid., 85.

28. Another example is: "The combats of Good & Evil <is Eating of the Tree of Knowledge The Combats of Truth & Error is Eating of the Tree of Life> [*& of Truth & Error which are the same thing*]" (E, 563). The combats of truth and error are like eating of the tree of life, because truth and error have both been given some kind of form in art.

29. Jerome J. McGann, "William Blake Illuminates the Truth," *Critical Studies* 1, no. 1 (1989): 56.

30. Ibid.

31. Milton's "errors" include his unenlightened view of women, his notion that human beings should wait for the culmination of history instead of bringing it about themselves, and his exaltation of a God of judgment. See, for the first two, Northrop Frye, *Fearful Symmetry: A Study of William Blake* (1947; reprint, Princeton, N.J.: Princeton University Press, 1969), 313–55; and for the second, Florence Sandler, "The Iconoclastic Enterprise: Blake's Critique of 'Milton's Religion,'" *Blake Studies* 5, no. 1 (1972): 13–58.

32. Frye observes that this is one of Blake's criticisms of Milton's vision of time in *Paradise Lost* (*Fearful Symmetry,* 338–39).

33. Erdman, *Prophet Against Empire,* 478.

Chapter 3. States and Individuals

1. Morton D. Paley, "The Figure of the Garment in *The Four Zoas, Milton,* and *Jerusalem,*" in *Blake's Sublime Allegory: Essays on "The Four Zoas," "Milton," and "Jerusalem,"* ed. Stuart Curran and Joseph Anthony Wittreich (Madison: University of Wisconsin Press, 1973), 123; Leopold Damrosch, Jr., *Symbol and Truth in Blake's Myth* (Princeton, N.J.: Princeton University Press, 1980), 166; Morris Eaves, *William Blake's Theory of Art* (Princeton, N.J.: Princeton University Press, 1982), 4.

2. Martin Heidegger, *Being and Time,* trans. John Macquarrie and Edward Robinson (London: SCM Press, 1962); Martin Buber, *I and Thou,* 2d ed., trans. Ronald Greger Smith (New York: Scribner's, 1958).

3. Elizabeth Grosz, *Sexual Subversions: Three French Feminists* (Sydney: Allen and Unwin, 1989), xvii.

4. For Levinas, see in particular *Ethics and Infinity* (Pittsburgh: Duquesne University Press, 1985); useful discussions of Levinas include Edith Wyschogrod, *Emmanuel Levinas: The Problem of Ethical Metaphysics* (The Hague: Martinus Nijhoff, 1974); and Andrius Valevičius, *From the Other to the Totally Other: The Religious Philosophy of Emmanuel Levinas* (New York: Peter Lang, 1988).

5. Jessica Benjamin, *The Bonds of Love: Feminism, Psychoanalysis, and the Problem of Domination* (New York: Pantheon Books, 1988), 20.

6. Margaret Whitford, Introduction to section 3 of *The Irigaray Reader,* by Luce Irigaray (Cambridge, Mass.: Basil Blackwell, 1991), 159. Irigaray's responses to Levinas include "Questions to Emmanuel Levinas" (*The Irigaray Reader,* 178–89) and "The Fecundity of the Caress," in *Face to Face with Levinas,* ed. Richard A. Cohen (Albany: State University of New York Press, 1986), 213–56.

7. Hannah Arendt, *The Origins of Totalitarianism* (New York: Harcourt and Brace, 1951), 458–59. For an account of Arendt's life and thought, see Elisabeth Young-Breuhl, *Hannah Arendt: For the Love of the World* (New Haven, Conn.: Yale University Press, 1982).

8. Hannah Arendt, *The Human Condition* (Chicago: University of Chicago Press, 1958), 7.

9. Ibid., 8.

10. Edward J. Rose, "Blake's Metaphorical States," *Blake Studies* 5, no. 1 (1972): 19.

11. Martin K. Nurmi, *Blake's "Marriage of Heaven and Hell": A Critical Study* (Kent, Ohio: Kent State University Press, 1957), 23. See also Stuart Crehan, *Blake in Context* (Atlantic Highlands, N.J.: Humanities Press, 1984).

12. Northrop Frye, "Notes for a Commentary on *Milton,*" in *The Divine Vision: Studies in the Poetry and Art of William Blake,* ed. Vivian de Sola Pinto (London: Victor Gollancz, 1957), 99–137.

13. Emanuel Swedenborg, *Heaven and Hell,* trans. George F. Dole (New York: Swedenborg Foundation, 1984), par. 155.

14. For discussions of Blake's doctrine of states and individuals, see Northrop Frye, *Fearful Symmetry: A Study of William Blake* (1947; reprint, Princeton, N.J.: Princeton University Press, 1969), 188–89, 333–37, 400; David V. Erdman, *Blake, Prophet Against Empire: A Poet's Interpretation of the History of His Own Times,* 3d ed. (Princeton, N.J.: Princeton University Press, 1977), 378, 401, 425–26, 436; S. Foster Damon, *A Blake Dictionary: The Ideas and Symbols of William Blake* (1965; reprint, Boulder, Colo.: Shambhala Press, 1979), s.v. "states"; and Susan Fox, *Poetic Form in Blake's "Milton"* (Princeton, N.J.: Princeton University Press, 1976), 23–24.

15. On Blake's "Public Address" and his picture of the Canterbury Pilgrims, see Karl Kiralis, "William Blake as an Intellectual and Spiritual Guide to Chaucer's *Canterbury Pilgrims,*" *Blake Studies* 1, no. 2 (1969): 139–77; Warren Stevenson, "Interpreting Blake's *Canterbury Pilgrims,*" *Colby Library Quarterly* 13 (1977): 115–26; and

Aileen Ward, "Canterbury Revisited: The Blake-Cromek Controversy," *Blake: An Illustrated Quarterly* 22, no. 3 (1988): 80–92.

16. On the relative priority of Blake's and Stothard's paintings, see Ward, "Canterbury Revisited."

17. Betsy Bowden, "The Artistic and Interpretive Context of Blake's *Canterbury Pilgrims," Blake: An Illustrated Quarterly* 13, no. 4 (1980): 165.

18. For a discussion of the textual history of this version, see E, 882.

19. Frye, "Notes," 106–7.

20. Hazard Adams, *Philosophy of the Literary Symbolic* (Tallahassee: Florida State University Press, 1983), 9, 104.

21. Bowden suggests that Blake's use of such approbative terms may sometimes be ironic ("Interpretive Context," 184).

22. Another example of *state* referring to an emotional condition is "Above Noah is the Church Universal represented by a Woman Surrounded by Infants *There is such a State in Eternity it is composed of the Innocent <civilized> Heathen & the Uncivilized Savage who having not the Law do by Nature the things containd in the Law*" (*VLJ;* E, 559; emphasis added).

23. W. J. T. Mitchell, "Blake's Visions of the Last Judgment" (Paper presented at the annual meeting of the Modern Language Association, December 28, 1975; published in *Blake Newsletter,* Summer 1976).

24. The literary evidence for Blake's return to Christianity exists in the long poem, probably ten years in the making, which he began as *Vala,* retitled as *The Four Zoas,* and never finished. "Before *Vala,*" G. E. Bentley, Jr., writes, "Blake seems to make a frontal attack on Christianity as a whole, as a force for evil which warps and restricts man's glorious free impulses. After 1800 he seems to have moved to the Christian camp, and to have concentrated his energies on exposing (and thereby destroying), not evil Christianity but the evil which had attached itself to Christianity" (*William Blake's "Vala"; or, The "Four Zoas": A Facsimile of the Manuscript, a Transcript of the Poem, and a Study of Its Growth and Significance* [Oxford: Clarendon Press, 1963], 188). Blake's enthusiasm for Christianity and forgiveness shows in such statements as "The Glory of Christianity is, To Conquer by Forgiveness" (*J* 52; E, 201).

25. Frye, *Fearful Symmetry,* 44.

26. Bentley, *Blake's "Vala,"* 189.

27. In *Narrative Unbound: Re-Visioning William Blake's "The Four Zoas"* (Barrytown, N.Y.: Station Hill Press, 1987), Donald Ault examines the radical heterogeneity of *The Four Zoas*, questioning the paradigms of coherence in Blake scholarship. In particular he challenges the practice of cross-referencing Blake's poems to minimize differences among them (xvi). In my analysis of states here and of the Spectre of Urthona in chapter 4, I have attempted to respect differences among Blake's treatments of these motifs in various contexts, while still assuming that Blake's use of the same word or name in various texts permits the critic to construe connections (though not identity) among their occurrences.

28. This passage is written over an erasure, but Erdman thinks Blake erased a previous error in copying; it is not an interpolation (E, 835).

29. This is the very last line on the page (89 of the MS) and, as Bentley notes, may be interpolated only in the sense that Blake wrote it in a sharper pen in order to fit it into the small space (*Blake's "Vala,"* 90).

30. Erdman notes that lines 11–16 are written over erasures (E, 819); Bentley, that these particular lines were written into a stanza break (*Blake's "Vala,"* 3).

31. Erdman notes that this was written over an erased "End of the First Night" (E, 826). Bentley notes the difference in Blake's handwriting; this is the modified copperplate hand he used for revisions (*Blake's "Vala,"* 19).

32. H. M. Margoliouth, ed., *William Blake's "Vala": Blake's Numbered Text* (Oxford: Clarendon Press, 1956), xiii, xxiv; Erdman, *Prophet Against Empire* 395–403; Andrew Lincoln, "The Revision of the Seventh and Eighth Nights of *The Four Zoas,*" *Blake: An Illustrated Quarterly* 18, no. 4 (1978): 115–33.

33. Paul Mann presents the argument that "manuscript" is the only appropriate name for *The Four Zoas* in "The Final State of *The Four Zoas,*" *Blake: An Illustrated Quarterly* 18, no. 4 (1985): 204–15.

34. Erdman, *Prophet Against Empire,* 397.

35. Gerald Newman, *The Rise of English Nationalism: A Cultural History 1740–1830* (New York: St. Martin's Press, 1983), 231–32.

36. Erdman, *Prophet Against Empire,* 400–401.

37. Ibid., 399; John Sutherland, "Blake and Urizen," in *Blake's Visionary Forms Dramatic,* ed. David V. Erdman and John E. Grant (Princeton, N.J.: Princeton University Press, 1970), 255.

38. Erdman and Bentley both notice that this line and the ones around it were written over erased and revised lines (E, 829; Bentley, *Blake's "Vala,"* 33). The page is reproduced in Cettina Tramantano Magno and David V. Erdman, eds., *"The Four Zoas" by William Blake: A Photographic Facsimile of the Manuscript with Commentary on the Illustrations* (Cranbury, N.J.: Associated University Presses, 1987), 147.

39. W. J. T. Mitchell, *Blake's Composite Art: A Study of the Illuminated Poetry* (Princeton, N.J.: Princeton University Press, 1978), 175. Mitchell uses Northrop Frye's description of the anatomy from *Anatomy of Criticism: Four Essays* (Princeton, N.J.: Princeton University Press, 1957), 309–10.

40. Bentley and Erdman both note that lines 11–19 were written in sideways on the left margin of p. 105, and that Blake later added lines 20–27 about the synagogue of Satan (E, 842; Bentley, *Blake's "Vala,"* 110–11).

41. Bentley, *Blake's "Vala,"* 122. The page is reproduced in Magno and Erdman, eds., *Four Zoas,* 221.

42. The reconstructed sequence of the pages of *The Four Zoas* suggests that individuality is associated with Jesus. Magno and Erdman discuss their reasons for resequencing these pages and comment on the sequence of illustrations of Christ on the pages preceding and following this one, as well as on this page's illustration: "The

grand *discovery* of these pages, the text makes known, is the potential identity of Los and Christ; and it is expressed by Christ's discovery of himself to others, of his willingness to die" (*"Four Zoas,"* 82; original emphasis).

43. Frye, *Fearful Symmetry,* 303.

44. Frye assumed that *The Four Zoas* was written first and later quarried for *Milton* and *Jerusalem* (*Fearful Symmetry,* 315). Bentley contends that "the traffic went both ways" (*Blake's "Vala,"* 165). While it is not easy to establish the priority of one version, it seems that Night the Eighth presents a simpler version of events that Blake later elaborated.

45. My commentary here is limited to the text of the Bard's Song. The ambiguity between intersubjective and intrapsychic pervades the illustrations too. For example, about plate 10 of *Milton* (a full-page illustration) Mitchell writes: "It is important to note that the three figures in plate 10 . . . are three distinct types (the 'Three Classes of Men') and also three aspects of one man (Reason, Pity, and Wrath)" ("Style and Iconography in the Illustrations of Blake's *Milton,*" *Blake Studies* 6, no. 1 [1973]: 65).

46. W. J. T. Mitchell, "Blake's Radical Comedy," in *Blake's Sublime Allegory,* ed. Curran and Wittreich, 290. Mitchell sees this temporal flexibility as one of Blake's chief virtues in the poem.

47. Frye, *Fearful Symmetry,* 376.

48. For example, Leonard Deen writes: "In *Paradise Lost,* the judgment falls on a Satan who in Milton's view is guilty and must be punished, but who in Blake's view is guilty and therefore cannot stand punishment. To act wrongly is [already] to suffer. . . . Now to suffer not only the original wrong but also its consequences, to be made responsible for the infinite ramifications of that wrong, is to suffer an infinitely multiplied loss. In Blake's eyes, then, the judgment in *Paradise Lost* is vengeance, and the vengeful justice Satan suffers makes him in turn an accuser and a seeker of vengeance" (*Conversing in Paradise: Poetic Genius and Identity-as-Community in Blake's Los* [Columbia: University of Missouri Press, 1983], 171).

49. Mitchell, "Style and Iconography," 66.

50. For a suggestive discussion of Blake's two- and three-part systems, see Mary Lynn Johnson, "'Separating What Has Been Mixed': A Suggestion for a Perspective on *Milton,*" *Blake Studies* 6, no. 1 (1973): 11–18.

51. Fox, *Poetic Form,* 140–41.

52. About the creation of Milton as the state of self-annihilation, John Middleton Murry writes: "This is, manifestly, a paradox. This State is not a State, in the former sense, at all. It is called a State only because it is a universal condition: the progress towards Self-annihilation. But there is, in fact, no progress towards Self-annihilation. . . . In regard to the pure Imaginative existence of the Identity, it is a State; in regard to selfhood, it is not a state" (*William Blake* [1933; reprint, New York: McGraw-Hill, 1964], 246).

53. Bloom comments on this passage: "The Seven Eyes, which are both historical cycles and stages within individual life, are not Individuals but Combinations thereof,

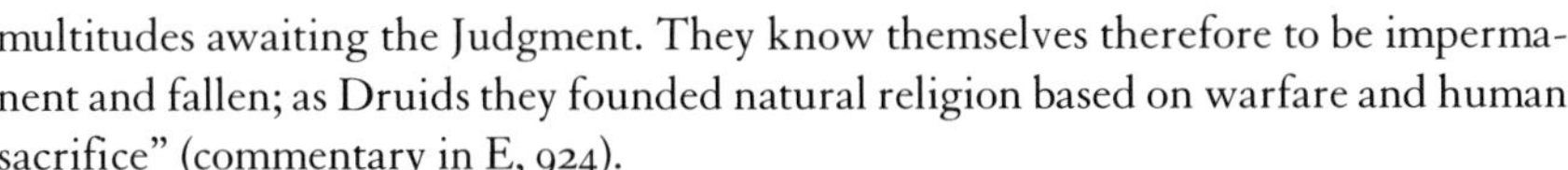

multitudes awaiting the Judgment. They know themselves therefore to be impermanent and fallen; as Druids they founded natural religion based on warfare and human sacrifice" (commentary in E, 924).

54. David V. Erdman, "The Suppressed and Altered Passages in Blake's *Jerusalem,*" *Studies in Bibliography* 17 (1964): 6–7.

55. Karl Kiralis, "The Theme and Structure of William Blake's *Jerusalem,*" *ELH* 23 (1956); reprinted in *The Divine Vision,* ed. Pinto, 148.

56. A summary of the disagreement is provided by Anne K. Mellor, "Blake's Portrayal of Women," *Blake: An Illustrated Quarterly* 16, no. 3 (1982–83):131–32.

57. Mitchell, *Blake's Composite Art,* 214.

58. An analysis of Albion's conversion in chapter 4 is provided by James Ferguson, "Prefaces to *Jerusalem,*" in *Interpreting Blake,* ed. Michael Phillips (London: Cambridge University Press, 1978), 185–93.

Chapter 4. Alterity and the Spectre of Urthona

1. Important feminist discussions of Blake include Alicia Ostriker, "Desire Gratified and Ungratified: William Blake and Sexuality," *Blake: An Illustrated Quarterly* 16, no. 3 (1982–83): 156–65; and Anne K. Mellor, "Blake's Portrayal of Women," *Blake: An Illustrated Quarterly* 16, no. 3 (1982–83): 148–55. An important discussion of Blake's tendency to emphasize male friendship and male homoeroticism in the late works is W. J. T. Mitchell, "Style and Iconography in the Illustrations of Blake's *Milton,*" *Blake Studies* 6, no. 1 (1973): 47–72.

2. Elizabeth Grosz, *Sexual Subversions: Three French Feminists* (Sydney: Allen and Unwin, 1989), 142.

3. Luce Irigaray, "Questions to Emmanuel Levinas," in *The Irigaray Reader,* ed. Margaret Whitford (Cambridge, Mass: Basil Blackwell, 1991), 181.

4. Northrop Frye, *Fearful Symmetry: A Study of William Blake* (1947; reprint, (Princeton, N.J.: Princeton University Press, 1969), 298.

5. Bentley approaches the shift in Blake's thought from a slightly different perspective as a shift from the mythology of the Zoas and their unity in the One Man Albion to the mythology of Los, Enitharmon, and the Spectre as members of the One Man Urthona. As Blake rewrote *Vala* as *The Four Zoas,* his cast of characters changed. "In Vala the central figure in Eternity is the Man . . . [but in] *The Four Zoas* [Los] seems to command more and more of Blake's sympathy and interest, until it almost seems as if he were the essence of The Man, and the Zoas, at least in Eternity, his subordinates" (Bentley, *Blake's "Vala,"* 189–90).

6. For example: Frye calls the Spectre of Urthona "clock time," that part of our existence that gets by in the world. He goes on to say, "The Spectre of Urthona is the isolated subjective aspect of existence in this world, the energy with which a man or any other living thing copes with nature. It is neither the selfhood, which is Satan, nor the

'vegetable' existence, which is Luvah; it is that aspect of existence in time which is linear rather than organic or imaginative" (*Fearful Symmetry,* 292); Paley calls him "Los's workaday self" in *The Continuing City: William Blake's "Jerusalem"* (Oxford: Clarendon Press, 1983), 244.

7. Geoffrey Keynes, "Blake's Spectre," *Book Collector* 28 (1979): 62.

8. Susan Fox, *Poetic Form in Blake's "Milton"* (Princeton, N.J.: Princeton University Press, 1976), 4.

9. Keynes, "Blake's Spectre," 60–62.

10. Fox, *Poetic Form,* 4.

11. For the date of "My Spectre," see David V. Erdman and Donald K. Moore, eds., *The Notebook of William Blake: A Photographic and Typographic Facsimile* (Oxford: Clarendon Press, 1973), 55. Blake produced fair copies of several other poems in the Pickering Manuscript.

12. Leopold Damrosch, Jr., interprets this couplet as expressing Blake's weariness of the demands of spousal affection (*Symbol and Truth in Blake's Myth* [Princeton, N.J.: Princeton University Press, 1980], 211).

13. In the MS Blake left two Nights entitled "Night the Seventh," traditionally referred to as VIIa and VIIb by Blake scholars. Frye and many others assumed that Blake wrote VIIa to replace VIIb, despite the evidence of stitchmarks that VIIb was written later. In the 1982 Erdman edition the two Nights have been spliced together. Erdman summarizes the textual debate in his notes (E, 836). The reader may consult *Blake: An Illustrated Quarterly* 12, no. 2 (1978) for further details. My analysis is almost entirely restricted to portions of VIIa.

14. Wayne Glausser, "The Gates of Memory in Night VIIa of *The Four Zoas,*" *Blake: An Illustrated Quarterly* 18, no. 4 (1985): 196–203. I rely on Glausser's article throughout this paragraph.

15. Hannah Arendt, *The Human Condition* (Chicago: University of Chicago Press, 1958), 237.

16. Glausser, "Gates of Memory," 201.

17. Brian Wilkie and Mary Lynn Johnson, *Blake's "Four Zoas": The Design of a Dream* (Cambridge, Mass.: Harvard University Press, 1978), 159–60.

18. Arendt, *The Human Condition,* 241.

19. John Sutherland, "Blake and Urizen," in *Blake's Visionary Forms Dramatic,* ed. David V. Erdman and John E. Grant (Princeton, N.J.: Princeton University Press, 1970), 251. I rely on Sutherland's analysis throughout this paragraph.

20. Arendt, *The Human Condition,* 237.

21. Morton D. Paley, *Energy and the Imagination: A Study of the Development of Blake's Thought* (Oxford: Clarendon Press, 1973), 252.

22. For analyses of Blake's treatment of the emanation and its relative equality with the Spectre, see Irene Tayler, "The Woman Scaly," *Bulletin of the Midwest Modern Language Association* 6 (1973): 74–87; Margaret Storch, "Blake and Women: Nature's Cruel Holiness," *American Imago* 38 (1981): 221–46; Susan Fox, "The Female as

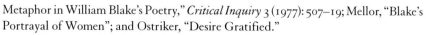

Metaphor in William Blake's Poetry," *Critical Inquiry* 3 (1977): 507–19; Mellor, "Blake's Portrayal of Women"; and Ostriker, "Desire Gratified."

23. Paley notes that the Spectre appears in each chapter of *Jerusalem*: in chapter 1, 6:1–11:7; in chapter 2, 33:1–11; in chapter 3, 74:1–13; in chapter 4, 91:3–58 (*Energy and the Imagination,* 252). However, the appearances in chapters 2 and 3 are not specifically the Spectre of Urthona and do not have the dramatic power of the encounters between Los and the Spectre of Urthona in chapters 1 and 4.

24. Thomas R. Frosch contends that Blake used forgiveness in *Jerusalem* much as he had in the early works, to reveal the hypocrisy of restrictions on sexuality, rather than, as I argue, to resolve a new set of issues about otherness. See Thomas R. Frosch, *The Awakening of Albion: The Renovation of the Body in the Poetry of William Blake* (Ithaca, N.Y.: Cornell University Press, 1974), 88–93.

25. See Janet Warner, "Blake's Figures of Despair: Man in His Spectre's Power," in *William Blake,* ed. Morton D. Paley and Michael Phillips (Oxford: Clarendon Press, 1973), 208–24.

26. David V. Erdman identifies the small "fairy" as Blake (*The Illuminated Blake* [Garden City, N.Y.: Doubleday, Anchor Books, 1974], 316).

27. The photographic reproduction in Erdman's edition of the Notebook reveals the revisions and second thoughts. This quatrain appears on page 8 of the Notebook. Blake revised the poem in the Notebook to read: "Each Man is in his Spectre's power / Untill the arrival of that hour, / When his Humanity awake / And cast his own Spectre into the Lake" (E, 810).

28. Morton D. Paley, "Cowper as Blake's Spectre," *Eighteenth-Century Studies* 1 (1968): 236–52. See also Paley, *The Continuing City,* 244–50.

29. Erdman, *The Illuminated Blake,* 372.

30. In *Milton* Blake twice compares Satan to a ruined building. In the Bard's Song, when Los and Enitharmon recognize Satan as Urizen, they also see him as a building: "The paved terraces of / His bosom inwards shone with fires, but the stones becoming opake! / Hid him from sight" (*M* 9:31–33; E, 103). Blake here reverses Milton's account of the building of Pandemonium in book 1 of *Paradise Lost.* Blake also likens Satan to a building at the close of the poem in the confrontation between Milton and Satan. The narrator speaks: "I also stood in Satans bosom & beheld its desolation! / A ruind Man: a ruind building of God not made with hands" (*M* 43:15–16; E, 139).

31. Peter Butter noted some inconsistency in the significance of Satan in *Milton* in "*Milton:* The Final Plates," in *Interpreting Blake,* ed. Michael Phillips (London: Cambridge University Press, 1978), 148–50.

32. Fox, *Poetic Form,* 162.

Chapter 5. Forgiveness in "The House of the Interpreter"

1. Standard discussions of typology include the *Jerome Biblical Commentary,* sec. 71; Jean Danielou, S.J., *From Shadows to Reality: Studies in the Biblical Typology of the*

Fathers, trans. Dom Walstan Hibberd (London: Burns and Oates, 1960); Thomas M. Davis, "The Traditions of Puritan Typology," in *Typology and Early American Literature,* ed. Sacvan Bercovitch (Amherst: University of Massachusetts Press, 1972), 11–45; Beryl Smalley, *The Study of the Bible in the Middle Ages* (Oxford: Clarendon Press, 1941); Paul Korshin, "The Development of Abstracted Typology in England, 1650–1820," in *The Literary Uses of Typology from the Late Middle Ages to the Present,* ed. Earl Miner (Princeton, N.J.: Princeton University Press, 1977), 147–203; Northrop Frye, *The Great Code: The Bible and Literature* (New York: Harcourt, 1982); and Erich Auerbach, "Figura," in *Scenes from the Drama of European Literature,* trans. Ralph Mannheim (New York: Meridian Books, 1959).

2. The evidence for two other points of contact between Blake and Byron remains sketchy. Blake illustrated a work called *The Seaman's Recorder,* which contains a picture entitled "Lord Byron in a Storm" and an account of Byron as a conventionally religious person—hardly one that would have inspired Blake to call Byron an "Elijah in the wilderness." For the evidence, see G. E. Bentley, Jr., "Byron, Shelley, Wordsworth, Blake, and *The Seaman's Recorder,*" *Studies in Romanticism* 9 (1980): 21–36. Also, Blake may have met Byron in 1818 at a party given by Lady Caroline Lamb, though there is no account of a conversation between them (*BR,* 248–50).

3. The text was readily available. Murray printed six thousand copies of the volume containing *Cain.* At least five pirated editions were published in London during 1822, including one published by Richard Carlile in nearby Fleet Street. Many reviewers quote the play liberally, including one-fifth to one-third of the total play. For the facts of publication and reviewing, see Truman Guy Steffan, *Lord Byron's "Cain": Twelve Essays and a Text with Variants and Annotations* (Austin: University of Texas Press, 1968), 3–25, 330–426; for Robinson's reading of *Cain,* see 310.

4. Byron, *Cain,* in *Poetical Works,* ed. Frederick Page, corrected by John Jump, 3d ed. (New York: Oxford University Press, 1970), 521.

5. E. E. Bostetter, "Byron and the Politics of Paradise," *PMLA* 75 (1960): 573.

6. Despite the fact that the author of the biblical Letter of Jude considered it canonical, the Book of Enoch lost its popularity in Judaism as the rabbis became disillusioned with apocalyptic literature. The destruction of the temple in A.D. 70 hastened their disillusionment (*Jerome Biblical Commentary*, s.v. "Apocryphal Old Testament"). For the story of its recovery, see the introductory essay to the Book of Enoch by H. F. D. Sparks in his edition of *The Apocryphal Old Testament* (Oxford: Clarendon Press, 1984), 170. Blake's illustrations to Enoch suggest that Blake tried to replace vengeance with forgiveness in that work as well, as noted by Allan R. Brown, "Blake's Drawings for The Book of Enoch," in *The Visionary Hand: Essays for the Study of Blake's Art and Aesthetics*, ed. Robert N. Essick (Los Angeles: Hennessey and Ingalls, 1973), 112. For discussion of the translation Blake read, see Peter Alan Taylor, "Blake's Text for the Enoch Drawings," *Blake Newsletter* 7, no. 4 (1974): 82–86. The quotation is from Enoch, in *The Apocryphal Old Testament*, ed. Sparks, 211.

7. Geoffrey Keynes, "Blake's Spectre," *Book Collector* 28 (1979): 62.

8. Byron, *Cain,* 543. Byron sent these last three lines to John Murray, after the manuscript had been sent, as "clinchers," according to Steffan, *"Cain,"* 251.

9. Byron, *Cain,* 544.

10. The opinion that Blake approves of Byron is shared by S. Foster Damon, *A Blake Dictionary: The Ideas and Symbols of William Blake* (1965; reprint, Boulder, Colo.: Shambhala Press, 1979), s.v. "Byron"; Northrop Frye, *Fearful Symmetry: A Study of William Blake* (1947; reprint, Princeton, N.J.: Princeton University Press, 1969), 199; Martin Bidney, "*Cain* and *The Ghost of Abel:* Contexts for Understanding Blake's Response to Byron," *Blake Studies* 8, no. 2 (1979): 161–65; Thomas Reisner, "*Cain:* Two Romantic Interpretations," *Culture* 31 (1970): 141; and Irene Tayler, "Blake Meets Byron on April Fool's," *English Language Notes* 16 (1978): 92. Tayler notes that Blake's colophon, "Wm Blake's Original Stereotype was 1788," may serve to remind the reader of Blake's activity during the year of Byron's birth (93). Tayler further points out the parallel between Elijah's despair—"he requested for himself that he might die" (1 Kings 19)—and the despair of Cain, which Blake attributed to Byron as well (90–91). Leslie Tannenbaum suggests that Byron, like Elijah, attacked the practice of nature worship, in "Lord Byron in the Wilderness: Biblical Tradition in Byron's *Cain* and Blake's *The Ghost of Abel,*" *Modern Philology* 72 (1975): 351. Edward Larissy usefully provides some historical background for Blake's curious division between "Jehovah Elohim" and "the Elohim of the Heathen" in "Blake and the Hutchinsonians," *Blake: An Illustrated Quarterly* 20, no. 2 (1986): 44–47.

11. David V. Erdman, *The Illuminated Blake* (Garden City, N.Y.: Doubleday, Anchor Books, 1974), 381; Tannenbaum, "Lord Byron," 356.

12. Erdman notes a textual problem here: the design suggests deletion signs for three of the *f*s to read "Life for Lie! Lie for Life" (E, 813); *The Illuminated Blake,* 381–82. Steffan notes the thematic parallel between Byron's Eve and Blake's Abel (*Cain*, 323).

13. Tannenbaum assumes that the figure is male, either Adam or Cain, and concludes that the "willingness to believe the figure is Cain will reveal the reader's willingness to accept Cain's repentance." Tannenbaum's commentary on the smaller illustrations in *The Ghost of Abel* shows their relation to the critique of divine justice in *Cain* in "Blake and the Iconography of *Cain,*" in *Blake in His Time,* ed. Robert N. Essick and Donald Pearce (Bloomington: Indiana University Press, 1978), 29–30. Erdman takes his drawing, at the poem's conclusion, as Eve exemplifying "Brotherhood & Love" and thus triumphing over the vengeance advocated by the Ghost (*The Illuminated Blake,* 383). Such a reading neglects the fact that, by the conclusion of the poem, Eve has found consolation in the Vision of Jehovah, in which Abel is still living.

14. The sketch itself shows Christ, not Jehovah, setting the mark on Cain by kissing him on the forehead. The iconography recalls the story of the Prodigal Son (Tannenbaum, "Iconography," 31). For an analysis of other parts of Blake's Genesis manuscript, see Piloo Nanavutty, "A Title Page in Blake's Illustrated Genesis Manuscript," in *The Visionary Hand,* ed. Essick, 127–46.

15. Tannenbaum, "Iconography," 26–27.

16. Two useful introductions to the textual and theological issues in Job are Marvin H. Pope, ed. and trans., *Job,* vol. 15 of the Anchor Bible, 3d ed. (Garden City, N.Y.: Doubleday, 1973); and *The Jerome Biblical Commentary,* ed. Raymond E. Brown, S.S.; Joseph A. Fitzmyer, S.J.; and Roland E. Murphy, O.Carm. (Englewood Cliffs, N.J.: Prentice-Hall, 1968), s.v. "Job." For Blake's knowledge of the higher criticism, see Leslie Tannenbaum, *Biblical Tradition and Blake's Early Prophecies: The Great Code of Art* (Princeton, N.J.: Princeton University Press, 1982), 8–24; and Jerome J. McGann, "The Idea of an Indeterminate Text: Blake's Bible of Hell and Dr. Alexander Geddes," *Studies in Romanticism* 25 (1986): 303–24.

17. Several motifs indicate Job's progress. Sir Geoffrey Keynes noticed that the sun sets as Job's captivity begins, and it rises with his change of heart (*Blake Studies: Notes on His Life and Works in Seventeen Chapters* [London: Rupert Hart-Davis], 148). As Joseph Wicksteed noted (in *Blake's Vision of the Book of Job* [New York: Dutton, 1910]), Job favors the left side in the early illustrations, a tendency common to all the characters Blake considers misguided. In the later plates, Job favors the right side. Wicksteed also noted a change in Job's image of God. At first, Job's God resembles Job himself, the righteous man resembling the rewarder of righteousness. But when Job suffers, Job's false God is revealed as Satan, an interpretation shared by Frye ("Blake's Reading of the Book of Job" in *William Blake: Essays for S. Foster Damon,* ed. Alvin H. Rosenfeld (Providence, R.I.: Brown University Press, 1969), 227. More recently, Diane Filby Gillespie has questioned Damon's assumption that Job progresses only once in his life; she sees, instead, an eternal cycle of error and vision (in "A Key to Blake's Job: Design XX," *Colby Library Quarterly* 19 [1983]: 59–68). And Damon's insistence that Job's pride must be humbled (in his *Blake's Job: William Blake's Illustrations of the Book of Job* [Hanover, N.H.: University Presses of New England for Brown University Press, 1966]) has been contested by Jenijoy LaBelle, who claims that Job's initial condition is not so much wickedness as naive self-righteousness (in "Words Graven with an Iron Pen: The Marginal Texts in Blake's *Job,*" in *The Visionary Hand,* ed. Essick, 538.

18. Bo Lindberg, *William Blake's Illustrations to the Book of Job* (Åbo, Finland: Åbo Akademi, 1973), figs. 113, 115, 119. Blake may have seen the medieval illustrations that relied on this typological reading; it is possible that Blake also knew patristic writing on the subject, which declares the companions to be hypocrites. Saint Gregory the Great denounced them as hypocrites (quoted in Lindberg, *Blake's Illustrations,* 244).

19. Blake probably knew the work of Alexander Geddes, who was Joseph Johnson's reviewer for books of biblical criticism from 1788 to 1793 (McGann, "Indeterminate Text," 309–11). Moreover, Blake may well have known Lowth's lectures on the Book of Job, even though they were originally written in Latin. They appeared in English translation in *The Christian Magazine* in 1767 and were summarized in Hugh Blair's *Lectures on Rhetoric and Belles Lettres* in 1783 (Tannenbaum, *Biblical Tradition,* 10–11). Moreover, Johnson published the two-volume English translation in 1787.

20. Robert Lowth, *De Sacra Poesi Hebraeorum,* trans. G. Gregory (1787; reprint, Hildesheim: Georg Olms, 1969), 2:372.

21. Ibid., 2:383, 372.

22. Frye, "Blake's Reading," 222; Lindberg, *Blake's Illustrations,* 241–43. Lindberg notes several other contemporary sources as well (241–42).

23. Keynes notes the resemblance of this design to "Elohim Creating Adam" (*Blake Studies,* 124).

24. Such a principle of simultaneity is familiar in Blake's prophecies; the principle has been articulated by Frye, *Fearful Symmetry,* 332, and by Susan Fox, *Poetic Form in Blake's "Milton"* (Princeton, N.J.: Princeton University Press, 1976), 6.

25. Andrew Wright, *Blake's Job: A Commentary* (Oxford: Clarendon Press, 1972), 41.

26. LaBelle, "Words Graven," 529; Ben F. Nelms, "Text and Design in *Illustrations of the Book of Job,*" in *Blake's Visionary Forms Dramatic,* ed. David V. Erdman and John E. Grant (Princeton, N.J.: Princeton University Press, 1970), 340–41.

27. Wicksteed, *Blake's Vision,* 122. Wicksteed speculates on the connection between a reversed Job and Blake's professional necessity of reversed writing.

28. Ibid., 121; Wright, *Blake's Job,* 41.

29. As Lindberg notes, *Blake's Illustrations,* 326.

30. Ibid., 331.

31. Ibid.

32. The plan was partly the idea of John Linnell, who had encouraged Blake by supporting him during his work on the Job illustrations and by buying them afterward. Linnell's plan was to continue supporting Blake by means of the Dante project.

33. Albert S. Roe (*Blake's Illustrations to the "Divine Comedy"* [Princeton, N.J.: Princeton University Press, 1953]), whose work on Blake's illustrations to Dante remains standard, also mentions that Blake thought Dante served the destructive Female Will, shown, for example, in Blake's illustration 91, "Beatrice addressing Dante from the Car" and in illustration 102, "The Queen of Heaven in Glory." As Milton Klonsky rightly observes, Blake thinks Dante has confused states and individuals in those states, "damning [individuals] for all eternity without hope of pardon or redemption" (*Blake's Dante: The Complete Illustrations to the "Divine Comedy"* [New York: Harmony Books, 1980], 11). Recently David Fuller has criticized Roe's method as too baldly allegorical, as reading Blake's own ideas into the Dante illustrations without regarding their common biblical sources (in "Blake and Dante," *Art History* 11 (1988): 349–73.

34. At the time Blake read Boyd, there was no English translation of the complete *Comedy*; Boyd's own complete translation of it appeared in 1802. The volume Blake read was Henry Boyd, *A translation of the "Inferno" of Dante Alighieri, in English verse with Historical Notes, and the Life of Dante, to which is added a specimen of a New Translation of the "Orlando Furioso" of Ariosto,* 2 vols. (Dublin: P. Byrne, 1785). For an assessment of Boyd, see C. P. Brand, *Italy and the English Romantics: The Italianate Fashion in Early Nineteenth-Century Britain* (New York: Cambridge University Press, 1957), 49; and William De Sua, *Dante into English* (Chapel Hill: University of North Carolina Press, 1964), 12, 23.

35. Boyd, *Translation of the "Inferno,"* 1:89, 105, 111, 122.

36. This incident is reported in Boyd, *Translation of the "Inferno,"* 1:117; Blake wrote, on the next page, a remark beginning "Dante was a Fool" (E, 634).

37. Brand, *Italy,* 180.

38. Mario Praz, *The Romantic Agony,* 2d ed. (New York: Oxford University Press, 1970), 69, 328.

39. Quoted in Brand, *Italy,* 189–90.

40. Ibid., 190.

41. Ibid., x.

42. Boyd, *Translation of the "Inferno,"* 2:377.

43. Ibid., 2:400.

44. In fact, Boyd himself seems to have been a particularly vengeful person. In commenting on the Trojan War, for example, Boyd writes, "It is a contest between barbarians, equally guilty of injustice, rapine, and bloodshed; and we are not sorry to see the vengeance of Heaven equally inflicted on both parties" (E, 633). For Boyd, the fact that the Greeks and Trojans are "criminals," that is, guilty of any crime, justifies any suffering inflicted on them as the just vengeance of heaven. Such lack of compassion for those labeled as criminals would logically underwrite harsh civil repression.

45. Boyd, *Translation of the "Inferno,"* 2:398–99.

46. Ibid., 2:382–83.

47. Thomas Aquinas, *Theological Texts,* ed. and trans. Thomas Gilby (Durham: Labyrinth Press, 1982), 118–19. Dante's sense of the fixity of the human soul in the state in which it died is a recurrent motif in the *Comedy;* witness, for example, the single lapse of Paolo and Francesca, which was followed immediately by their deaths. Witness also Buonconte of *Purgatory* 5, whose eternal salvation is assured only because he died with the first syllable of Mary's name on his lips. By contrast, Blake's attitude toward an afterlife is one that includes the possibility of growth and change. For example, Blake protests Emanuel Swedenborg's doctrine of posthumous fixity. When Swedenborg writes, "He who is in Evil in the World, the same is in Evil after he goes out of the World; . . . it cannot be removed afterwards," Blake responds, "Cursed Folly!" (E, 610). In making the assumption that Blake takes the division between life and death seriously, I depart from Roe's approach, which has influenced later discussions of the Dante illustrations. Klonsky and Butlin follow Roe in assuming that Blake equates the posthumous Inferno invented by Dante with the created material world in which we live before our deaths. Roe, *Blake's Illustrations,* 54 et passim; Klonsky, *Blake's Dante,* 11 et passim; and Martin Butlin, *The Paintings and Drawings of William Blake,* 2 vols. (New Haven, Conn.: Yale University Press, 1981), 2:554. Therefore, Roe and the others assume that Blake disregards the posthumous nature of Dante's *Inferno,* merely likening individual inhabitants of the *Inferno* to miscellaneous concepts articulated in Blake's own works, for example, comparing Filippo Argenti to the Spectre cast in the lake. My assumption is that Blake made a systematic critique of Dante by taking

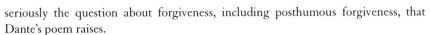

seriously the question about forgiveness, including posthumous forgiveness, that Dante's poem raises.

48. Roe, *Blake's Illustrations,* 50.

49. Klonsky, *Blake's Dante,* 137; Roe, *Blake's Illustrations,* 49.

50. Fuller, "Blake and Dante," 353.

51. Klonsky, *Blake's Dante,* 137.

52. Blake originally wrote that this God had a throne in Paradise, too, but he erased that word (Butlin, *Paintings,* 812.3).

53. The inverted triangle formed by the three suns echoes plate 76 of *Jerusalem,* "Albion Adoring Christ," where Christ is crucified on an Oak of Suffering in an inverted triangle. See Roe, *Blake's Illustrations,* 175.

54. All quotations from Dante follow the translation of Henry Francis Cary, *The Vision; or Hell, Purgatory, and Paradise of Dante Alighieri* (New York: American News, 1814). Blake used the Cary translation while working on the Dante illustrations because he thought it was the best one available (*BR,* 475). For an assessment of eighteenth- and nineteenth-century translations of Dante, see De Sua, *Dante into English,* 1–50. For information about Blake's friendship with Cary, see Keynes, *Blake Studies,* 101–2.

55. Klonsky criticizes the Christ here depicted: "Christ stares straight before him, almost without expression, as if not deigning to become aware of [Dante's] presence" (*Blake's Dante,* 160). But this Jesus looks at the reader, not at Dante, in order to enact the spread of mutual forgiveness which Dante has failed to do.

56. Morton D. Paley, *The Continuing City: William Blake's "Jerusalem"* (Oxford: Clarendon Press, 1983), 226.

57. Klonsky identifies it as a circle, not as a sun, despite the rays (*Blake's Dante,* 139); Roe identifies it as the sun but does not remark on it (*Blake's Illustrations,* 64).

58. See "The Lovers Punished," in *Flaxman: Designs for Dante,* ed. Bill Tate (Truchas, N.M.: Tate Gallery, 1968), 15.

59. Klonsky notes that four "good angels" appear behind Minos's throne (*Blake's Dante,* 139); perhaps this is another way that Blake offers a different perspective (or a different viewer or viewers) on Dante's judgments.

60. Boyd wrote, "Would [the reader] feel what vice is in itself . . . let him enter into the passions of Lear, when he feels the ingratitude of his children; of Hamlet, when he learns the story of his father's murder; . . . and he will know the difference of right and wrong much more clearly than from all the moralists that ever wrote" (E, 634). In response, Blake wrote: "The grandest Poetry is Immoral the Grandest characters Wicked Very Satan. Capanius [*sic*] Othello a murderer. Prometheus. Jupiter. Jehovah, Jesus a wine bibber Cunning & Morality are not Poetry but Philosophy the Poet is Independent & Wicked the Philosopher is Dependent & Good Poetry is to excuse Vice & shew its reason & necessary purgation" (E, 634).

61. Roe, *Blake's Illustration,* 132–33.

62. Henry Fuseli's depiction of this subject is equally condemning of Dante's kicking Bocca degli Abati. See "Dante on the Ice of Cocytus," reproduced in Klonsky, *Blake's Dante,* 9.

63. Ibid., 152.

Conclusion. Forgiveness and Literary Form

1. Leslie Tannenbaum, *Biblical Tradition and Blake's Early Prophecies: The Great Code of Art* (Princeton, N.J.: Princeton University Press, 1982), 120.

2. Saint Augustine of Hippo, *Quaestio in Heptateuchum,* sec. 2:74, in *Patrologia Latina,* ed. J. Migne (Paris: N.p., n.d.), 34:625.

3. Jean Danielou, S.J., *From Shadows to Reality: Studies in the Biblical Typology of the Fathers,* trans. Dom Walstan Hibberd (London: Burns and Cates, 1960).

4. Morris Eaves, *William Blake's Theory of Art* (Princeton, N.J.: Princeton University Press, 1982), 4.

5. I have been helped in my reading of readerly issues in *Milton* by Harold Bloom's books *The Anxiety of Influence: A Theory of Poetry* (New York: Oxford University Press, 1973); *Kabbalah and Criticism* (New York: Seabury, 1975); *A Map of Misreading* (New York: Oxford, 1975); *Poetry and Repression: Revisionism from Blake to Stevens* (New Haven, Conn.: Yale University Press, 1976); and *Agon: Towards a Theory of Revisionism* (New York: Oxford University Press, 1982); and by Harold Fisch, "Blake's Miltonic Moment," in *William Blake: Essays for S. Foster Damon,* ed. Alvin H. Rosenfeld (Providence, R.I.: Brown University Press, 1969), 38–55; Peter Alan Taylor, "Providence and the Moment in Blake's *Milton,*" *Blake Studies* 4, no. 1 (1971): 43–60; Florence Sandler, "The Iconoclastic Enterprise: Blake's Critique of 'Milton's Religion,'" *Blake Studies* 5, no. 1 (1972): 44–47; Joseph A. Wittreich, Jr., *Angel of Apocalypse: Blake's Idea of Milton* (Madison: University of Wisconsin Press, 1975); Irene Taylor, "Say First! What Mov'd Blake? Blake's *Comus* Designs and *Milton*" in *Blake's Sublime Allegory: Essays on "The Four Zoas," "Milton," and "Jerusalem,"* ed. Stuart Curran and Joseph A. Wittreich, Jr. (Madison: University of Wisconsin Press, 1973), 233–58; and Susan Fox, "The Female as Metaphor in William Blake's Poetry," *Critical Inquiry* 3 (1977): 507–19. There have been four book-length studies on Blake's *Milton:* Susan Fox's *Poetic Form in Blake's "Milton"* (Princeton, N.J.: Princeton University Press, 1976); John Howard's *Blake's "Milton": A Study in the Selfhood* (Rutherford, N.J.: Fairleigh Dickinson University Press, 1976); David E. James's *Written Within and Without: A Study of Blake's "Milton"* (Las Vegas: Peter Lang, 1977); and Mark Bracher's *Being Form'd: Thinking Through Blake's "Milton"* (Barrytown, N.Y.: Station Hill Press, 1985).

6. Thomas A. Vogler, "Re: Naming MIL/TON," in *Unnam'd Forms: Blake and Textuality,* ed. Nelson Hilton and Thomas A. Vogler (Berkeley and Los Angeles: University of California Press, 1986), 141–76.

7. Erdman suggests when Blake writes that Milton arrived "on my left foot falling

on the tarsus" (*M* 17:49; E, 110), he puns on Saul of Tarsus, who became Saint Paul (*The Illuminated Blake* [Garden City, N.Y.: Doubleday, Anchor Books, 1974], 226). Bloom interprets Milton's arrival there as an alteration in Blake's stance (E, 915). And Hazard Adams suggests that creativity and language reside in the legs of Albion, at the base of culture, in *Philosophy of the Literary Symbolic* (Tallahassee: Florida State University Press, 1983), 109.

8. Saint Cyril of Jerusalem, Lecture 3, sec. 6, trans. E. H. Gifford, in *Nicene and Post-Nicene Fathers,* 7:15.

9. Bloom suggests that the allusions mean that "Urizen is seeking to baptize Milton into the moral law, lest a new Incarnation come into the fullness of prophetic vision" (E, 916).

10. Fox, *Poetic Form,* 159.

11. Joanne Witke, "*Jerusalem:* A Synoptic Poem," *Comparative Literature* 22 (1970): 265–78; *Jerome Biblical Commentary,* 41:21.

12. Harvey K. McArthur, *The Quest Through the Centuries: The Search for the Historical Jesus* (Philadelphia: Fortress Press, 1966), 85–101, 160.

13. *Jerome Biblical Commentary,* 41:8.

14. Northrop Frye, *Fearful Symmetry: A Study of William Blake* (1947; reprint, Princeton, N.J.: Princeton University Press, 1969), 357.

15. W. J. T. Mitchell, *Blake's Composite Art: A Study of the Illuminated Poetry* (Princeton, N.J.: Princeton University Press, 1978), 215.

16. McArthur, *Quest,* 104.

17. Ibid., 104; Tannenbaum, *Biblical Tradition,* 14.

18. Morton D. Paley, "'A New Heaven Is Begun': Blake and Swedenborgianism," in *Blake and Swedenborg: Opposition Is True Friendship,* ed. Harvey F. Bellin and Darrell Ruhl (New York: Swedenborg Foundation, 1985), reprinted in *Blake: An Illustrated Quarterly* 12, no. 2 (1979): 28.

19. Charles Altieri, "Expressivist Ethics," in *Literature and the Question of Philosophy,* ed. Anthony J. Cascardi (Baltimore: Johns Hopkins University Press, 1987), 134–66.

Selected Bibliography

Abbey, Charles J., and John H. Overton. *The English Church in the Eighteenth Century.* 2 vols. London: Longmans, Green, 1878 and 1899.

Adams, Hazard. *Philosophy of the Literary Symbolic.* Tallahassee: Florida State University Press, 1983.

Altizer, Thomas J. J. *The New Apocalypse: The Radical Christian Vision of William Blake.* East Lansing: Michigan State University Press, 1967.

Arendt, Hannah. *The Human Condition.* Chicago: University of Chicago Press, 1958.

———. *The Origins of Totalitarianism.* New York: Harcourt and Brace, 1951.

Aristotle. *Nicomachean Ethics.* Translated by David Ross. Revised by J. O. Urmson. Oxford: Oxford University Press, 1984.

Aubrey, Bryan. *Watchmen of Eternity: Blake's Debt to Jacob Boehme.* Lanham, Md.: University Presses of America, 1986.

Ault, Donald D. *Narrative Unbound: Re-Visioning William Blake's "The Four Zoas."* Barrytown, N.Y.: Station Hill Press, 1987.

Bandy, Melanie. *Mind Forg'd Manacles: Evil in the Poetry of Blake and Shelley.* University: University of Alabama Press, 1981.

Bataille, Georges. "William Blake." In *Literature and Evil* (1957), translated by Alastair Hamilton. New York: Urizen Books, 1981.

Benjamin, Jessica. *The Bonds of Love: Feminism, Psychoanalysis, and the Problem of Domination.* New York: Pantheon Books, 1988.

Bentley, G. E., Jr. *Blake Books.* Rev. ed. Oxford: Clarendon Press, 1977.

———. *Blake Records.* Oxford: Clarendon Press, 1969.

———, ed. *William Blake's "Vala; or, The Four Zoas": A Facsimile of the Manuscript, a Transcript of the Poem, and a Study of Its Growth and Significance.* Oxford: Clarendon Press, 1963.

Blake, William. *The Complete Poetry and Prose of William Blake.* Rev. ed. Edited by David V. Erdman. Berkeley and Los Angeles: University of California Press, 1982.

———. *The Notebook of William Blake: A Photographic and Typographic Facsimile.* Edited by David V. Erdman and Donald K. Moore. Oxford: Clarendon Press, 1973.

Blake: An Illustrated Quarterly 12, no. 2 (1978). Special Issue on *Four Zoas,* Night VII.

Bloom, Harold. *Blake's Apocalypse: A Study in Poetic Argument.* Garden City, N.Y.: Doubleday, 1963.

———. *Ruin the Sacred Truths: Poetry and Belief from the Bible to the Present.* Cambridge, Mass.: Harvard University Press, 1989.

———. *The Visionary Company: A Reading of English Romantic Poetry.* Rev. ed. Ithaca, N.Y.: Cornell University Press, 1971.

Boehme, Jakob. *The Works of Jacob Boehme, the Teutonic Theosopher; to Which Is Prefixed the Life of the Author. With Figures, Illustrating His Principles, Left by William Law.* 4 vols. London: n.p., 1764–81.

Bottrall, Margaret. *The Divine Image: A Study of Blake's Interpretation of Christianity.* Rome: Edizioni di Storia e Letteratura, 1950.

Bowden, Betsy. "The Artistic and Interpretive Context of Blake's *Canterbury Pilgrims.*" *Blake: An Illustrated Quarterly* 13, no. 4 (1980): 164–90.

Brand, C. P. *Italy and the English Romantics: The Italianate Fashion in Early Nineteenth-Century Britain.* New York: Cambridge University Press, 1957.

Brown, Raymond E., S.S.; Joseph A. Fitzmyer, S.J.; and Roland E. Murphy, O.Carm. *The Jerome Biblical Commentary.* Englewood Cliffs, N.J.: Prentice-Hall, 1968.

Butlin, Martin. *The Paintings and Drawings of William Blake.* 2 vols. New Haven, Conn.: Yale University Press, 1981.

Cary, Henry Francis. *The Vision; or, Hell, Purgatory, and Paradise of Dante Alighieri.* New York: American News, 1814.

Cascardi, Anthony J., ed. *Literature and the Question of Philosophy.* Baltimore: Johns Hopkins University Press, 1987.

Clubbe, John, and Ernest J. Lovell, Jr. *English Romanticism: The Grounds of Belief.* DeKalb: Northern Illinois University Press, 1983.

Cohen, Richard A., ed. *Face to Face with Levinas.* Albany: State University of New York Press, 1986.

Cooke, Michael G. *Acts of Inclusion: Studies Bearing on an Elementary Theory of Romanticism.* New Haven, Conn.: Yale University Press, 1979.

Cooper, Andrew M. "Blake's Escape from Mythology: Self-Mastery in *Milton.*" *Studies in Romanticism* 20 (1981): 85–110.

Copleston, Frederick, S.J. *A History of Philosophy.* Vols. 1–7. London: Burns, Oates, and Washbourne, 1951–65. Vol. 8. Westminster, Md.: Newman Press, 1966. Vol. 9. London: Search Press, 1975.

Cox, Stephen D. *"The Stranger Within Thee": Concepts of the Self in Late Eighteenth-Century Literature.* Pittsburgh: University of Pittsburgh Press, 1980.

Cragg, Gerald R. *Reason and Authority in the Eighteenth Century.* Cambridge: Cambridge University Press, 1964.

Crehan, Stuart. *Blake in Context.* Atlantic Highlands, N.J.: Humanities Press, 1984.

Curran, Stuart, and Joseph Anthony Wittreich, Jr., eds. *Blake's Sublime Allegory: Essays on "The Four Zoas," "Milton," and "Jerusalem."* Madison: University of Wisconsin Press, 1973.

Damon, S. Foster. *A Blake Dictionary: The Ideas and Symbols of William Blake.* 1965. Reprint. Boulder, Colo.: Shambhala Press, 1979.

———. *Blake's Job: William Blake's Illustrations of the Book of Job.* Hanover, N.H.: University Presses of New England for Brown University Press, 1966.

Damrosch, Leopold, Jr. *Symbol and Truth in Blake's Myth.* Princeton, N.J.: Princeton University Press, 1980.

Davies, J. G. *The Theology of William Blake.* 1948. Reprint. Hamden, Conn.: Archon Books, 1966.

Deen, Leonard. *Conversing in Paradise: Poetic Genius and Identity-as-Community in Blake's Los.* Columbia: University of Missouri Press, 1983.

De Sua, William. *Dante into English.* Chapel Hill: University of North Carolina Press, 1964.

Dorfman, Deborah. *Blake in the Nineteenth Century: His Reputation as a Poet from Gilchrist to Yeats.* New Haven, Conn.: Yale University Press, 1969.

Eaves, Morris. *William Blake's Theory of Art.* Princeton, N.J.: Princeton University Press, 1982.

Erdman, David V. *Blake, Prophet Against Empire: A Poet's Interpretation of the History of His Own Times.* 3d ed. Princeton, N.J.: Princeton University Press, 1977.

———. "Blake's Early Swedenborgianism: A Twentieth-Century Legend." *Comparative Literature* 5 (1953): 247–57.

———. "The Suppressed and Altered Passages in Blake's *Jerusalem.*" *Studies in Bibliography* 17 (1964): 1–54.

———, ed. *The Illuminated Blake.* Garden City, N.Y.: Doubleday, Anchor Books, 1974.

Erdman, David V., and John E. Grant, eds. *Blake's Visionary Forms Dramatic.* Princeton, N.J.: Princeton University Press, 1970.

Erdman, David V., and Donald K. Moore, eds. *A Concordance to the Writings of William Blake.* 2 vols. Ithaca, N.Y.: Cornell University Press, 1967.

Essick, Robert N., ed. *The Visionary Hand: Essays for the Study of Blake's Art and Aesthetics.* Los Angeles: Hennessey and Ingalls, 1973.

Essick, Robert N., and Donald Pearce, eds. *Blake in His Time.* Bloomington: Indiana University Press, 1978.

Ferber, Michael. *The Social Vision of William Blake.* Princeton, N.J.: Princeton University Press, 1985.

Foot, Philippa. *Virtues and Vices and Other Essays in Moral Philosophy.* Berkeley and Los Angeles: University of California Press, 1978.

Fox, Susan. "The Female as Metaphor in William Blake's Poetry." *Critical Inquiry* 3 (1977): 507–19.

———. *Poetic Form in Blake's "Milton."* Princeton, N.J.: Princeton University Press, 1976.

Frankena, William K. *Ethics.* Englewood Cliffs, N.J.: Prentice-Hall, 1963.

Frosch, Thomas R. *The Awakening of Albion: The Renovation of the Body in the Poetry of William Blake.* Ithaca, N.Y.: Cornell University Press, 1974.

Frye, Northrop. *Anatomy of Criticism: Four Essays.* Princeton, N.J.: Princeton University Press, 1957.

———. *Fearful Symmetry: A Study of William Blake.* 1947. Reprint. Princeton, N.J.: Princeton University Press, 1969.

———. "Notes for a Commentary on *Milton.*" In *The Divine Vision: Studies in the Poetry and Art of William Blake,* edited by Vivian de Sola Pinto. London: Victor Gollancz, 1957.

Fuller, David. "Blake and Dante." *Art History* 11 (1988): 349–73.

Gaull, Marilyn. *English Romanticism: The Human Context.* New York: Norton, 1988.

Geach, Peter. *The Virtues: The Stanton Lectures, 1973–1974.* Cambridge: Cambridge University Press, 1977.

Gilchrist, Alexander. *The Life of William Blake with Selections from His Poems and Other Writings.* 2 vols. 1880. Reprint. Totowa, N.J.: Rowman and Littlefield, 1973.

Gillham, D. G. *William Blake.* London: Cambridge University Press, 1973.

Glausser, Wayne. "*Milton* and the Pangs of Repentance." *Blake: An Illustrated Quarterly* 13, no. 4 (1980): 192–99.

Godwin, William. *Enquiry Concerning Political Justice.* 1798. Edited by K. Codell Carter. Oxford: Clarendon Press, 1971.

Grant, John E. "The Female Awakening at the End of Blake's *Milton:* A Picture Story, with Questions." In *Milton Reconsidered: Essays in Honor of Arthur E. Barker,* edited by John Karl Franson. Salzburg Studies in English Literature, no. 49, 1976.

Grant, Philip Bernard. "Blake's *The Everlasting Gospel:* An Edition and Study." Ph.D. dissertation, University of Pennsylvania, 1976.

Grimes, Ronald L. *The Divine Imagination: William Blake's Major Prophetic Visions.* Metuchen, N.J.: Scarecrow Press, 1972.

Grosz, Elizabeth. *Sexual Subversions: Three French Feminists.* Sydney: Allen and Unwin, 1989.

Hagstrum, Jean H. *William Blake, Poet and Painter.* Chicago: University of Chicago Press, 1964.

Hall, Carol Louise. *Blake and Fuseli: A Study in the Transmission of Ideas.* New York: Garland, 1985.

Harper, George Mills. *The Neoplatonism of William Blake.* Chapel Hill: University of North Carolina Press, 1961.

Hauerwas, Stanley. *Against the Nations: War and Survival in a Liberal Society.* Minneapolis: Winston Press, 1985.

———. *A Community of Character: Toward a Constructive Christian Social Ethic.* Notre Dame, Ind.: University of Notre Dame Press, 1981.

Hauerwas, Stanley, with Richard Bondi and David B. Burrell. *Truthfulness and Tragedy: Further Investigations in Christian Ethics.* Notre Dame, Ind.: University of Notre Dame Press, 1977.

Hauerwas, Stanley, and Alasdair MacIntyre, eds. *Revisions: Changing Perspectives in Moral Philosophy.* Notre Dame, Ind.: University of Notre Dame Press, 1983.

Hilles, Frederick W., and Harold Bloom, eds. *From Sensibility to Romanticism: Essays Presented to Frederick A. Pottle.* New York: Oxford University Press, 1965.

Hilton, Nelson. *Literal Imagination: Blake's Vision of Words.* Berkeley and Los Angeles: University of California Press, 1983.

Hilton, Nelson, and Thomas A. Vogler, eds. *Unnam'd Forms: Blake and Textuality.* Berkeley and Los Angeles: University of California Press, 1986.

Howard, John. *Blake's "Milton": A Study in the Selfhood.* Rutherford, N.J.: Fairleigh Dickinson University Press, 1976.

———. *Infernal Poetics: Poetic Structures in Blake's Lambeth Prophecies.* Rutherford, N.J.: Fairleigh Dickinson University Press, 1984.

Huehns, Gertrude. *Antinomianism in English History, with Special Reference to the Period 1640–1660.* London: Cresset Press, 1951.

Irigaray, Luce. *The Irigaray Reader.* Edited by Margaret Whitford. Cambridge, Mass.: Basil Blackwell, 1991.

John, Donald. "Blake and Forgiveness." *Wordsworth Circle* 17 (1986): 74–80.

Johnson, Mary Lynn. "'Separating What Has Been Mixed': A Suggestion for a Perspective on *Milton.*" *Blake Studies* 6, no. 1 (1973): 11–18.

Jonas, Hans. *The Gnostic Religion.* 2d ed. Boston: Beacon Press, 1963.

Kant, Immanuel. *Fundamental Principles of the Metaphysic of Morals.* Translated by Thomas K. Abbott. New York: Liberal Arts Press, 1949.

———. *Religion Within the Limits of Reason Alone.* Translated by Theodore M. Greene and Hoyt H. Hudson. New York: Harper and Row, 1960.

Kazin, Alfred. Introduction to *The Portable Blake.* New York: Viking Press, 1946.

Keynes, Geoffrey. Introduction and commentary to *The Marriage of Heaven and Hell,* by William Blake. New York: Oxford University Press, 1975.

Kiralis, Karl. "William Blake as an Intellectual and Spiritual Guide to Chaucer's *Canterbury Pilgrims.*" *Blake Studies* 1, no. 2 (1969): 139–77.

Klonsky, Milton. *Blake's Dante: The Complete Illustrations to the "Divine Comedy."* New York: Harmony Books, 1980.

Kolnai, Aurel. "Forgiveness." *Proceedings of the Aristotelian Society* 74 (1973–74): 91–106. Reprinted in *Ethics, Value, and Reality: Selected Papers of Aurel Kolnai.* Indianapolis: Hackett, 1978.

Lavater, Johann Caspar. *Aphorisms on Man.* 1788. A facsimile reproduction of William Blake's copy of the 1st English edition, edited by R. J. Shroyer. Delmar, N.Y.: Scholars' Facsimiles and Reprints, 1980.

Levinas, Emmanuel. *Collected Philosophical Papers.* Translated by Alphonso Lingis. Dordrecht: Martinus Nijhoff, 1987.

———. *Ethics and Infinity.* Pittsburgh: Duquesne University Press, 1985.

———. *Totality and Infinity: An Essay on Exteriority.* Translated by Alphonso Lingis. Pittsburgh: Duquesne University Press, 1969.

Lindberg, Bo. *William Blake's Illustrations to the Book of Job.* Åbo, Finland: Åbo Akademi, 1973.

Locke, John. *An Essay Concerning Human Understanding.* Edited by Peter H. Nidditch. Oxford: Clarendon Press, 1975.

Lockridge, Laurence S. *The Ethics of Romanticism.* Cambridge: Cambridge University Press, 1989.

Lowth, Robert. *De Sacra Poesi Hebraeorum.* 2 vols. Translated by G. Gregory. Reprint. Hildesheim: Georg Olms, 1969.

Lyons, John O. *The Invention of the Self: The Hinge of Consciousness in the Eighteenth Century.* Carbondale, Ill.: Southern Illinois University Press, 1978.

McArthur, Harvey K. *The Quest Through the Centuries: The Search for the Historical Jesus.* Philadelphia: Fortress Press, 1966.

McGann, Jerome J. "The Idea of an Indeterminate Text: Blake's Bible of Hell and Dr. Alexander Geddes." *Studies in Romanticism* 25 (1986): 303–25.

———. "William Blake Illuminates the Truth." *Critical Studies* 1, no. 1 (1989): 43–60.

MacIntyre, Alasdair. *After Virtue: A Study in Moral Theory.* 2d ed. Notre Dame, Ind.: University of Notre Dame Press, 1984.

———. *A Short History of Ethics.* London: Routledge and Kegan Paul, 1967.

Magno, Cettina Tramantano, and David V. Erdman, eds. *"The Four Zoas" by William Blake: A Photographic Facsimile of the Manuscript with Commentary on the Illustrations.* Cranbury, N.J.: Associated University Presses, 1987.

Mann, Paul. "The Final State of *The Four Zoas.*" *Blake: An Illustrated Quarterly* 18, no. 4 (1985): 205–15.

Margoliouth, H. M., ed. *William Blake's "Vala": Blake's Numbered Text.* Oxford: Clarendon Press, 1956.

Mellor, Anne K. "Blake's Portrayal of Women." *Blake: An Illustrated Quarterly* 16, no. 3 (1982–83): 148–55.

Mitchell, W. J. T. *Blake's Composite Art: A Study of the Illuminated Poetry.* Princeton, N.J.: Princeton University Press, 1978.

———. "Blake's Visions of the Last Judgment." Paper at meeting of the Modern Language Association, December 28, 1975; *Blake Newsletter,* Summer 1976.

———. "Dangerous Blake." *Studies in Romanticism* 21 (1982): 410–16.

———. "Style and Iconography in the Illustrations of Blake's *Milton.*" *Blake Studies* 6, no. 1 (1973): 47–71.

Morton, A. L. *The Everlasting Gospel: A Study in the Sources of William Blake.* 1957. Reprint. New York: Haskell House, 1966.

Murdoch, Iris. *The Sovereignty of Good.* 1970. Reprint. London: Ark Paperbacks, 1985.

Murray, E. B. "Thel, *Thelyphthora,* and the Daughters of Albion." *Studies in Romanticism* 20 (1981): 275–97.

Niebuhr, Reinhold. *An Interpretation of Christian Ethics.* 1935. Reprint. New York: Seabury Press, 1979.

Nurmi, Martin K. *Blake's "Marriage of Heaven and Hell": A Critical Study.* Kent, Ohio: Kent State University Press, 1957.

Nussbaum, Martha C. *The Fragility of Goodness: Luck and Ethics in Greek Tragedy and Philosophy.* Cambridge: Cambridge University Press, 1986.

O'Hear, Anthony. "Guilt and Shame as Moral Concepts." *Proceedings of the Aristotelian Society* 77 (1976–77): 73–86.

Ostriker, Alicia. "Desire Gratified and Ungratified: William Blake and Sexuality." *Blake: An Illustrated Quarterly* 16, no. 3 (1982–83): 156–65.

Pagliaro, Harold. *Selfhood and Redemption in Blake's Songs.* University Park: Pennsylvania State University Press, 1987.

Paley, Morton D. *The Continuing City: William Blake's "Jerusalem."* Oxford: Clarendon Press, 1983.

———. *Energy and the Imagination: A Study of the Development of Blake's Thought.* Oxford: Clarendon Press, 1970.

———. "'A New Heaven Is Begun': Blake and Swedenborgianism." In *Blake and Swedenborg: Opposition Is True Friendship,* edited by Harvey F. Bellin and Darrell Ruhl. New York: Swedenborg Foundation, 1985. Reprinted in *Blake: An Illustrated Quarterly* 12, no. 2 (1979): 64–90.

———. "The Truchsessian Gallery Revisited." *Studies in Romanticism* 16 (1977): 165–77.

———. "William Blake, the Prince of the Hebrews, and the Woman Clothed with the Sun." In *William Blake: Essays in Honor of Sir Geoffrey Keynes,* edited by Morton D. Paley and Michael Phillips. Oxford: Clarendon Press, 1973.

Phillips, Michael, ed. *Interpreting Blake.* Cambridge: Cambridge University Press, 1978.

Pincoffs, Edmund L. *Quandaries and Virtues: Against Reductivism in Ethics.* Lawrence: University of Kansas Press, 1986.

Plowman, Max. *An Introduction to the Study of Blake.* 2d ed., 1927. Reprint. London: Frank Cass, 1967.

Pope, Marvin H., ed. and trans. *Job.* Vol. 15 of the Anchor Bible. 3d ed. Garden City, N.Y.: Doubleday, 1973.

Praz, Mario. *The Romantic Agony.* 2d ed. New York: Oxford University Press, 1970.

Punter, David. "Blake: 'Active Evil' and 'Passive Good.'" In *Romanticism and Ideology: Studies in English Writing, 1765–1830,* by David Aers, Jonathan Cook, and David Punter. London: Routledge and Kegan Paul, 1981.

Raphael, D. D. *British Moralists,* 1650–1800. 2 vols. Oxford: Clarendon Press, 1969.

Ricoeur, Paul. *The Symbolism of Evil.* Translated by Emerson Buchanan. Boston: Beacon Press, 1967.

Roe, Albert S. *Blake's Illustrations to the "Divine Comedy."* Princeton, N.J.: Princeton University Press, 1953.

Rorty, Amelie Oksenberg, ed. *Essays on Aristotle's Ethics.* Berkeley and Los Angeles: University of California Press, 1980.

———, ed. *Explaining Emotions.* Berkeley and Los Angeles: University of California Press, 1980.

Rose, Edward J. "Blake and the Double: The Spectre as *Doppelgänger.*" *Colby Library Quarterly* 13 (1977): 127–39.

———. "Blake's Metaphorical States." *Blake Studies* 4, no. 1 (1971): 9–31.

Rosenfeld, Alvin H., ed. *William Blake: Essays for S. Foster Damon.* Providence, R.I.: Brown University Press, 1969.

Sandler, Florence. "The Iconoclastic Enterprise: Blake's Critique of 'Milton's Religion.'" *Blake Studies* 5, no. 1 (1972): 13–58.

Selby-Bigge, L. A., ed. *British Moralists, Being Selections from Writers Principally of the Eighteenth Century.* 2 vols. Library of Liberal Arts, no. 152. Indianapolis: Bobbs-Merrill, 1964.

Sparks, H. F. D. Introductory essay to the Book of Enoch. In *The Apocryphal Old Testament,* edited by H. F. D. Sparks. Oxford: Clarendon Press, 1984.

Steffan, Truman Guy. *Lord Byron's "Cain": Twelve Essays and a Text with Variants and Annotations.* Austin: University of Texas Press, 1968.

Stevenson, Warren. "Interpreting Blake's *Canterbury Pilgrims.*" *Colby Library Quarterly* 13 (1977): 115–26.

Storch, Margaret. "Blake and Women: 'Nature's Cruel Holiness.'" *American Imago* 38 (1981): 221–46.

———. "The 'Spectrous Fiend' Cast Out: Blake's Crisis at Felpham." *Modern Language Quarterly* 44 (1983): 115–35.

Studies in Romanticism 21, no. 3 (1982). Special issue on Blake.

Swedenborg, Emanuel. *Heaven and Hell.* Translated by George F. Dole. New York: Swedenborg Foundation, 1984.

———. *True Christian Religion: Containing the Universal Theology of the New Church.* Translated by John C. Ager. 2 vols. 1795. Reprint. New York: Swedenborg Foundation, 1963.

Tannenbaum, Leslie. *Biblical Tradition and Blake's Early Prophecies: The Great Code of Art.* Princeton, N.J.: Princeton University Press, 1982.

Tate, Bill, ed. *Flaxman: Designs for Dante.* Truchas, N.M.: Tate Gallery, 1968.

Tayler, Irene. "The Woman Scaly." *Bulletin of the Midwest Modern Language Association* 6 (1973): 74–87.

Taylor, Gabriele. *Pride, Shame, and Guilt: Emotions of Self-Assessment.* Oxford: Clarendon Press, 1985.

Thompson, E. P. *The Making of the English Working Class.* New York: Random House, Vintage Books, 1963.

Valevičius, Andrius. *From the Other to the Totally Other: The Religious Philosophy of Emmanuel Levinas.* New York: Peter Lang, 1988.

Wallace, James D. *Virtues and Vices.* Ithaca, N.Y.: Cornell University Press, 1978.

Ward, Aileen. "Canterbury Revisited: The Blake-Cromek Controversy." *Blake: An Illustrated Quarterly* 22, no. 3 (1988): 80–92.

———. "'Sr Joshua and His Gang': William Blake and the Royal Academy." *Huntington Library Quarterly* 52 (1989): 75–95.

Wilkie, Brian, and Mary Lynn Johnson. *Blake's "Four Zoas": The Design of a Dream.* Cambridge, Mass.: Harvard University Press, 1978.

Wilson, Mona. *The Life of William Blake.* 1927. Rev. ed. London: Rupert Hart-Davis, 1948.

Witke, Joanne. "*Jerusalem:* A Synoptic Poem." *Comparative Literature* 22 (1970): 265–78.

Wyschogrod, Edith. *Emmanuel Levinas: The Problem of Ethical Metaphysics.* The Hague: Martinus Nijhoff, 1974.

Young-Breuhl, Elisabeth. *Hannah Arendt: For the Love of the World.* New Haven, Conn.: Yale University Press, 1982.

Youngquist, Paul. *Madness and Blake's Myth.* University Park: Pennsylvania State University Press, 1989.

Index

Titles and page numbers of illustrations are in boldface.